જી ♦ ભ

# Adolescent Pregnancy and Parenting

*Findings From a*
*Racially Diverse Sample*

જી ♦ ભ

# Research Monographs in Adolescence
Nancy L. Galambos/Nancy A. Busch-Rossnagel, Editors

৪০ ◆ ৪৩

# Adolescent Pregnancy and Parenting

## Findings From a Racially Diverse Sample

৪০ ◆ ৪৩

**Patricia L. East**
*University of California, San Diego School of Medicine*
**Marianne E. Felice**
*University of Maryland School of Medicine*

Routledge
Taylor & Francis Group

LONDON AND NEW YORK

First published 1996 by
Lawrence Erlbaum Associates, Inc.

2 Park Square, Milton Park, Abingdon, Oxon OX14 4RN
711 Third Avenue, New York, NY 10017, USA

*Routledge is an imprint of the Taylor & Francis Group, an informa business*

First issued in paperback 2016

**Library of Congress Cataloging-in-Publication Data**

East, Patricia, 1958–
    Adolescent pregnancy and parenting : findings from a racially diverse sample / Patricia L. East, Marianne E. Felice.
        p. cm. — (Research monographs in adolescence)
    Includes bibliographical references.
    ISBN 0-8058-1470-1 (cloth : alk. paper)
    1. Teenage pregnancy—California—San Diego—Longitudinal studies. 2. Teenage mothers—California—San Diego—Longitudinal studies. 3. Teenage parents—California—San Diego—Longitudinal studies. 4. Unmarried mothers—California—San Diego—Longitudinal studies. I. Felice, Marianne E. II. Title. III. Series.
HQ759.4.E25 1996
362.7'083—dc20
                        96-13153
                        CIP

ISBN 978-0-8058-1470-5 (hbk)
ISBN 978-1-138-96596-6 (pbk)

We dedicate this book to our spouses, William Ganelin (PLE)
and John M. Giles, III (MEF), who have always been supportive
of our academic careers and our interest in children and adolescents.
We realize that the time we spent on this project and on this book
often took away from the time we could have spent with them.

ಔ  ◆  ಚ

In loving memory of William J. East, who set me
on my path (PLE).

# Contents

� ◆ ᘓ

# Preface

ʚ ◆ ɞ

This book reports on the pregnancies and parenting in an ethnically diverse sample of more than 200 adolescent women. Adolescents were studied prenatally and at regular 6-month intervals for 3 1/2 years postpartum. Most of the teens were poor, unmarried, first-time mothers who resided within Southeast San Diego, a poor urban area approximately 10 miles north of the U.S.–Mexico border. This study began in 1987 as part of a comprehensive adolescent pregnancy and parenting program at the University of California, San Diego (UCSD)Medical Center and continued until 1993. Our purpose in writing this book was to offer researchers, practitioners, program directors, teachers, and graduate and medical students a better understanding of teenage pregnancy and parenthood within the following five domains: adolescent prenatal care and postpartum maternal and infant health outcomes, immediate repeat pregnancy, adolescent mothers' parenting, the role of the adolescent's mother in teenage mothers' parenting, and the baby's father. These emphases were chosen for various reasons. Some reflected our personal interests, some we felt were not adequately addressed in the literature but were a big part of the picture, some reflected a strength of our data set, and some had policy ramifications that we thought were especially topical. In examining these areas, we tried to be practical in what we could synthesize from the already large literature and in what we could realistically address in each chapter. Thus, we strove to put forth a collection of informative, nonredundant, yet fairly comprehensive studies on adolescent pregnancy and parenting as opposed to focusing exclusively on only one single aspect of the phenomenon.

What will become quickly apparent to the more experienced reader is that this book is clearly the union of a pediatrician–adolescent medicine specialist (MEF) and a developmental psychologist (PLE). Although the pediatrician half of this writing team focused mostly on the medical-health issues and the developmental psychologist stayed mainly within the bounds of the adolescent's socio-familial domain, this was truly a collaborative effort wherein we each contributed to all aspects of the book. We believe this work reflects a truly interdisciplinary approach, and we hope this enhanced the book. In our opinion, this was clearly "a collaboration that worked,"[1] and we encourage our respective colleagues to do likewise.

Many funding agencies have supported our research over the last several years. The project on which this book is based was funded by the U.S. Department of Health and Human Services, Office of Adolescent Pregnancy Programs (OAPP; Grant APH-000-150). We wish to thank, in particular, Dr. Patrick Sheeran, Dr. Karen Smith Thiel, Dr. Dennis McBride, and Ms. Barbara Rosenberg of OAPP, who gave generously their time and expertise to the UCSD Teen OB Follow-Up Study and for their dedicated efforts in support of programs for adolescent mothers and their children.

We are also grateful to support from the National Institute of Child Health and Human Development (R29-HD29472 to Dr. East) and the Maternal and Child Health Bureau (MCJ-980 to Dr. Felice) for their support while writing this book. This project was also facilitated by a grant from the NIH National Center for Research Resources (M01-RR00827) to the UCSD Medical Center's General Clinical Research Center.

Thanks are due to many colleagues who have helped sharpen our ideas about this field. We especially thank Dorothy R. Hollingsworth, MD, our collaborator in the Department of Reproductive Medicine, University of California, San Diego, who inspired this project. We proudly acknowledge the project's two case managers, Carol Anne Drastal, MPH, RN and Karen L. Matthews, LCSW, MPH, who generously shared their expertise and insights into the young mothers in our sample and who spent enormous amounts of time on all aspects of this project. We also appreciate the input of many extraordinary adolescent medicine professionals who were part of this research project from its inception: Vincent Mason, MD, Yuko Matsuhashi, MD, Maria Morgan, MD, Lynn Rice, RN, CPNP, and Nancy Williams, RN. Paul G. Shragg, of the UCSD Medical Center Clinical Research Center, provided invaluable and always instructive tips on managing our large data set, and Glenn Sobeck of the UCSD Medical Center Library tenaciously tracked down numerous reference articles for this book. In addition, we thank the following individuals for their superb efforts at subject follow-up, data collection, and data entry: Beth Baker, MSW, Grace Barca, Carolyn Bushman, Donna Charielle, MSW, Katy Engelhorn and Maria Lara-Carvalho. This book would not have been possible without them. Dr. Nancy L. Galambos, the series co-editor, provided many valuable and insightful comments on previous drafts of this book. The faults that remain are ours. We are indebted to her for her professionalism and patience. Finally, we thank the many adolescent mothers who graciously participated in this project for the first 3 1/2 years of their children's lives. We continue to learn from them and to be inspired by them.

—*Patricia L. East*
—*Marianne E. Felice*

---

[1] LeBaron, S., & Zeltzser, L. (1985). Pediatrics and psychology: A collaboration that works. *Journal of Developmental and Behavioral Pediatrics, 6*, 157-161.

# Chapter 1

## Introduction and Background

&#8766;   &#9670;   &#8731;

Adolescent childbearing has emerged as one of the most significant social problems facing the United States today. The latest estimates show that approximately 1 million teens become pregnant each year (Alan Guttmacher Institute, 1994b; Centers for Disease Control [CDC], 1993; Henshaw, 1993; Moore, 1993; National Center for Health Statistics [NCHS], 1993). Among these million teens, approximately half will give birth, slightly over one third will opt for abortions, and the remainder (14%) will have miscarriages or stillbirths. Despite being an advanced and relatively affluent country, teens in the United States have higher rates of pregnancy and childbearing than any other industrialized nation including those with comparable levels of sexual activity (Henshaw, Kenney, Somberg, & Van Vort, 1989; Jones et al., 1985). This disturbing trend is even more apparent among younger adolescents: Girls 15 and younger are five times more likely to give birth in the United States than in other Western nations (Moore, Wenk, Hofferth, & Hayes, 1987).

In response to the alarming rates of teenage pregnancy and childbearing, the Adolescent Family Life Act (AFL) was federally legislated in 1981. The AFL had at its core the purpose of alleviating the negative consequences of pregnancy and childbearing for the adolescent parent and her offspring (Mecklenburg & Thompson, 1983). A secondary goal of the act was to increase our knowledge about the educational, psychosocial, and economic consequences of adolescent pregnancy and childbearing for the adolescent mothers, their children, and their families. The University of California, San Diego (UCSD) Teen Obstetric (OB) Follow-Up Study began in 1987 as a grant-funded AFL demonstration program. The original goal of the Teen OB Follow-Up Study was to research factors related to adolescent prenatal care and maternal and infant health outcomes, and factors associated with short-interval repeat pregnancy among teenage mothers. This goal was later broadened to include researching issues related to the qualities of adolescent mothers' parenting and the role of the infant's father in the postpartum period. Analysis of these issues form the core of this book.

A secondary aim of the Teen OB Follow-Up Study was to address these issues while highlighting potential differences and similarities for adolescents of different racial and cultural backgrounds. The current sample includes, in particular, a large percentage of Hispanic adolescents—most of whom recently immigrated from Mexico—thus providing much needed data on the medical and psychosocial sequelae of adolescent pregnancy and childbearing for this ethnic population. Evidence indicates that Hispanic adolescent mothers have different medical and psychosocial problems than do White or Black teens (Felice, Shragg, James, & Hollingsworth, 1986, 1987), and that their recent immigrant status—common among many California Hispanics—makes them particularly vulnerable to receiving inadequate prenatal care and, consequently, to experiencing poor infant and maternal health outcomes. This is particularly significant given that, in California, Hispanic teenagers have a higher birthrate than do White and Black teenage women: In 1990, the birthrate for Hispanic 15- to 19-year-olds was 112.3 per 1,000 women, the birthrate of comparably aged Black teens was 101.0 per 1,000 women, and the birthrate of comparably aged White teens was 73.9 per 1,000 women (CDC, 1993). Moreover, in recent years, Hispanics have increased at a fivefold rate faster than the rest of the U.S. population (U.S. Bureau of the Census, 1988), totaling 20.1 million in 1985, or 8.2% of the U.S. population. Although the influx of Hispanics is concentrated mostly in California, which is 34% Hispanic, Texas (21%), Florida (12%), and New York (10%) also have sizeable percentages of Hispanic residents (U.S. Bureau of the Census, 1988). Thus, throughout this book we try to describe in particular the pregnancy and parenting experiences of our Hispanic adolescent subjects, most of whom recently—and oftentimes illegally—immigrated to the United States.

Before describing the methods and sample of the study, an update is provided on recent trends in adolescent pregnancy and childbearing within the United States, within the state of California, and within the city of San Diego.

## TRENDS IN ADOLESCENT PREGNANCY AND CHILDBEARING

### The United States

As stated previously, 1 million teenage women become pregnant in the United States every year, the vast majority unintentionally. Although the rate of teenage pregnancy has increased dramatically among all teens since the early 1970s, among sexually active adolescents, pregnancy rates have actually decreased 19% over the last two decades (Alan Guttmacher Institute, 1994b). This decline in pregnancy among sexually active teens is due in large part to better use of contraceptives. Recent estimates show that approximately 12% of all teenage girls (aged 15–19) become pregnant each year, whereas 21% of those who have had sexual intercourse (aged 15–19) become pregnant annually (Alan Guttmacher Institute, 1994b).

Regarding births resulting from teenage pregnancies, the percentage of teenage women who gave birth rose almost 19% from 1988 to 1990 (the last year for which statistics are currently available; Alan Guttmacher Institute, 1994b). The abortion rate among teens has remained fairly stable since the late 1970s, with approximately 43 teens per 1,000 opting for abortion. However, over that same time period, abortion rates have declined steadily among sexually experienced adolescent women, both because a lower proportion of teenagers became pregnant and because a lower proportion of pregnant teenagers choose to have an abortion (Alan Guttmacher Institute, 1994b; Henshaw, 1993; NCHS, 1993).

Racial differences exist in both the prevalence of adolescent pregnancy and adolescent childbearing (East & Felice, 1994; Henshaw et al., 1989; Hollingsworth & Felice, 1986; Moore, Simms, & Betsey, 1986). For example, Black teenagers have historically had a higher pregnancy rate than their Hispanic and White peers: 19% of all Black women aged 15 to 19 become pregnant each year, compared to 13% of Hispanics and 8% of Whites (Alan Guttmacher Institute, 1994b; NCHS, 1993). The higher pregnancy rate among Blacks is due to higher rates of sexually experienced individuals and because Blacks are considerably less likely than Whites and Hispanics to use a contraceptive or to use it effectively (NCHS, 1993). Every year, 32% of sexually experienced Black teenage women, compared with 26% of Hispanics and 15% of Whites, become pregnant (Alan Guttmacher Institute, 1994b). Similar to the pregnancy rate, the birthrate among Black adolescents in 1990 was almost four times that of White adolescents: 252 Black teens gave birth per 1,000 women versus 96 White teens per 1,000 women (Alan Guttmacher Institute, 1994b; NCHS, 1993). The birthrate of Hispanics fell in between, with 215 Hispanic teens per 1,000 giving birth (see Fig. 1.1).

What is particularly striking, however, is that since the mid-1980s, the birthrates for Latino and Black teenagers (aged 15–19) have increased at a significantly faster rate than that for teens overall (Alan Guttmacher Institute, 1994b). As shown in Table 1.1, the birthrate among Latina teenage women increased 45% since the mid-1980s; among Black teens the birthrate increased 31%. In contrast, among Whites, Asians, and teens of another ethnicity, there was only a 1% to 2% increase in the teenage birthrate. In recent years (1990–1993), Hispanics have surpassed Blacks in teenage birthrates.

## Teenage Pregnancy and Birthrates Within California

Overall, one in eight babies in California is born to a teenager, who is typically unwed and poor (NCHS, 1993). In 1988, California had the highest number of births, abortions, and pregnancies to women aged 15 to 19 than any other state for which data were available (Henshaw, 1993). When considering the rates of births, abortions, and pregnancies per 1,000 women aged 15 to 19, California had the highest teenage pregnancy rate and the highest teenage abortion rate. The state's teenage birthrate, however, was only slightly above the national rate because the state has such a high teenage abortion rate (Alan Guttmacher Institute, 1994b).

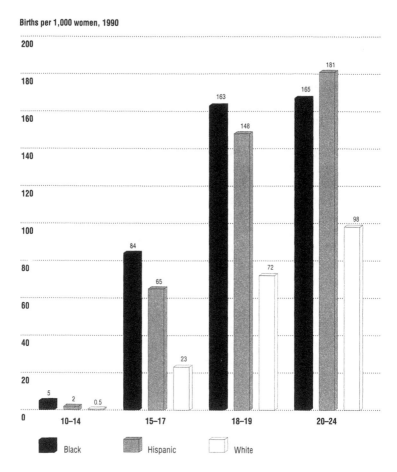

FIG. 1.1. Racial differences in birthrates. Reproduced with the permission of the Alan Guttmacher Institute from the Alan Guttmacher Institute, *Sex and America's Teenagers,* New York (1994b).

Table 1.1
Increased Birthrates Among 15- to 19-Year-Olds by Race/Ethnicity of Mother (Per 1,000 Women)

| Birthrates | 1983 | 1993 | % Change |
|---|---|---|---|
| Latino | 85.1 | 123.2 | +44.8 |
| African American | 75.0 | 97.9 | +30.5 |
| White | 35.6 | 36.2 | +1.7 |
| Asian and other | 30.3 | 30.6 | +1.0 |

*Source.* Alan Guttmacher Institute (1994b).

Births to Hispanic teenagers have increased dramatically in California since the mid-1980s, nearly doubling since 1980 (California Department of Health Services, 1994). Although birthrates for White, Black, and Asian teens dipped slightly in both 1990 and 1993, birthrates rose steadily among California's Hispanics. As shown in Table 1.2, in 1993, Hispanic teens comprised 60% of all teenage births in California; Whites accounted for 23%, Blacks accounted for 11%, and Asians and others accounted for 6% of all teenage births (Alan Guttmacher Institute, 1994a). The steady increase in the teenage birthrate among Hispanics is thought to stem from the chronic poverty of many of the state's Latinos. Poverty is pervasive among California's Hispanics due to the fact that many Latinos are recent immigrants into the country and many are not U.S. citizens. Although lack of citizenship does not preclude paid employment, such jobs are typically low pay and often involve hard, manual labor (California Department of Health Services, 1994).

When considering births to same-race women of all ages in California in 1986, Blacks had the highest percentage of teenage births, with 19% of all live births among Blacks occurring among teenagers (women age 19 or younger; Brindis & Jeremy, 1988). Hispanics had the second highest percentage of teenage births, with 15% of all live births among Hispanics occurring among teens. Eight percent of all White births were to teenagers. Within California, 11% of all births were to teenage women (Brindis & Jeremy, 1988).

## San Diego: The Ecological Setting

Understanding the geographic, demographic, and socioeconomic characteristics of the area helps illuminate the context within which our sample of teenage mothers live and puts the findings of this book into perspective. The city of San Diego, primarily a military base and tourist site, has consistently been ranked as the seventh largest city in the United States (U.S. Bureau of the Census, 1990, 1992), with more than 2.6 million residents in 1992. San Diego County covers a geographic area of more than 4,200 square miles, roughly equivalent in square miles to the state of Rhode Island, and shares a southern international border with Mexico. The county's population is growing at a rate of 3% per year, compared to the 2.2% growth rate of California, which is currently one of the fastest growing states in the nation. San Diego County has a particularly large child population (with 26% of the region's population 18 years of age or younger), and a large retired (12%) and military (6%) population base. San Diego County continues to have one of the least affordable major housing markets in the United States, and a higher Consumer Price Index than the national average (United Way of San Diego County, 1993).

In 1992, ethnic populations (Latino, Black, Asian/Pacific Islander, American Indian) comprised 35% of the county's total population, with Hispanics the predominate ethnic minority comprising 21% of the county population, Asians the next largest at 7%, and Blacks the third largest at 6%. The percentage of the Latino population is probably greatly underestimated, however, because undocumented aliens are not included in the census.

Table 1.2
Percentage of Births to Teenage Mothers in California
by Race/Ethnicity of Mother

| Race/Ethnicity | 1980 % | 1985 % | 1990 % | 1993 % |
|---|---|---|---|---|
| Hispanic | 40 | 43 | 54 | 60 |
| Non-Hispanic White | 40 | 36 | 28 | 23 |
| Black | 15 | 15 | 12 | 11 |
| Asian and other | 5 | 6 | 6 | 6 |

*Source.* Alan Guttmacher Institute (1994a).

In 1992, more than 11% of the county's residents were living in poverty. Although the overall poverty rate did not change significantly between 1980 and 1990, the number of children living in extreme poverty in San Diego County during that time increased by 57%. Approximately 18% of all county children are classified as "extremely poor" (i.e., in a family of three earning less than $694 per month) and receive Aid to Families with Dependent Children (AFDC) benefits (United Way of San Diego County, 1993). Statistics show that approximately 70,000 students in the county (approximately 17% of all children enrolled in public school) speak little or no English. Of this total, approximately 80% are Latino; the remaining students are primarily Vietnamese, Filipino, Cambodian, and Laotian.

## Teenage Pregnancy and Birthrates Within San Diego

In 1994, there were 5,369 births to teenage mothers in San Diego County, or about 15 births to adolescent girls each day. One hundred and five births were to mothers under 15 years of age or younger (2%); 33% of such births were to 15- to 17-year-olds, and; 65% were to 18- to 19-year-olds (San Diego County Department of Health Services, personal communication, 1995). The San Diego County birthrate for women aged 15 to 19 has hovered around 43.6 per 1,000 women since the early 1980s, slightly lower than the overall state birthrate of 53.2 per 1,000 women (Brindis & Jeremy, 1988). However, given the large population of San Diego County, it has consistently had the second highest number of births to teenage women in California, typically second only to Los Angeles County (Brindis & Jeremy, 1988).

Most of the county's teenage births are to Latina mothers (56%); Whites comprise 28% of all teenage births and Blacks comprised only 11% of all county teenage births (San Diego County Department of Health Services, personal communication, 1995). The teenage birthrates among 12- to 19-year-olds are 80 and 64 per 1,000 women for Hispanics and Blacks, respectively, and are nearly four times higher than the rate for Whites (18 per 1,000).

Let us turn now to a brief description of the methods used in the UCSD Teen OB Follow-Up Study. These methods are also elaborated further in chapters 2 through 6.

# THE UCSD TEEN OB FOLLOW-UP STUDY

## Sample

Participants for this study were 208 adolescent mothers (M age at delivery = 17.2 years; range = 14–18.8). Most adolescents described themselves as members of an ethnic/racial minority, with 40% of subjects identifying themselves as Hispanic (n = 84), 32% as Black (n = 66), 20% as Non-Hispanic-White (n = 42), and 8% from another or not reported race (n = 16). All subjects were followed prenatally and at 6-month intervals for 3½ years postpartum. Participants were recruited from one of two health care sites: the Teen OB Clinic at the UCSD Medical Center; or four surrounding community prenatal clinics within 20 miles of the UCSD Medical Center. Characteristics for the total sample and for the two recruitment sites are shown in Table 1.3.

Table 1.3
Sample Characteristics By Recruitment Site

| Sample Characteristic | Total Sample | Recruitment Site | | Recruitment Site Difference |
|---|---|---|---|---|
| | | Teen OB Clinic | Community Clinics | |
| Total | 208 | 109 | 99 | |
| Mean age at delivery | 17.18 | 17.01 | 17.37 | $t = 2.59^{**}$ |
| Standard deviaiton | (1.03) | (1.05) | (0.98) | |
| Race | | | | $\chi^2 (3) = 15.65^{**}$ |
| Number Hispanic (%) | 84 (40%) | 32 (29%) | 52 (53%) | |
| Number Black (%) | 66 (32%) | 44 (40%) | 22 (22%) | |
| Number White (%) | 42 (20%) | 21 (19%) | 21 (21%) | |
| Number other (%) | 16 (8%) | 12 (11%) | 4 (4%) | |
| Number married at intake (%) | 40 (19%) | 12 (11%) | 28 (28%) | $\chi^2 (1) = 9.29^{**}$ |
| Mean grade in school at intake | 9.66 | 9.62 | 9.71 | $t < 1$ |
| Standard deviation | (1.76) | (1.70) | (1.85) | |
| Mean years of education completed by teen's mother | 10.50 | 10.84 | 10.08 | $t = 2.38^{*}$ |
| Standard deviation | (2.00) | (1.81) | (2.15) | |
| Percent receiving governmental assistance | 30% | 40% | 19% | $\chi^2 (1) = 10.18^{**}$ |
| Gravida[a] | | | | $\chi^2 (3) = 11.10^{*}$ |
| 1 (%) | 73% | 67% | 79% | |
| 2 (%) | 18% | 26% | 10% | |
| ≥ 3 (%) | 5% | 6% | 3% | |

[a] Data on nine adolescents' gravida status (number of times pregnant) were missing.
* p < .05. **p < .01.

The UCSD Teen OB Clinic is a hospital-based collaborative program of the Departments of Pediatrics and Reproductive Medicine at the UCSD Medical Center, a tertiary-level care hospital located near downtown San Diego. The clinic was first established in 1979 and provides comprehensive prenatal and postpartum health care to young women aged 11 to 18. One hundred twenty-seven pregnant adolescents who presented consecutively to the Teen OB Clinic for prenatal care from October 1987 to January 1989 were recruited into the study. Eighteen of these teens were omitted from all analyses because they received extensive, aggressive individual prenatal and postpartum intervention as part of a special county-funded program. The experiences and outcomes of such young women would be expected to be different from the other adolescents involved in this study. Thus, the data of 109 adolescents recruited from the UCSD Teen OB Clinic were used for analyses. All teens at this site were recruited into the study at their first prenatal visit and had, thus, previously decided to continue with their pregnancies. The rate of program participation was very high (98%), with only two adolescents refusing to participate. Forty percent of teens recruited from the Teen OB Clinic were Black, 29% were Hispanic, 19% were Non-Hispanic-White, and the remainder (11%) were of another racial background (Southeast Asian, Filipino, American Indian). The mean age of participants at delivery was 17 years, with an age range of 14 to 18.8 years.

The second type of recruitment site were prenatal community clinics within 20 miles of the UCSD Medical Center. These clinics were all part of a countywide collaborative perinatal project with strong ties to the UCSD Medical Center. Ninety-nine teens were recruited from such community clinics at varying stages of their pregnancies and not necessarily at their first prenatal visit (unlike at the UCSD Teen OB Clinic). The rate of participation was also very high (> 80%) at these sites. More than half of the teens from community clinics described themselves as Hispanic (53%), 22% as Black, and 21% as Non-Hispanic-White. The mean age of teens at delivery was 17.4 years, with an age range of 14.7 to 18.8 years. All adolescents from both the UCSD Teen OB Clinic and from the surrounding community clinics delivered their babies at the UCSD Medical Center, thereby receiving identical perinatal and neonatal medical care.

Terms used to describe the ethnic/racial background of the current sample were purposefully chosen as *Hispanic*, *Black*, and *White*. Descriptors such as Mexican American and African American were not used because they do not accurately reflect the ethnic background of this study's participants. Most of the Hispanic adolescents were not U.S. citizens: 75% of this sample's Hispanics were Mexican nationals residing illegally within the United States at the time of their prenatal care. Moreover, two Hispanic teens were from Puerto Rico. Although most of the Black adolescents described their heritage as descending from Africa, two Black teens recently immigrated from the Caribbean, and one teen described her race as Black but her heritage was not African. Thus, the terms *Hispanic*, *Black*, and *White* are used throughout this book to describe the race and ethnicity of this study's participants.

## Subjects' Marital, Educational, and Financial Characteristics

As shown in Table 1.3, approximately one in five teens was married at intake and their mean highest grade level completed was ninth grade. For most participants (73%), this was their first pregnancy, although for almost a quarter of the sample (23%), this was at least their second pregnancy. Thirty percent of teens or their families were receiving some form of governmental assistance at intake or at their first prenatal visit (e.g., AFDC, WIC, food stamps, MediCal [California's form of Medicaid]). The low number of teens receiving public assistance at the time of clinic registration is probably a reflection of the large number of Hispanic teens who were undocumented immigrants and fearful of using government subsidies; this does not suggest that these teens were not low income. By 6 months postpartum, 78% of all teens were receiving some form of governmental assistance (AFDC, food stamps, WIC) and 44% were using governmental assistance as their primary means of income, although these figures may also underrepresent those eligible for assistance.

As can be observed in Table 1.3, there were several differences between the adolescents recruited from the hospital-based Teen OB Clinic and the adolescents recruited from the surrounding community prenatal clinics. Teens who received their prenatal care at the UCSD Teen OB Clinic were significantly more likely to be younger, Black, unmarried, from a higher socioeconomic status (SES; as indexed by the teen's mother's level of education), receiving some form of governmental assistance, and Gravida 2 or higher. (The difference in age may not be clinically significant, however, given that both groups were, on average, 17 and 17.4 years.) In contrast, teens recruited through the community clinics were more likely to be older, Hispanic, married, from a lower SES background, receiving no form of governmental assistance, and Gravida 1. The only similarity between the adolescents recruited from the two clinic sites was their mean grade level in school.

Further analyses revealed, however, that all but one of these recruitment site differences (participants' age) were largely a function of the different racial compositions of the two sites and were not a function of the recruitment site per se.[1] Given this, teens recruited from the UCSD Teen OB Clinic and teens recruited from the surrounding community clinics were merged to form this study's core sample of 208 adolescents. (Participants' age, which was associated with recruitment site, did not vary by race of adolescent. This is discussed further later.)

## Differences in Participant Characteristics By Race

Many racial differences were evident for participants' sociodemographic characteristics. These differences are shown in Table 1.4 for the 84 Hispanic teens, the 66 Black teens, and the 42 White teens. (The group of 16 teens who comprised the

---

[1]To determine if the differences in the sample characteristics between the two recruitment sites would be nonsignificant once racial effects were accounted for, an analysis of variance was computed using race and recruitment site as the independent variables and the six sample characteristics listed in Table 1.3 as the dependent variables. Results of the ANOVAs showed that site effects were nonsignificant for all six sample characteristics once racial effects had been accounted (all $Fs \leq 1.57$, ns).

Table 1.4
Racial Differences in Participants' Background Characteristics

| Sample Characteristic | Hispanic (n = 84) | Black (n = 66) | White (n = 42) | Racial Difference |
|---|---|---|---|---|
| Mean age at delivery | 17.14 | 17.18 | 17.29 | $F (2,188) < 1$ |
| Standard deviation | (1.00) | (1.03) | (1.06) | |
| Percent married at intake[+] | 29%[a,b] | 6%[a] | 13%[b] | $F (2,188) = 6.88**$ |
| Mean grade in school at intake | 9.07[a,b] | 10.24[a] | 9.80[b] | $F (2,188) = 8.53**$ |
| Standard deviation | (1.75) | (1.24) | (2.12) | |
| Mean years of education completed by teen's mother | 8.89[a,b] | 11.63[a] | 11.68[b] | $F (2,188) = 59.16**$ |
| Standard deviation | (2.00) | (1.81) | (2.15) | |
| Percent receiving governmental assistance | 20% | 61% | 26% | $\chi^2 (2) = 28.33**$ |
| Gravida | | | | $\chi^2 (2) = 7.13*$ |
| 1 (%) | 82% | 67% | 86% | |
| 2+ (%) | 18% | 33% | 14% | |

Note. Means with the same letter superscript in the same row are significantly different.

[+] Coded as 1 = married, 0 = unmarried to compute the F statistic.

*$p < .05$. **$p < .001$. [a]Hispanic–Black contrast. [b]Hispanic–White contrast.

"other" racial category was deemed too small for reliable analysis and too hetero-geneous to be informative and, thus, was not included in these analyses.) Although there were no racial differences in participants' age, Hispanic teens were most likely to be married while pregnant, Whites next most likely, and Blacks least likely to be married while pregnant. Regarding mean grade level in school, Black teens had completed more schooling than had Hispanic teens. White teens fell in the middle, with an average grade level significantly higher than that of Hispanics, but not significantly different from that of Blacks. Because there were no racial differences in adolescents' mean age, this would suggest the possibility that White and Hispanic teens were more likely to have been held back a grade than their Black peers. Subsequent analyses confirmed this, with a trend for more Hispanic adolescents (35%) and White adolescents (24%) to have repeated a grade than Black adoles-cents [18%; $\chi^2(2) = 5.27, p < .06$].

Racial differences were also apparent for the educational background of partici-pants' families. The mothers of White adolescents and the mothers of Black adolescents had completed significantly more schooling than had the mothers of Hispanic adolescents. This most likely reflects the fact that many Hispanics residing in San Diego County are illegal immigrants from Mexico for whom the option of continuing their education or returning to school once they have crossed the U.S.–Mexico border is not available. This difference may also reflect country-spe-cific factors such as laws about school attendance, with fewer years of schooling required in Mexico than is required in the United States. Regarding financial support, Black teens were significantly more likely to already be on welfare or receiving some form of governmental assistance while pregnant than were White or Hispanic teens. As stated previously, this difference found for receipt of governmental assistance is likely to be due to the illegal immigrant status of many Hispanic subjects for whom access to the many forms of governmental financial assistance is not available. This finding may also be attributed to the greater likelihood that Black teens were already teen mothers at intake: 21% of Black teens had previously had children; 15% of Hispanic teens and only 5% of White teens had previously had children. (Although the difference in these percentages was not statistically significant; $\chi^2[2] = 2.65$, ns.

## Overview of Design

As part of the Teen OB Follow-Up Study, several measures were compiled on and about the adolescent women, their families, their infants, and the fathers of the infants. These measures were obtained via interview with the adolescent, self-report on questionnaires, and from medical records at the following eight times of assessment: at intake (which was the first prenatal visit for Teen OB clients and, prenatally but not necessarily at the first prenatal visit for participants recruited from the community clinics), and at 6, 12, 18, 24, 30, 36, and 42 months postpartum. Follow-up rates are shown in Table 1.5. Follow-up was not related to mothers' age nor race, with consistent percentages of all racial groups participating at each assessment point. As shown in Table 1.5, most assessments were conducted within 3 months of the scheduled follow-up, and children's mean ages were approximately at the scheduled time of follow-up (i.e., 6.7 months, 12.3 months, 18.3 months, 24.3 months, 30.7 months, and 36.7 months). Because less than 64% of the 208 participants completed the 42-month assessment ($n = 134$), and because of

Table 1.5
Sample at Each Follow-Up (Excluding the 42-Month Follow-Up)

|  | 6 months | 12 months | 18 months | 24 months | 30 months | 36 months |
|---|---|---|---|---|---|---|
| Total | 193 | 168 | 161 | 171 | 164 | 143 |
| Follow-up rate | 93% | 81% | 77% | 82% | 79% | 69% |
| Mean age of infant | 6.66 | 12.30 | 18.34 | 24.31 | 30.74 | 36.67 |
| Standard deviation | (1.41) | (1.39) | (2.65) | (1.44) | (2.02) | (1.85) |
| Percent +/- 3 months | 100% | 98% | 98% | 96% | 90% | 90% |
| Mother's race | H B W O | H B W O | H B W O | H B W O | H B W O | H B W O |
| Total | 84 61 35 13 | 74 53 29 12 | 72 52 25 12 | 77 52 30 12 | 67 46 39 12 | 60 43 29 11 |
| Percent of total sample | 44 32 18 7 | 44 36 17 7 | 45 32 16 7 | 45 30 18 7 | 41 28 24 7 | 42 30 20 8 |

Note. H indicates Hispanic; B indicates Black; W indicates White, and; O indicates an Other race.

potential selectivity problems associated with low follow-up (Stahler & DuCette, 1991), this last assessment point was not included in any analyses of this book. Finally, because the issues addressed in each chapter used different measures, all relevant measures are described separately in each chapter. It should be noted, however, that all participants were assured of the confidentiality of their responses, and that teens were not paid for their participation. Instead, the participants were given gifts as tokens of our appreciation of their time and effort in participating (e.g., baby items such as baby shampoo, baby food, and baby powder, and items for women, such as shampoo, make-up, and nail polish).

## OVERVIEW OF CHAPTERS

In the following chapters, we report on aspects of the teenagers' prenatal care, maternal and infant health outcomes, their parenting, and their partners. In each chapter, we include analyses that examine the similarities and differences among Hispanic, Black, and White adolescents in their pregnancy and parenting outcomes. For example, in chapter 2, "Prenatal Care and Maternal and Infant Health Outcomes," we focus on adolescents' general health during their pregnancies and their infants' neonatal outcomes. We address to what extent the pregnancy characteristics of all adolescents in the sample (e.g., gestational age, weight gain during pregnancy) relate to their infants' neonatal outcomes (e.g., infant birthweight, Apgar scores), and whether pregnancy and neonatal health outcomes vary by mothers' age, race, or marital status. We also discern how drug use during pregnancy relates to pregnancy and neonatal complications.

In chapter 3, "Short-Interval Repeat Pregnancy," we examine the mothers who became pregnant again within 6 months postpartum (15% of the sample) and the mothers who became pregnant again within 18 months postpartum (35%). Subsequent pregnancies of adolescent mothers have been related to even more adverse health, social, and economic consequences than a first birth, including a higher incidence of low birthweight babies and a higher rate of infant mortality (Darabi, Graham, & Philliber, 1982; McCormick, Shapiro, & Stanfield, 1984). These risks of subsequent pregnancy are even greater when the pregnancy takes place within 6 months of an earlier birth (Atkin & Alatorre-Rico, 1992; McCormick et al., 1984). Using data from this study, we sought to identify the prenatal, postpartum, and infant characteristics that might be related to immediate repeat pregnancy, which we defined as within 6 months postpartum.

In chapter 4, "Qualities of Adolescent Mothers' Parenting," we focus on qualities of adolescent mothers' parenting. We determine the interrelations among adolescent mothers' parenting attitudes, parenting commitment, parenting knowledge, parenting involvement, parenting confidence, and parenting stress, and the potential differences in these parenting qualities by mothers' age, race, and parity, and age and gender of child. We also discern how such qualities of adolescent mothers' parenting are consequential for their children's behavioral adjustment.

Chapter 5, "The Role of Grandmothers in Adolescent Mothers' Parenting and Children's Outcomes," takes a closer look at adolescent mothers' parenting and children's outcomes as a function of grandmothers' coresidence, the extent of grandmother-provided child-care assistance and grandmother–adolescent conflict. In this sample, 40% of teens resided with their mothers at some point within 2 years following delivery. We examine how coresidence varies by mothers' age, race, and marital status, and to what extent coresidence is linked with grandmothers' assistance with child care and grandmother–adolescent conflict. We also investigate the links between grandmothers' coresidence, grandmother-provided child care, and grandmother–adolescent conflict and qualities of adolescent mothers' parenting (e.g., their parenting stress, parenting confidence, and involvement with their children's care) and their children's behavioral outcomes.

In chapter 6, "The Partners of Adolescent Mothers," we focus on the "forgotten partner" in the pregnancy (Sander & Rosen, 1987), the father of the infant. Similar to other studies (Buhlmann, Felice, Shragg, & Hollingsworth, 1988; Hardy, Duggan, Masynk, & Pearson, 1989; Robinson, 1988), approximately half of the current sample of adolescent mothers had partners who were 20 years of age or older and, thus, not necessarily teenagers themselves. We capitalize on this feature of the sample and compare adolescent fathers to adult fathers on a number of characteristics including their financial commitment to the mother and child, their level of relationship commitment to the mother, and their involvement in child care in the postpartum period. We found many similarities between adult and adolescent fathers, yet some differences also emerged between older and younger fathers. We also examined how fathers' financial commitment, relationship commitment to the teen, and child care involvement were related to their children's behavioral adjustment as assessed at 3 years of age.

Finally, in chapter 7, "Summary and Conclusions," we summarize our findings and share with the reader the lessons we learned from the current project. We discuss the implications of the study's results and how the current findings can be used to inform programs and policies related to pregnant and parenting teenagers. The limitations and strengths of the study are noted, and suggestions are offered for future research and for future intervention programs.

# Chapter 2

## Prenatal Care and Maternal and Infant Health Outcomes

80 ◆ 03

Adolescent pregnancies are more likely to result in a poor outcome for both mother and baby than pregnancies in adult women. Adolescent mothers are at increased risk for mortality and pregnancy-induced hypertension, and their babies are at increased risk for prematurity, low birthweight, and mortality in the first year of life (Brown, Fan, & Gonsoulin, 1991; Friede et al., 1987; Hayes, 1987; McAnarney et al., 1978). It is unclear whether the adverse outcomes are a result of biological or environmental factors—an issue that is currently a topic of controversy in the teen pregnancy literature (Fraser, Brockert, & Ward, 1995; Goldenberg & Klerman, 1995; Hughes & Simpson, 1995).

Biologically, several factors have been theorized to explain poor pregnancy outcome in adolescents, including a low gynecological age (conception within 2 years of menarche; Erkan, Rimer, & Stine, 1971; Zlatnik & Burmeister, 1977), incomplete growth in height (Scholl, Hediger, Ances, & Cronk, 1988), and low prepregnancy weight and poor weight gain (Haiek & Lederman, 1989). But only low prepregnancy weight and poor weight gain have been consistently associated with low birthweight infants (Goldenberg & Klerman, 1995). Many environmental factors have been associated with poor birth outcomes including poverty, unmarried status, low educational levels, and inadequate prenatal care (Ahmad, 1990; Ketterlinus, Henderson, & Lamb, 1990); pregnant adolescents are more likely to be poor, single, uneducated (Trussell, 1988) and are less likely to receive early prenatal care (Kinsman & Slap, 1992). Perhaps in adolescents it is a combination of both biological and social factors that lead to poor outcomes.

In this chapter, we present outcome data for both mothers and babies with attention to both biological and environmental factors. For example, we examine a number of prenatal maternal characteristics, such as the incidence of specific pregnancy complications, pregnancy weight gain, prenatal drug use, and quality

**14**

of prenatal care. The major neonatal outcomes studied were prematurity, low birthweight, and neonatal functioning as assessed by 1-and 5-minute Apgar scores. We examined all of these factors as a function of mothers' age, race, and marital status.

# METHOD

## Overview of Sample

As noted in chapter 1, the mean age of the teens at delivery was 17.2 years with an age range of 14.7 to 18.8 years. Approximately one in five of the teens was married at the time of the first prenatal visit, and 30% were receiving some form of governmental assistance (AFDC, WIC, food stamps, MediCal). As stated previously, this low number of teens receiving public assistance at intake does not suggest that the teens in this study were not low income but, rather, may reflect the large number of Hispanics who are undocumented immigrants and hesitant to use governmental subsidies. For 75% of the sample, this was their first pregnancy. For the most part, teens were young, unmarried, and pregnant for the first time.

## Measures

All of the health-related data discussed in this chapter were obtained by medical chart review. This was conducted by either the study nurse or a trained medical student soon after the teen gave birth. After the nurse or medical student reviewed the patient's and her baby's hospital chart, the nurse or medical student completed a lengthy questionnaire that asked about specific health conditions of the teen and her baby. The assessment and reliability of particular data are discussed further later.

# RESULTS

## Prenatal Care Issues

Because it has been well documented that optimal obstetrical and neonatal health outcomes are directly correlated with the provision of appropriate prenatal care, particularly among low-income, minority, and young women (Felice et al., 1981; McAnarney et al., 1978; Scholl, Hediger, & Belsky, 1994), it is important to note that most of the teenagers in this study received comprehensive and interdisciplinary care from medical, obstetrical, nursing, social work, and nutrition specialists. All deliveries were at the same tertiary care hospital with ready availability of sophisticated perinatal services including obstetrical and neonatal intensive care as needed.

As seen in Table 2.1, 65% of the teenagers initiated prenatal care in the first or second trimester (before 25 weeks gestation). The mean number of prenatal visits was 9.2 with nearly half the young women having more than 9 visits. This relatively early entry into

Table 2.1
Descriptive Statistics Associated With Pregnancy
and Neonatal Characteristics of the Sample

| Characteristic | Mean | % |
|---|---|---|
| Trimester[a] sought prenatal care | 2.13 | 19% first trimester |
| | | 46% second trimester |
| | | 34% third trimester |
| | | 1% no care |
| No. of prenatal visits | 9.23 | 45% > 9 visits |
| | | 25% 7–9 visits |
| | | 20% 4–6 visits |
| | | 10% 3 or fewer |
| Weight gained | 34.53 lbs ± 15.79 (SD) | |
| Weeks gestation (Dubowitz) | 39.19 weeks; range = 24–43 wks | |
| Baby's birthweight (in grams) | 3,276 | 6% < 2,500 gms |
| | | 18% < 2,900 and ≥ 2,500 |
| | | 48% < 3,500 ≥ 2,900 |
| | | 18% ≥ 3,500 |
| Apgar 1 | 7.73 | 30% 9 (no10s) |
| | | 57% 7,8 |
| | | 7% 5,6 |
| | | 6% ≤ 4 |
| Apgar 5 | 8.75 | 84% 9, 10 |
| | | 14% 7, 8 |
| | | 1.5% 5, 6 |
| | | 0.5% ≤ 4 |

[a] The mean was derived using codes of 1, 2, and 3 for the first, second, and third trimesters, respectively.

prenatal care and frequent visits are probably a reflection of the adolescent-friendly nature of the prenatal programs that were particularly sensitive to cultural and age appropriate issues.

## Neonatal Outcomes

The major neonatal outcomes studied were prematurity, low birthweight, and neonatal distress. Prematurity was defined as a birth at or less than 37 weeks using Dubowitz criteria (Dubowitz, Dubowitz, & Goldberg, 1970) that incorporates established age norms of physical and neuromotor characteristics of the newborn to estimate gestational age. Low birthweight was defined as less than 2,500 grams. Neonatal distress was defined as an Apgar score of 5 or less at 5 minutes after birth.

One infant died within hours of birth due to prematurity. The infant's mother tested positive for drug use at delivery and reported using heroin occasionally throughout her pregnancy. Although there were no maternal mortalities at birth, one teen contracted hemolytic uremic syndrome at delivery and went on permanent kidney dialysis immediately after delivery. She died 12 months later.

As seen in Table 2.1, the mean gestational age was 39.19 weeks with a range of 24 to 43 weeks. The mean birthweight was 3,276 grams with only 6% of the sample weighing less than 2,500 grams. In fact, in this patient group, nearly one fifth of the babies weighed 3,500 grams or more. In 98% of the infants, the Apgar score at 5 minutes was 7 or greater. In general, these figures suggest that as a whole the infants were healthy, normal size, and full-term.

## Weight Gain

All the pregnant teenagers had access to dietitians experienced with adolescents and pregnancy. All the girls were referred for WIC services as soon as possible after the initial screening. Although the Food and Nutrition Board of the Institute of Medicine (IOM, 1990) recommends that pregnant women gain between 22 and 27 pounds (10–12 kilograms) during pregnancy, it is controversial as to how much weight pregnant teenagers should gain (Meserole, Worthington-Roberts, Rees, & Wright, 1984). The total weight gained during pregnancy was determined by asking each girl at her first prenatal visit what her weight was before she became pregnant and then subtracting that weight from the weight recorded at the last prenatal visit prior to delivery. This method of patient report has been found to be fairly accurate, particularly in average weight teens (Stevens-Simons, Roghmann, & McAnarney, 1992).

In the 93 patients for whom weight gain data were available, the mean weight gain was 34.53 pounds (+/– 15.79 pounds) with a range of –12 pounds to +72.5 pounds. Two teenagers lost weight: one lost 12 pounds and the other lost 9 pounds. Twenty-two percent of the sample gained less than 20 pounds and 51% gained more than 35 pounds, findings that are consistent with previous reports from this clinic (Felice et al., 1986). Table 2.2 presents a comparison of the girls who had poor weight gain (< 20 lbs) with all the others. It is clear from this table that low weight gain was associated with poor neonatal outcome. Girls who gained less than 20 pounds had significantly smaller babies, with lower Apgar scores at 5 minutes, and higher levels of prematurity (25% were premature). Teens with poor weight gain tended to be younger than the others and to have fewer prenatal visits, which may contribute further to the poor outcome. Neither marital status nor race were linked to weight gain.

## Medical Complications of Teen Mothers

Table 2.3 presents a list of the prevalence of prenatal, labor, and delivery complications by race of mother. For some data analyses we have used the total number of pregnancy complications listed here, rather than individual complications. The definition of each complication (not previously described) is as follows:

Table 2.2
Weight Gained During Pregnancy and Adolescents' Demographic, Prenatal,
and Neonatal Characteristics

| Outcomes | Gained ≤ 20 lbs (n = 20) | Gained > 20 lbs (n = 73) | F (1,91) |
|---|---|---|---|
| Age at delivery | 16.48 | 17.07 | 5.13* |
| | (1.19) | (0.98) | |
| Percent Married | 5% | 8% | $\chi^2$ (1) < 1 |
| Race | | | |
| Percent African American | 24% | 76% | $\chi^2$ (2) < 1 |
| Percent Hispanic | 19% | 81% | |
| Percent Caucasian | 20% | 80% | |
| Trimester sought care | 2.25 | 2.32 | < 1 |
| | (0.72) | (0.62) | |
| No. of prenatal visits | 7.15 | 9.18 | 4.70* |
| | (3.70) | (3.71) | |
| No. of pregnancy complications | 3.00 | 2.66 | < 1 |
| | (2.25) | (1.49) | |
| Gestational age (Dubowitz) | 38.08 | 39.34 | 7.26** |
| | (3.56) | (0.99) | |
| Percent Premature (<37 weeks) | 25% | 2% | $\chi^2$ (1) = 14.31*** |
| Apgar 1 | 7.20 | 7.67 | 1.81 |
| | (2.12) | (1.57) | |
| Apgar 5 | 8.35 | 8.82 | 7.36** |
| | (1.14) | (0.51) | |
| Birthweight (grams) | 2,832 | 3,355 | 17.37*** |
| | (693) | (431) | |
| Percent Low birthweight (< 2,500 grams) | 25% | 0% | $\chi^2$ (1) = 19.29*** |

Note. Standard deviations are in parenthesis.
*$p < .05$. **$p < .01$. ***$p < .001$.

| | |
|---|---|
| Anemia: | Hematocrit < 35% |
| Goiter: | Palpable thyroid > 6.5 cm |
| RH Negative: | Presence of RH antibodies at first visit screen |
| Rubella Negative: | Seronegative screen at first visit |
| Urinary Tract Infection (UTI): | Growth of > 100,000 colonies of one strain of organism |
| Hypertension: | Blood pressure > 140/90 or an increase in systolic pressure by ≥ 20 mmHg or an increase in diastolic pressure ≥ 15 mmHg |

Pregnancy Induced
Hypertension (PIH): Hypertension as defined above after 24 weeks gestation with proteinuria and edema

Respiratory Infection: Symptoms of rhinorrhea, pharyngitis, sinusitis, or cough

Other Infections: Sexually transmitted diseases (STDs), skin infections, etc. exclusive of respiratory infections

Trauma: History of a significant traumatic episode during pregnancy necessitating a visit to the physician (e.g., automobile accident, assault, fall, etc.)

Vaginal Bleeding: Vaginal bleeding of any cause anytime during the pregnancy

Placenta Previa: Vaginal bleeding secondary to placental tissue being at or over the internal os (opening) of the cervix

**Table 2.3**
**Prevalence of Prenatal, Labor and Delivery Complications
by Race of Mother**

| | Hispanic (n = 84) | Black (n = 66) | White (n = 42) |
|---|---|---|---|
| Prenatal Complication | | | |
| Anemia | 43 | 56 | 39 |
| Goiter | 0 | 4 | 0 |
| RH negative* | 3 | 8 | 13 |
| Rubella negative | 8 | 8 | 8 |
| UTI | 12 | 17 | 18 |
| Hypertension | 11 | 10 | 11 |
| PIH | 7 | 10 | 8 |
| Respiratory infection | 17 | 23 | 21 |
| Other infectious disease** | 43 | 71 | 55 |
| Trauma | 1 | 2 | 5 |
| Labor and Delivery | | | |
| Vaginal bleeding | 7 | 15 | 8 |
| Placenta previa | 0 | 0 | 0 |
| C-Section | 10 | 12 | 11 |
| Prematurity[a] | 5 | 7 | 8 |
| Low birthweight[b] | 7 | 5 | 7 |

Note. Numbers represent percentages of adolescents experiencing the complication. See definition of complications in text.

* $\chi^2$ (2) = 4.68, p < .10.

** $\chi^2$ (2) = 9.59, p = .008.

[a]Defined as less than 37 weeks.

[b]Defined as less than 2,500 grams.

As noted, there were no significant differences among the three racial groups for prevalence of complications except other infectious diseases. In this category, more Black teenagers had infectious diseases than the other two groups ($p < .01$). Approximately 40% to 60% of each group was anemic. Approximately 12% of all deliveries resulted in a Caesarian (C) Section (usually for cephalopelvic disproportion or failure to progress in labor). This C-Section rate has remained relatively stable for pregnant teenagers seen at the UCSD Medical Center over the past decade (Felice et al., 1986).

The prematurity rates and low birthweight rates were very low for all three racial groups ranging from 5% to 8%, including Black teens who are usually reported to have high rates of prematurity and low birthweights in other studies (Alo, Howe, & Nelson, 1993; McAnarney & Hendee, 1989; Wegman, 1993). For example, in all first births to Baltimore adolescents in 1983, the frequency of low birthweight in Black babies was more than double that of White babies (16% vs. 7%; Hardy & Zabin, 1991). This was not true in this San Diego population. We have speculated that the reason for this fortunate outcome is that so many of the girls received early and comprehensive prenatal care, which has been shown to be the single most important preventive measure to reduce poor infant outcome (Wegman, 1993).

## Correlations Among Pregnancy Characteristics and Neonatal Outcomes

Table 2.4 shows the correlations among selected pregnancy characteristics and neonatal outcomes. There are no surprising findings in these correlations. For example, infants whose mothers had a high number of medical complications spent more days in the special care nursery ($r = .34$, $p < .001$); babies with higher gestational ages at birth had higher birthweights ($r = .57$, $p < .001$). It is interesting to note, however, that young maternal age was associated with later prenatal care, less weight gain during pregnancy, and babies who spent more days in special care. Too, a low SES (as indexed by the number of years of schooling completed by the teen's mother) was related only to fewer prenatal visits. We speculate that this correlation may be a reflection of the inadequate transportation services available to poorer patients. San Diego County covers a geographic area roughly equivalent in square miles to the state of Rhode Island. Public transportation is minimal and access to an automobile is essential. Perhaps patients from low SES missed more appointments because they could not always find transportation to the clinic site for their scheduled appointments (Siegel, Thomas, Coulter, Tuthill, & Chipman, 1971).

## Pregnancy and Neonatal Characteristics by Race of Mother

Table 2.5 presents some pregnancy and neonatal characteristics by the race of the mother. In this table, substance use was indexed as follows: cigarette smoking during pregnancy was coded as: 1 = none; 2 = less than one pack per day; 3 = approximately one pack per day; and 4 = more than one pack per day. Alcohol use during pregnancy

## Table 2.4
### Correlations Among Pregnancy Characteristics and Neonatal Outcomes

| | Age | SES | Trimester of Care | No. of visits | Weight gained | No. of preg. compl. | Weeks gest. | Birthweight | Apgar 1 | Apgar 5 |
|---|---|---|---|---|---|---|---|---|---|---|
| 1. Age at delivery | | | | | | | | | | |
| 2. SES+ | -.09 | | | | | | | | | |
| 3. Trimester of care | -.16* | -.02 | | | | | | | | |
| 4. No. pren. visits | .14* | -.14* | -.47*** | | | | | | | |
| 5. Weight gained | .18** | .03 | -.02 | .23** | | | | | | |
| 6. No. of preg. comp. | .07 | .04 | .11 | -.05 | -.18** | | | | | |
| 7. Weeks gest. | .12 | -.05 | .11 | .22** | .26*** | -.09 | | | | |
| 8. Birthweight | .01 | .01 | .02 | .31*** | .41*** | -.18* | .57*** | | | |
| 9. Apgar 1 | -.08 | -.09 | .02 | .08 | .03 | -.11 | .34*** | .15* | | |
| 10. Apgar 5 | -.01 | -.05 | .03 | .07 | .21** | -.06 | .64*** | .32*** | .69*** | |
| 11. Days special care nursery | -.18** | .09 | .11 | -.17* | -.39*** | .34*** | -.57*** | -.53*** | -.23*** | -.35*** |

Note. Bonferroni-adjusted probability values were used to gauge statistical significance.

+ Indexed by number of years of education completed by adolescent's mother.

*p < .05.   **p<.01.   ***p<.001.

21

Table 2.5
Pregnancy and Neonatal Characteristics by Race of Mother

| | Hispanic (n = 84) | Black (n = 66) | White (n = 42) | F (2,188) |
|---|---|---|---|---|
| **Pregnancy Characteristics** | | | | |
| Age at delivery | 17.14 | 17.18 | 17.29 | < 1 |
| Percent married at intake[+] | 29%$^{ab}$ | 6%$^{a}$ | 13%$^{b}$ | 6.88*** |
| SES[++] | 8.89$^{ab}$ | 11.63$^{a}$ | 11.68$^{b}$ | 59.16*** |
| Trimester sought prenatal care | 2.23 | 2.20 | 1.86 | 2.59 |
| No. prenatal visits | 9.58 | 8.77 | 10.11 | < 1 |
| Weight gained during pregnancy | 37.21 | 32.21 | 35.26 | < 1 |
| **Drug Use During Pregnancy** | | | | |
| Cigarette use | 1.10$^{b}$ | 1.27$^{c}$ | 1.49$^{b,c}$ | 6.47** |
| Alcohol use | 1.08 | 1.03 | 1.10 | < 1 |
| Marijuana | 0.07$^{b}$ | 0.19$^{c}$ | 0.50$^{b,c}$ | 3.83* |
| Cocaine | 0.05 | 0.16 | 0.16 | < 1 |
| Crack | 0.00 | 0.12 | 0.00 | 1.76 |
| Crystal | 0.13$^{b}$ | 0.05$^{c}$ | 0.62$^{b,c}$ | 5.96** |
| Speed | 0.00 | 0.00 | 0.07 | 2.18 |
| PCP | 0.13 | 0.00 | 0.12 | 1.72 |
| **Neonatal Outcomes** | | | | |
| No. pregnancy compl. | 2.20 | 2.23 | 2.15 | < 1 |
| Weeks gestation | 39.37 | 38.98 | 39.12 | < 1 |
| Birthweight (gms.) | 3325 | 3168$^{c}$ | 3421$^{c}$ | 2.98* |
| Apgar 1 | 7.95 | 7.48 | 7.51 | 1.95 |
| Apgar 5 | 8.81 | 8.59 | 8.77 | 1.20 |
| Days in special care nursery | 0.76 | 1.98 | 4.93 | 1.67 |

Note. Means with the same letter superscript in the same row are significantly different.

[+]Coded as 0 = unmarried, 1 = married to compute the F statistic.

[++]Indexed by number of years of education completed by adolescent's mother.

*$p < .05$. **$p < .01$. ***$p < .001$.

[a]Hispanic–Black contrast.

[b]Hispanic–White contrast.

[c]Black–White contrast.

was coded as: 1 = *none*; 2 = *occasionally* (2–3 times per month); 3 = *weekly*; and 4 = *daily*. Drug use (i.e., of marijuana, cocaine, crack, crystal, speed, PCP) during pregnancy was coded as: 0 = *never used*; 1 = *used once or twice during pregnancy*; 2 = *occasionally* (about once a month or once every 2 months); 3 = *frequently* (about twice a month); and 4 = *often* (weekly or daily).

In this sample, there were no significant differences among the three racial groups in age at delivery, trimester initiating care, number of prenatal visits, or weight gain during the pregnancy. However, Hispanic girls were more likely to be married and to have lower socioeconomic backgrounds as indexed by mother's education ($p < .001$). These findings are consistent with previous reports from this clinic (Felice et al., 1986, 1987). There were no differences in neonatal outcomes for the three groups except that the Black infants weighed less at birth than the White infants, a common finding in many studies (Wegman, 1993). However, even the Black babies in this study were clearly more than 2,500 grams.

## Substance Use

All teenage girls were asked about their cigarette, alcohol, and illicit drug use at the first prenatal visit and at several times during the course of prenatal care. These questions were asked in a caring, nonjudgmental way by experienced nursing and/or social work staff as well as by physicians. Using these self-report data, we note that very few adolescents admitted to illicit drug use and that cigarette and alcohol use were in low amounts. These self-reports of substance use were lower than most other reports on pregnant teenagers in the literature (Gillmore, Butler, Lohr, & Gilchrist, 1992; Kokotailo, Adger, Duggan, Repke, & Joffe, 1992). We appreciate the limitations of substance use data based on self-report (Zuckerman, Amaro, & Cabral, 1989); however, a recent study on a similar but separate sample from the UCSD Teen OB Clinic (Hall et al., 1993) using a standardized self-report instrument and urine sample assays taken at intake and at delivery also showed very low substance use prevalence rates during pregnancy. In fact, results in that study showed substantially lower prevalence of substance use during pregnancy when compared to lifetime prevalence. We believe that the pregnant adolescents in this study, like some adolescents in other settings (Pletsch, 1988), were aware of the risks to themselves and their infants if they engaged in drug use, so they chose not to do so. It is also possible that our teens were simply not high risk for substance abuse. For those pregnant teens who did engage in substance use (licit or illicit), non-Hispanic White teens were more likely than Black or Hispanic teens to smoke cigarettes, to use marijuana, and to use crystal while pregnant. This is consistent with previous reports from this clinic (Felice et al., 1986, 1987).

Table 2.6 shows correlations among teens' substance use during pregnancy and their pregnancy and neonatal outcomes. Some findings of note are that crack and cocaine use during pregnancy were particularly deleterious for length of gestation and neonatal functioning (i.e., 5-minute Apgar scores). Also of note is that, as shown in the upper-half of Table 2.6, both licit and illicit drug use were highly intercorrelated. This is quite common among drug-using adolescents (Newcomb & Bentler, 1989) and pregnant teens (Kokotailo et al., 1992). Substance use was not, however, correlated with age of the adolescent or SES (not shown in Table 2.6). Thus, the correlations found to be significant with drug use are not likely to be confounded by young maternal age or low SES, a finding also reported by McCarthy and Hardy (1993). Drug use during pregnancy was also not correlated with trimester of prenatal care or weight gain during pregnancy (not shown). However, there was a negative correlation between marijuana use and number of prenatal visits ($r = -.15, p < .05$).

Table 2.6

Correlations Among Drug Use During Pregnancy and Neonatal Outcomes

| | 1 | 2 | 3 | 4 | 5 | 6 | 7 | 8 |
|---|---|---|---|---|---|---|---|---|
| Drug Use | | | | | | | | |
| 1. Cigarettes | | | | | | | | |
| 2. Alcohol | .27*** | | | | | | | |
| 3. Marijuana | .54*** | .36*** | | | | | | |
| 4. Cocaine | .52*** | .10 | .70*** | | | | | |
| 5. Crack | .46*** | -.02 | .60*** | .73*** | | | | |
| 6. Crystal | .32*** | .23*** | .67*** | .45*** | — | | | |
| 7. Speed | .28*** | .55*** | .37*** | .42*** | — | .26*** | | |
| 8. PCP | .03 | -.03 | -.02 | .51*** | — | .53*** | -.01 | |
| Outcomes | | | | | | | | |
| 9. No. preg. compl. | .19*** | .23*** | .16* | .11 | .06 | .14* | -.01 | .17* |
| 10. Weeks gestation | .16 | .03 | -.16 | -.24*** | -.43*** | .11 | — | -.01 |
| 11. Birthweight | .12 | .02 | -.06 | -.19** | -.31*** | -.15* | -.00 | .03 |
| 12. Apgar 1 | -.15* | -.07 | -.12 | -.15* | -.24*** | .08 | .06 | .08 |
| 13. Apgar 5 | -.23*** | .01 | -.24*** | -.37*** | -.59*** | .05 | .03 | .05 |
| 14. Days special care nurs. | .05 | .03 | -.02 | -.03 | — | -.03 | — | -.03 |

Note. Some correlations could not be reliably computed due to insufficient variance. Bonferroni-adjusted probability values were used to gauge statistical significance.

*p < .05.  **p < .01.  ***p < .001.

## Marital Status

Table 2.7 lists pregnancy and neonatal characteristics by mother's marital status at registration for prenatal care. Although most characteristics were similar for the two groups, married adolescents appeared to fare better than unmarried teens in key areas. Specifically, married teens were older than unmarried teens ($p < .05$), but this may not have clinical significance because the mean age of both groups was a little over 17 years. The infants of the married teens had higher Dubowitz scores ($p < .05$), but again this may not have clinical significance because both groups of infants were over 39 weeks gestation. However, it is important to note that the infants of unmarried teens were more likely to spend more days in the special care nursery ($p < .02$).

Marital status is a difficult issue to analyze in terms of outcome in adolescent pregnancy. It is generally agreed that unmarried women are less likely to receive adequate prenatal care (Wegman, 1993), resulting in poor outcomes for infants such as infant mortality, low birthweight, prematurity, or any of the conditions that will cause an infant to be admitted to the special care nursery. Perhaps marriage results in economic stability for a mother, but this may be only a temporary condition for adolescents. In one study of middle-class White adolescent mothers (Lamb, Elster, Peters, Kahn, & Tavare, 1986), the couples who were married at conception earned more than the teenagers who were not married, but they were usually high school dropouts, which subsequently limits lifetime earning potential. But this may not be true for all adolescents. One could speculate that a pregnant 15-year-old would receive more support (financially and emotionally) if she stayed at home with her mother during a pregnancy than if she married her 17-year-old boyfriend. In this sample, married adolescents were more likely to be Hispanic (see Table 2.5). Perhaps these young women enjoyed a better economic life by being married than by staying home in a large poor family. In previous years, nonmarital childbirth was common among the young and the poor, and was more often seen in Black births than in White births. But nonmarital births are continuously rising in the United States and many adult women of all races and socioeconomic levels are choosing to have infants outside of marriage. Nearly 30% of all births in the United States in 1991 were to unmarried mothers (Wegman, 1993), potentially influencing future neonatal outcome data.

## Predictors of Pregnancy and Neonatal Outcome

Tables 2.8 and 2.9 show results of hierarchical multiple regression analyses used to predict pregnancy and neonatal outcomes, respectively. In order to examine the relative importance for pregnancy and neonatal outcomes, predictors were grouped into domains of adolescents' sociodemographic characteristics, prenatal care, and prenatal drug use. The sociodemographic variables (age at delivery, SES, governmental assistance [coded as 0 = *receiving no assistance*; 1 = *receiving some form of*

Table 2.7
Pregnancy and Neonatal Characteristics by Mother's Marital Status at Intake

|  | Unmarried (n = 165) | Married (n = 37) | t (1,201) |
|---|---|---|---|
| Age at delivery | 17.10 | 17.50 | 2.06* |
| SES[a] | 10.80 | 9.18 | 4.48** |
| Trimester sought prenatal care | 2.15 | 2.06 | < 1 |
| No. of prenatal visits | 9.06 | 10.52 | 1.53 |
| Weight gained during preg. | 33.57 | 37.78 | < 1 |
| Drug Use During Pregnancy |  |  |  |
| Cigarette use | 1.25 | 1.11 | 1.78+ |
| Alcohol use | 1.08 | 1.03 | 1.42 |
| Other substance use | 0.11 | 0.03 | < 1 |
| Outcomes |  |  |  |
| No. of pregnancy complications | 2.26 | 2.09 | < 1 |
| Weeks gestation (Dubowitz) | 39.13 | 39.64 | 2.02* |
| Birthweight (gms.) | 3,266 | 3,355 | < 1 |
| Apgar 1 | 7.67 | 7.94 | < 1 |
| Apgar 5 | 8.23 | 8.83 | < 1 |
| Days in special care nursery | 3.52 | 0.16 | 2.41* |

[a]Indexed by number of years of education completed by adolescent's mother.
+$p < .10$. *$p < .05$. **$p < .001$.

assistance at intake], and marital status [coded as 0 = unmarried; 1 = married]) were entered on the first step, prenatal care variables (trimester sought care and number of prenatal visits) were entered on the second step, and drug use during pregnancy (of cigarettes, alcohol, and marijuana) were entered on the third step. The total number of pregnancy complications and gestational age (Dubowitz maturity) were the two dependent variables for pregnancy outcomes (Table 2.8), and infant birthweight and 5-minute Apgar scores were the dependent variables for neonatal outcomes (Table 2.9).

Results indicated that, for the total number of pregnancy complications, prenatal drug use was the largest positive predictor, contributing 30% of the total variance in pregnancy complications ($p < .001$). A more mature gestational age was predicted by good prenatal care, which contributed 8% of the total variance ($p < .05$), and lack of prenatal drug use, which accounted for 7% of the variance in gestational age ($p < .05$). In the current study, young maternal age was not found to be associated with an increased risk of preterm delivery, as was reported by Scholl et al. (1994) in their meta-analysis of more than 20 studies.

Using the same model to predict neonatal outcomes (Table 2.9), we found that adolescents' sociodemographic variables contributed 8% of the total variance in infant birthweight ($p < .01$), with an older age at delivery positively related to a

Table 2.8
Predictors of Pregnancy Outcomes

| Step and Predictor | Pregnancy Complications[a] | | | Gestational Age[b] | | |
|---|---|---|---|---|---|---|
| | B | t | R² of step | B | t | R² of step |
| Step 1 | | | .02 | | | .05 |
| Age at delivery | .07 | — | | .13 | — | |
| SES[c] | −.06 | — | | .06 | — | |
| Governmental assistance[d] | −.03 | — | | −.09 | — | |
| Marital status[e] | −.16 | — | | −.04 | — | |
| Step 2 | | | .05 | | | .08* |
| Trimester frist sought care | .19 | 1.91+ | | .25 | 2.25* | |
| No. of prenatal visits | −.01 | — | | .29 | 2.47* | |
| Step 3 | | | .30*** | | | .07* |
| Cigarette use during pregnancy | .36 | 3.13** | | −.16 | — | |
| Alcohol use during pregnancy | .43 | 4.32*** | | .14 | — | |
| Marijuana use during pregnancy | −.14 | — | | −.16 | — | |
| F (df) | F (9,180) = 5.00*** | | | F (9,180) = 2.33* | | |
| Total R² | | | .37*** | | | .20* |

[a]Total number of pregnancy complications.
[b]Coded in weeks and assessed using the Dubowitz method.
[c]Assessed as the number of years of education completed by adolescent's mother.
[d]Coded as 0 = receiving no governmental assistance and 1 = receiving some form of governmental assistance.
[e]Coded as 0 = unmarried at intake and 1 = married at intake.
+$p$ <.10. *$p$ < .05. **$p$ < .01. ***$p$ < .001.

higher infant birthweight. Good prenatal care also was a significant predictor of high infant birthweight, contributing 12% of the variance ($p$ < .01), as was lack of prenatal drug use, which accounted for 7% of the variance in infant birthweight ($p$ < .05). Cumulatively, all factors accounted for 27% of the variance in infants' birthweight ($p$ < .01). The only statistically significant predictor of 5-minute Apgar scores was prenatal drug use, with frequent marijuana use associated with poor neonatal functioning ($p$ < .05). All of the predictors accounted for 20% of the total variance in the Apgar score.

Thus, results from hierarchical multiple regressions indicated that prenatal drug use was highly predictive of pregnancy complications, and substandard prenatal care and drug use during pregnancy were predictive of young gestational age. Regarding neonatal outcomes, young maternal age, infrequent prenatal care, and prenatal drug use (particularly alcohol) were predictive of low infant birthweight, and marijuana use during pregnancy was the only significant predictor of poor neonatal functioning.

Table 2.9
Predictors of Neonatal Outcomes

| Step and Predictor | Infant Birth Weight | | | Apgar 5 | | |
|---|---|---|---|---|---|---|
| | B | t | $R^2$ of step | B | t | $R^2$ of step |
| Step 1 | | | .08** | | | .05 |
| Age at delivery | .25 | 2.56** | | .06 | — | |
| SES[a] | .17 | — | | .06 | — | |
| Governmental assistance[b] | .00 | — | | −.15 | — | |
| Marital status[c] | .03 | — | | −.02 | — | |
| Step 2 | | | .12** | | | .02 |
| Trimester first sought care | .14 | 1.91+ | | .10 | — | |
| No. of prenatal visits | .38 | 3.44*** | | .15 | — | |
| Step 3 | | | .07* | | | .13** |
| Cigarette use during pregnancy | −.16 | — | | −.15 | — | |
| Alcohol use during pregnancy | −.23 | 2.24* | | .13 | — | |
| Marijuana use during pregnancy | −.10 | — | | −.29 | 2.12* | |
| F (df) | $F_{(9,180)} = 3.33$** | | | $F (9,180) = 2.02$* | | |
| Total $R^2$ | | | .27** | | | .20** |

[a] Assessed as the number of years of education completed by adolescent's mother.

[b] Coded as 0 = receiving no governmental assistance and 1 = receiving some form of governmental assistance.

[c] Coded as 0 = unmarried at intake and 1 = married at intake.

+$p < .10$.  *$p < .05$.  **$p < .01$.  ***$p < .001$.

## SUMMARY

In this group of 208 racially diverse pregnant adolescents who received comprehensive, interdisciplinary and age-appropriate prenatal care, the vast majority of mothers and infants experienced excellent outcomes. There was, however, one infant death and one maternal death. Differences among the three major racial groups reveal that Hispanic teens were more likely to be married but also to be of lower SES based on teens' mothers' level of education; more Black adolescents were likely to have an infectious disease during their pregnancy; and more White adolescents were likely to smoke cigarettes and marijuana and to use crystal during their pregnancies. Correlational data offer the clinically reassuring information that early prenatal care and frequent visits result in fewer pregnancy complications, mature infants, and healthy birthweights. Multiple regression data indicate that cigarette and alcohol use during pregnancy are predictive of a high number of pregnancy complications, and that young maternal age, poor prenatal care, and alcohol use are predictive of a low infant birthweight.

# Chapter 3

## Short-Interval
## Repeat Pregnancy

ଚ୨ ◆ ଓ୫

Almost 30% of all first-time adolescent mothers have a second child within 2 years after their first delivery (Hayes, 1987; Mott, 1986; Zelnik, 1980). Subsequent pregnancies of adolescent mothers have been related to even more adverse health consequences than a first birth, including a higher incidence of low birthweight, premature, and stillborn infants, and a higher rate of infant mortality (Jekel, Harrison, Bancroft, Tyler, & Klerman, 1975; McCormick et al., 1984). Jekel et al. reported that subsequent infants born to women in their teens have a rate of neonatal death almost 9 times that of firstborn infants of teenage mothers. Twenty-seven percent of the subsequent infants in the Jekel et al. study were low birthweight, or below 2,500 grams, which was over twice the number of low birthweight firstborn infants. Furthermore, 32% of subsequent infants of low birthweight died compared to 9% of low birthweight firstborn infants (Jekel et al., 1975). For the mother, subsequent childbearing brings unfavorable educational and economic outcomes, such as a decreased likelihood of school completion and higher rates of unemployment and welfare dependency for several years following the childbearing (Furstenberg, 1976a, 1976b; Moore & Waite, 1977; Mott, 1986; Polit & Kahn, 1986; Trussell & Menken, 1978; Upchurch & McCarthy, 1989). Women whose first birth occurs during the teenage years tend to have larger families, and family size is a strong predictor of welfare recipiency (Moore, Hofferth, Wertheimer, Waite, & Caldwell, 1981). A teen with two children is much more likely than even a teen with one child to drop out of school and to go on welfare (Maynard & Rangarajan, 1994).

The adverse health, educational, and economic consequences of subsequent pregnancy are even greater when the pregnancy takes place within 12 months of an earlier birth (McCormick et al., 1984; Mott, 1986). One of the factors possibly leading to the higher rates of prematurity and perinatal death among infants conceived soon after delivery is that the young mother may not have had enough time to prepare physiologically and nutritionally for a new pregnancy (Jekel et al., 1975). Moreover, most repeat pregnancies occurring within 1 year of a previous birth are unplanned and unintended (Ford, 1983; Mott, 1986; Trussell & Menken, 1978), possibly making the adverse consequences of repeated childbearing for mothers even more undesirable. The unintended nature of closely spaced repeated pregnancies are perhaps reflected in the higher abortion rates of subsequent pregnancies among adolescent women. Linares and colleagues reported that the most common pregnancy outcome following a live birth for teenagers with a history of two or more previous pregnancies was abortion, with 44% of such women opting to terminate their pregnancies (Linares, Leadbeater, Jaffe, Kato, & Diaz, 1992). Miscarriage was the next most common outcome, with 31% of teens having a miscarriage, and only 25% carried the subsequent pregnancy to term.

Given the suboptimal outcomes associated with rapid subsequent pregnancy and childbearing among adolescent mothers, it would be useful to identify characteristics of adolescents who are at greatest risk of rapid repeat pregnancies, that is, pregnancies occurring within 18 months of a previous birth. Previous research in this area has been quite consistent, with studies showing that being married and not returning to school are the greatest risk factors for short-interval subsequent childbearing among adolescents (Atkin & Alatorre-Rico, 1992; Darabi et al., 1982; Dempsey, 1972; Ford, 1983; Jekel, Klerman, & Bancroft, 1973; Koenig & Zelnik, 1982; Linares et al., 1992; Mott, 1986; Stevens-Simon, Parson, & Montgomery, 1986). In fact, Jekel et al. reported that postpartum school attendance by adolescent mothers was a stronger predictor of remaining not pregnant at 15 months postpartum than use of birth control. Several investigators have noted, however, that marriage and school return may represent proxies for lifestyle choices, such that young mothers who marry, do not return to school and have a second infant right away hold more traditional gender-role orientations in which motherhood and marriage are highly valued to the exclusion of other roles (Jekel et al., 1973; Linares et al., 1992; Stevens-Simon et al., 1986). Thus, not returning to school may not be so much a risk factor for repeat pregnancy, but an outcome of the desire to bear children. In contrast, young mothers who do not marry, return to school, and who do not have a second pregnancy may have life goals and motivations other than childbearing and marriage.

Rapid repeat pregnancy has also been associated with a young age at first childbearing, with women who first give birth at 16 or younger more likely to bear a second child within 2 years than women who have their first child at 17 or older (Mott, 1986; Trussell & Menken, 1976). The younger the girl is at her first delivery, the more likely she is to have two, three, or four children by the time she is 20 (Henshaw et al., 1989). Pace of subsequent childbearing also varies for women of different ethnic backgrounds, with Hispanic women more likely than either White or Black women to have a second birth quickly (Mott, 1986). However, Hispanic women, compared to White or Black women, report larger desired family sizes, lower educational expectations, are more likely to be married at their first childbearing, and are more likely to report that the first birth was intended (Atkin & Alatorre-Rico, 1992; Felice et al., 1987; Mott, 1986). Thus, Hispanic adolescent mothers would appear to hold more traditional values about motherhood and childbearing than either White or Black teen mothers. In one of the few studies to examine characteristics of the infant as potential predictors of incidence of repeat pregnancy, Darabi et al. (1982) found that the gender of the infant of the previous birth was associated with repeat pregnancy, with the mothers of girls more likely (although not statistically significant) to be pregnant again within 2 years postpartum than the mothers of boys.

Based on the studies just cited, we identified 10 specific sociodemographic characteristics of the adolescent assessed at intake, four prenatal and baby characteristics, and nine 6-month postpartum characteristics of the adolescent that might be predictive of a short-interval repeat pregnancy. Adolescents' sociodemographic characteristics assessed at intake included the following: race, age, marital status, living situation (with male partner or not living with male partner), whether receiving governmental assistance, teens' mothers' educational attainment, grade at intake, ever repeat a grade, whether dropped out of school prior to the pregnancy, and age at first sexual intercourse. The four prenatal and baby characteristics included: trimester sought prenatal care, number of prenatal visits, number of pregnancy complications, and baby's sex. The nine 6-month postpartum characteristics were: return to school by 6 months postpartum, current school status, marital status, living with a male partner or not living with a male partner, receipt of governmental assistance, and child-care assistance from the teen's mother, friends or relatives, the father of the baby, and total child-care assistance (child-care assistance totaled across all providers).

## METHOD

### Pace of Repeat Pregnancy

We examined repeat pregnancy at two postpartum intervals: within 6 months of a previous birth (which we termed *immediate* repeat pregnancy) and between 6 and 18 months postpartum (which we termed *short-interval* repeat pregnancy). We selected to study immediate repeat pregnancy (i.e., within 6 months postpartum) because this time interval has been associated with particularly unfavorable psychosocial and health outcomes for both mother and baby (Jekel et al., 1975; McCormick et al., 1984). We examined repeat pregnancy within 18 months postpartum so as to be comparable with most of the other studies in this area that have examined repeat pregnancy within 2 years of a previous birth (e.g., Atkin & Alatorre-Rico, 1992; Mott, 1986; Polit & Kahn, 1986; Stevens-Simon et al., 1986).

Incidence of subsequent pregnancy and its timing was assessed initially by self-report and then confirmed by medical chart review. For example, if a teen reported at the 6-month, 12-month, or 18-month follow-up interview that she was pregnant or that she believed she was pregnant, the teen's medical records were examined for confirmation. Most teens were still being seen in the UCSD Adolescent Medicine Clinic, so their medical records were readily available. Reliability of the incidence of repeat pregnancy was 98%, with two adolescents not reporting a pregnancy documented on their chart and one teen reporting a false pregnancy. Once a repeat pregnancy was confirmed, the teen was interviewed again using a structured format of 34 questions. This was the "repeat pregnancy" interview and included questions on pregnancy resolution (e.g., whether the subsequent pregnancy was aborted, miscarried, or carried to term), partner information (e.g., whether the father of the subsequent pregnancy was the same as or different from the father of the previous pregnancy), and the teens' living situation at the time of the second conception. With these data, we are able to address whether abortions and miscarriages are more likely when a subsequent pregnancy occurs immediately as opposed to within 18 months of a previous birth, as reported by Linares et al. (1992).

## Subjects

Of the 208 adolescent mothers in this study, 151 (73%) were Gravida 1 at intake. Only Gravida 1 adolescents were included in analyses of this chapter for two reasons. First, the predictors associated with a third or fourth pregnancy are likely to be different from those associated with a second pregnancy (Atkin & Alatorre-Rico, 1992; Matsuhashi, Felice, Shragg, & Hollingsworth, 1989). Second, the number of women who were Gravida 2 or higher who had a repeat pregnancy between 6 and 18 months postpartum was too small for reliable analysis ($n = 10$). Of the 151 Gravida 1 mothers, 22 (15%) had a repeat pregnancy within 6 months postpartum, 31 (21%) had a repeat pregnancy between 6 months and 18 months postpartum, and 98 teens (65%) did not have a subsequent pregnancy by 18 months postpartum (see Table 3.1). Gravida status at intake was not associated with timing of repeat pregnancy ($\chi^2 = 2.99$, ns, see Table 3.1). The fact that, cumulatively, 35% of the current sample of Gravida 1 teens (or 53 out of 151) had a subsequent pregnancy by 18 months postpartum is slightly high given that other studies have reported repeat pregnancy rates of 7% at 6 months postpartum (Zelnik, 1980) and 19% at 2 years postpartum (Atkin & Alatorre-Rico, 1992; Stevens-Simon et al., 1986). Yet other studies have reported 28-month repeat pregnancy rates as high as 45% (McAnarney et al., 1978) depending on the follow-up intervention implemented. The relatively high repeat rate of the current sample may be due to the fact that the current sample included teens who were married, a group known to have higher rates of repeat pregnancies (Atkin & Alatorre-Rico, 1992). Or possibly, the relatively robust and healthy status of the first baby could have made a repeat pregnancy and childbearing more desirable. In any case, the current analyses included only repeat pregnancies following a live birth; other studies have included repeat pregnancies subsequent to abortion (Zelnik, 1980). Individuals who choose to abort have significantly lower cumulative risks of a subsequent pregnancy (at 2 years postpartum) than those who have live births (Zelnik, 1980).

Table 3.1
Timing of Repeat Pregnancy by Gravida Status at Intake

| Timing of Repeat Pregnancy | Gravida Status | | |
|---|---|---|---|
| | 1 | > = 2 | Missing Gravida Data |
| Within 6 mos. postpartum | 22 | 12 | 1 |
| Between 6 and 18 mos. postpartum | 31 | 10 | 3 |
| No repeat pregnancy by 18 mos. postpartum | 98 | 26 | 5 |
| Total N | 151 | 48 | 9 |

Note. Gravida status (number of times pregnant) was not associated with timing of a repeat pregnancy. [$\chi^2$ (df=2) = 2.99, ns].

## Procedure

The variables used as predictors of a repeat pregnancy were obtained by structured interview with the adolescent conducted at the intake assessment (at the first prenatal visit or at some time during the pregnancy) and at 6 months postpartum, and by information cited on the medical record of the birth and delivery. All interview questions were asked in a caring, nonjudgmental manner by experienced nurses or social workers and clarification was provided if a teen did not understand a question or a response option. The interviews were conducted individually in a small, private office in the clinic suites of the prenatal care clinic. The intake interview was 120 questions and took approximately 1 hour to complete. The 6-month postpartum interview was approximately 100 questions and required about 45 minutes to complete. The postpartum interviews were conducted in the teen's place of residence at a time of her convenience. All of the 151 Gravida 1 teens completed the 6-month interview.

## RESULTS

To determine whether the adolescent's sociodemographic characteristics (assessed at intake), the prenatal and baby characteristics, and the 6-month postpartum characteristics of the adolescent were associated with timing of a subsequent pregnancy, chi-square analyses and multivariate analysis of variance were computed using the three categories of timing of a repeat pregnancy as the classification variable (i.e., within 6 months, between 6 and 18 months, and no repeat pregnancy diagnosed by 18 months postpartum). Results indicated that none of the adolescent's background sociodemographic characteristics (assessed at intake) and none of the prenatal and baby characteristics were associated with timing of a repeat pregnancy. However, five of the nine 6-month postpartum characteristics were significantly associated with timing of a subsequent pregnancy (see Table 3.2). Results indicated that teens who became pregnant within 6 months postpartum were significantly more likely to have not returned to school and to have dropped

Table 3.2
Characteristics at 6 Months Postpartum Associated
With Timing of a Repeat Pregnancy

| Characteristics at 6 months postpartum | Timing of Repeat Pregnancy | | | $\chi^2$ (df=2) |
| --- | --- | --- | --- | --- |
| | Within 6 mos (n = 22) | Between 6 and 18 mos (n = 31) | No repeat pregnancy by 18 mos (n = 98) | |
| Returned to school | | | | 2.12** |
|   Yes | 19% | 64% | 59% | |
|   No | 81% | 36% | 41% | |
| School status | | | | 13.63** |
|   In school or graduated | 18% | 64% | 58% | |
|   Dropped out | 82% | 36% | 41% | |
| Marital status | | | | 0.63 |
|   Married | 24% | 24% | 22% | |
|   Nonmarried | 76% | 76% | 78% | |
| Live with male partner | | | | 6.35* |
|   Yes | 57% | 38% | 23% | |
|   No | 43% | 62% | 77% | |
| Governmental assistance | | | | 6.95* |
|   Receive | 59% | 39% | 30% | |
|   Do not receive | 41% | 61% | 70% | |
| Child-care support from teen's mother | | | | 21.37*** |
|   None or some | 45% | 65% | 81% | |
|   A lot | 55% | 35% | 12% | |

*$p < .05.$   **$p < .01.$   ***$p < .001.$

out of school at the 6-month follow-up than those who became pregnant between 6 and 18 months postpartum and those who had not become pregnant by 18 months postpartum. Contrary to findings from other studies, using the current sample, marital status was not associated with timing nor incidence of repeat pregnancy, but living with a male partner was more prevalent among women who became pregnant again within 6 months postpartum than among other women. Receipt of governmental assistance during the 6-month postpartum period was also associated with timing of a repeat pregnancy, with 59% of those who had an immediate repeat pregnancy receiving some form of assistance, a figure twice as high as those who had not become pregnant by 18 months postpartum (30%). Finally, child-care assistance received from the adolescent's mother was highly associated with timing of a repeat pregnancy, with the adolescents who became pregnant within 6 months over four times as likely to report receiving "a lot" of child-care assistance from their mothers (55%) than adolescents who had not become pregnant by 18 months postpartum (12%). Child-care assistance from the father of the first baby, from a friend or relative, and total child-care assistance (perceived support totaled across all three types of providers) were inconsequential for timing of a subsequent pregnancy.

Follow-up contrasts indicated that in all cases where a significant effect was found, those who became pregnant by 6 months postpartum were significantly different from the other two groups. No significant differences were found between adolescents who became pregnant between 6 and 18 months and adolescents who had not become pregnant by 18 months. Results from logistic regression analysis, in which immediate repeat pregnancy (i.e., within 6 months postpartum) was predicted using the characteristics found to be different for the three groups, indicated that adolescents who at 6 months postpartum had not returned to school, had dropped out of school, were living with a male partner, were receiving some form of governmental assistance, and were receiving large amounts of child-care support from their mothers were more than twice as likely to become pregnant again by 6 months postpartum than other women (odds ratio = 2.11; 95% confidence interval: 2.89–1.69, $p < .01$).

To determine whether pregnancy characteristics of the repeat pregnancy differed as a function of the timing of the repeat pregnancy, chi-square analyses and $t$ tests were computed on the following characteristics of the second pregnancy: pregnancy resolution (i.e., carry to term, abortion, miscarriage), month sought prenatal care for the second pregnancy, use of cigarettes, alcohol, marijuana, and crystal during the second pregnancy, whether the partner involved in the second pregnancy was the same as or different than the father of the first baby, and the total number of pregnancies conceived within 18 months postpartum. Results, shown in Table 3.3, indicated that when compared to adolescents who became pregnant after 6 months postpartum, adolescents who became pregnant within 6 months postpartum sought prenatal care significantly later during their second pregnancies, used more alcohol and marijuana during their second pregnancies, and had significantly more pregnancies by 18 months postpartum. The two groups did not differ in cigarette use or crystal use (although there was a trend for more frequent crystal use in teens who became pregnant again within 6 months postpartum) or in whether the partner involved in the second pregnancy was the same as or different than the father of the first baby.[1] Pregnancy resolution also did not differ significantly by timing of the repeat pregnancy. The most common pregnancy resolution for teens who became pregnant within 6 months was to abort (46%); whereas, only 29% of teens who became pregnant after 6 months postpartum chose to abort (see Table 3.3). The miscarriage rate was not higher for women who became pregnant within 6 months of giving birth (18%), although this rate was slightly higher than the national estimate for U.S. women age 19 or younger, which was 14% in 1990 (Alan Guttmacher Institute, 1994b).

---

[1]The partner involved in the second pregnancy was, however, significantly more likely to be different than the father of the first baby if the second pregnancy was conceived within 12 to 18 months postpartum. The percentages of different partners involved in the second pregnancy by timing of repeat pregnancy were: within 6 months postpartum: 19%; between 6 and 12 months postpartum: 18%; and between 12 and 18 months postpartum: 71%; $\chi^2(2) = 7.50, p < .05$.

Table 3.3
Pregnancy Characteristics by Timing of Repeat Pregnancy

| Pregnancy Characteristics[a] | Timing of Repeat Pregnancy | | Test Statistic |
|---|---|---|---|
| | Within 6 mos | Between 6 and 18 mos | |
| | (n = 22) | (n = 31) | |
| Pregnancy resolution | | | $\chi^2 = 2.28$ |
| Carried to term | 36% | 55% | |
| Aborted | 46% | 29% | |
| Miscarried | 18% | 16% | |
| Month sought prenatal care | 5.83 | 3.77 | $t = 3.09^{**}$ |
| Standard deviation | (2.39) | (2.27) | |
| Cigarette use during pregnancy[b] | 0.08 | 0.24 | $t = 1.32$ |
| Standard deviation | (0.28) | (0.44) | |
| Alcohol use during pregnancy[b] | 0.24 | 0.00 | $t = 2.06^*$ |
| Standard deviation | (0.63) | (0.00) | |
| Marijuana use during pregnancy[b] | 0.23 | 0.00 | $t = 2.04^*$ |
| Standard deviation | (0.60) | (0.00) | |
| Crystal use during pregnancy[b] | 0.59 | 0.10 | $t = 1.75^+$ |
| Standard deviation | (1.41) | (0.55) | |
| Partner Involved in Second Pregnancy | | | $\chi^2 = 1.65$ |
| Same as first pregnancy | 81% | 61% | |
| Different than first pregnancy | 19% | 39% | |
| Total number of pregnancies within 18 mos postpartum | 1.49 | 1.14 | $t = 2.95^{**}$ |
| Standard deviation | (0.66) | (0.41) | |

[a]Of the second pregnancy.
[b]Response options ranged from 0 = none, 1= occasionally (2–3 times during pregnancy); 2 = frequently (1–2 times per month); 3 = once a week; 4 = daily.
$^+p < .10.$  $^*p < .05.$  $^{**}p < .01.$

## DISCUSSION

Rapid and repeated childbearing during adolescence has been associated with negative educational and economic outcomes for the young mother and with poor health outcomes for her infant. Despite these real causes of concern, it is important to remember that many teenagers do not experience short-interval repeat pregnancies, and when they do, not all of these pregnancies result in live births. In the current sample, 65% of all first time mothers had not experienced a subsequent pregnancy by 18 months postpartum, and among those who did, less than half (47%) carried to term, or 17% of all first-time mothers in this sample. Thus, although certainly a potentially problematic situation, rapid and repeated childbearing was relatively uncommon in this sample.

Nevertheless, 35% of this study's sample of first-time teen mothers had a second pregnancy by 18 months postpartum. Given the limited resources now available for social programs, it would be useful to target such resources to those most at risk of a short-interval pregnancy. Interestingly, and similar to other studies (Darabi et al., 1982; Polit & Kahn, 1986), we found that characteristics of the young women assessed at intake and several infant and prenatal care characteristics failed to discriminate which adolescents would have an immediate or short-interval repeat pregnancy. Immediate repeat pregnancy was, however, associated with a number of characteristics present at 6 months postpartum in the areas of education, welfare dependency, living situation, and child-care assistance. Because such characteristics occurred during the same time interval as the repeat pregnancy, it is not possible to surmise direction of effects, that is, that such characteristics caused the repeat pregnancy. The results are, nevertheless, informative because they help to shed light on the conditions that co-occur with rapid repeat pregnancy.

Not returning to school during the 6 months following birth was associated with an immediate repeat pregnancy. Failure to return to school cannot be said to predict immediate repeat pregnancy, however, because it may itself have been caused by the repeat pregnancy. Additional results indicated that twice as many women who became pregnant within 6 months after birth had dropped out of school (82%) as compared to women who had no repeat pregnancy by 18 months postpartum (41%). A declared dropped out status may reveal more than just a failure to return to school but a conscious decision not to return to school in the near future, if at all. Thus, the young mothers who considered their educational careers terminated by 6 months postpartum were likely to also be pregnant at that time. Darabi et al. (1982), using time-ordered event data, concluded that school return was more likely to precede postponing a second pregnancy than the reverse. Stevens-Simon et al. (1986) found that if a second pregnancy could be prevented, young mothers eventually returned to school. These findings and others (e.g., Atkin & Alatorre-Rico, 1992; Darabi et al., 1982; Jekel et al., 1973) reporting an association between postpartum school enrollment and a reduced likelihood of repeat pregnancy suggest that school return is critical for secondary pregnancy prevention.

Receipt of governmental assistance was also found to be associated with immediate repeat pregnancy. Although this finding could be interpreted to suggest that the teenagers in this sample were reinforced for having subsequent births by receipt of governmental subsidies, an argument could also be made that governmental assistance was more crucial for women who found themselves pregnant again after 6 months of giving birth. In fact, findings from the Baltimore Longitudinal Study show that welfare assistance was more prevalent among women who had rapid, repeated childbearings and among women with young children, but that most of these young mothers were not welfare dependent by the time their youngest child was age 5 (Furstenberg, Brooks-Gunn, & Morgan, 1987b). Thus, teenage mothers who have many young children and limited schooling may have no other options except welfare to support themselves and their families in the early parenting period.

The finding that marital status was not associated with immediate repeat pregnancy but living with a male partner was parallels findings by Darabi et al. (1982).

Marital status often reflects living situation, but living situation is a more inclusive variable, incorporating cohabitating unmarried male partners. Living with a male partner, whether married or not, reflects an ongoing sexual relationship and, therefore, consistent exposure to the risk of immediate repeat pregnancy. It is not surprising, then, that in this sample, living with a male partner best captured this risk.

Large amounts of child-care assistance provided by the teen's mother was also significantly related to immediate repeat pregnancy. It is difficult to suggest intervention applications for child-care assistance from the adolescent's mother given that such support has been shown to have many favorable implications for the adolescent, her parenting, and her infant (Crockenberg, 1987b; Furstenberg & Crawford, 1978; Spieker & Bensley, 1994; see also chapter 5 for a review of this literature). Yet, it may be that in providing large amounts of child-care assistance, the adolescents' mothers are not allowing their daughters to shoulder the true responsibilities and challenges of parenthood. As suggested by Furstenberg (1980), large amounts of grandmother support may be a double-edged sword, easing the teen's transition to parenthood by providing child-care instruction and assistance, but also potentially thwarting and complicating the ultimate transition to a family of procreation and the establishment of an independent household where the teen mother is matriarch. High grandmother support that is provided over a long period may not, therefore, be entirely advantageous to the adolescent or to the adolescent's child (Chase-Lansdale, Brooks-Gunn, & Zamsky, 1994; Unger & Cooley, 1992). Findings from this study suggest a heretofore not previously studied negative effect of high grandmother assistance: a greater likelihood of rapid repeat pregnancy. Having primary responsibility for their children's caretaking acted as a fairly effective contraceptive against an immediate second pregnancy for many teens in this sample.

Further results indicated that when compared to women who became pregnant after 6 months postpartum, adolescents who become pregnant within 6 months following a previous birth sought prenatal care later during their second pregnancies, had more frequent alcohol and marijuana use during their second pregnancies, and had more cumulative pregnancies by 18 months postpartum. This is consistent with results found by Stevens-Simon, Roghmann, and McAnarney (1990) and Scholl et al. (1994), who reported that teenagers who had rapid successive pregnancies were more likely than teenagers who had only one child during adolescence to receive inadequate prenatal care for their subsequent pregnancies. Because teens who have numerous and rapid pregnancies are more likely to have inadequate prenatal care and to engage in behaviors that negatively affect fetal growth, they are at a compounded risk of poor maternal and infant health outcomes. These are causes of concern and underscore the at-risk nature of rapid subsequent pregnancies among adolescents.

It has been well documented that programs that redirect adolescent mothers back to school before they become pregnant again, while providing close and intensive psychosocial postpartum follow-up, are most successful in preventing immediate subsequent pregnancy and repeated childbearing (see Stevens-Simon et al., 1986, for a review). Conversely, programs that supply only enhanced contraceptive services often fail. As a case in point, Maynard and Rangarajan (1994) launched a massive effort at reducing the number of repeat pregnancies among teenagers. Approximately 3,000 first-time teenage mothers (in Chicago and in Newark and Camden, New Jersey) were given extensive education about contraception and the contraceptive of their choice free. In addition, they were provided transportation for their doctors' visits and received free child care. Thirty months later, 66% of the targeted teens had given birth or were pregnant again—the same percentage of adolescents in a comparison group ($N = 3,000$) who received no services. The authors concluded that knowledge and access had little to do with preventing repeat pregnancy among teens. In a study using a similar study population as the current sample, 44% of a sample of Gravida 2 mothers reported that they became pregnant a second time because they wanted a baby, as opposed to Gravida 1 mothers who were more likely to report that the pregnancy was an accident, that it "just happened" (Matsuhashi et al., 1989). This suggests that many young women who become pregnant more than once appear to do so intentionally. With these findings in mind, perhaps secondary pregnancy prevention programs would be well-directed to simultaneously focus on a young woman's educational goals as well as on her desires and motivations for having or not having more children.

# Chapter 4

## Qualities of Adolescent Mothers' Parenting

ഇ ♦ ജ

The quality of adolescent mothers' parenting has been the focus of much research (see, e.g., reviews by Bierman & Streett, 1982; Brooks-Gunn & Furstenberg, 1986a; Elster, McAnarney, & Lamb, 1983; Furstenberg, Brooks-Gunn, & Morgan, 1987a; Osofsky, Hann, & Peebles, in press; Panzarine, 1988; Phipps-Yonas, 1980; Roosa, Fitzgerald, & Carlson, 1982b; Schellenbach, Whitman, & Borkowski, 1992). Most studies examining the quality of adolescent mothers' parenting have focused on adolescents' *behavior* in the context of mother–infant interactions, and compared adolescent mothers to adult mothers (e.g., Conger, McCarty, Yang, Lahey, & Burgess, 1984; Garcia-Coll, Vohr, Hoffman, & Oh, 1986; Levine, Garcia-Coll, & Oh, 1985; McAnarney, Lawrence, Riccuiti, Polley, & Szilagyi, 1986; Roosa, Fitzgerald, & Carlson, 1982a; Teberg, Howell, & Wingert, 1983). Regarding the latter trend, the general conclusion of these studies is that adolescent mothers, when compared to adult mothers, are reportedly less sensitive, less verbal, and less responsive to their infants' interactional cues. However, most studies do not control for the socioeconomic factors associated with early child-bearing. When such controls are implemented, few differences emerge between the parental behavior of teenage mothers and adult mothers (Baldwin & Cain, 1980; Elster et al., 1983; Klerman, 1993; McAnarney et al., 1986; Panzarine, 1988). Moreover, by examining only group level differences between adolescent mothers and adult mothers, it is not possible to learn of the potential for variation within groups of adolescent mothers (East, Matthews, & Felice, 1994). Indeed, it is important to recognize that not all adolescent mothers parent alike. Some teenagers lack the maturity and sense of responsibility to adequately nurture their children, whereas others adjust well to the stresses of parenting and provide favorable caregiving.

The other trend ascribed to studies of adolescent mothers—that of examining exclusively their behaviors—overlooks the importance of the psychological components of parenting, such as adolescents' parenting attitudes and values, perceived parenting confidence, and commitment to the parenting role. Such psychological dimensions of parenting are significant for the way adolescents approach and carry out basic parenting tasks and for the way they interact with their children. For example, mothers who have unfavorable parenting attitudes, such as a high perceived value of physical punishment and inappropriate child expectations, are likely to use harsh and rejecting discipline strategies (Fox, Baisch, Goldberg, & Hochmuth, 1987). These strategies have been linked with child anger, low self-esteem, and social withdrawal (Crockenberg, 1985, 1987a; Fox et al., 1987; Rohner, 1975). In contrast, mothers who have dramatic and intense feelings of inadequacy and failure in the parenting role are likely to withdraw physically and emotionally from their children (Colletta, 1983; Frommer & O'Shea, 1973; Main & Goldwyn, 1984). Such maternal withdrawal has been linked with angry and resistant infant behaviors (Crockenberg, 1981; Field, Healy, Goldstein, & Guthertz, 1990; Main & Goldwyn, 1984) and to subsequent problematic mother–child relationships (Zahn-Waxler, Kochanska, Krupnick, & McKnew, 1990).

In this chapter, we address the shortcomings of previous studies on adolescent parenting by examining potential sources of within-group variation on the psychological qualities of adolescent mothers' parenting. Specifically, we focus on the following five dimensions of parenting: mothers' parenting attitudes, perceived parenting confidence, perceived parenting stress, parenting knowledge, and commitment to the parenting role. In addition, we examine an often overlooked aspect of teenage parenting, mothers' extent of involvement in the caretaking of their children. Each of these parenting qualities has been identified by theorists as key components for effective childrearing and for adaptive child development (Baumrind, 1978; Goodnow, 1984; Lancaster, Altmann, Rossi, & Sherrod, 1986; Maccoby & Martin, 1983; Zelkowitz, 1982). In examining these six dimensions of parenting, we first determined how they were interrelated, that is, whether a pattern of relationships emerge with respect to adaptive parenting. It was expected that positive parenting attitudes, low parenting stress, positive maternal self-confidence, high parenting knowledge, high parenting commitment, and high maternal involvement will be interrelated. Second, we examined whether such qualities of parenting varied by mothers' race, age, parity, and marital status, and age and gender of child. Finding differences in teen mothers' parenting as a function of these factors would highlight sources of within-group variability among adolescent mothers. For example, primiparous adult mothers have been found to be less self-confident about their parenting than multiparous adult mothers (Westbrook, 1978). Whether this difference is also evident among teenage mothers is not known. Adolescent mothers may become more competent parents as they have more children and become more experienced in parenting. Alternately, they may become more harsh and punitive in their parenting as the stresses associated with having more children increase. Qualities of adolescent mothers' parenting may also vary by maternal age. As suggested by Hardy and Zabin (1991), all too often little attention is given to the different development status of adolescents, with the outcomes of very young mothers (i.e., younger than 15) unlike those of older teenage mothers (i.e., over 18). Regarding differences due to race, Wasserman, Rauh, Brunelli, Garcia-Castro, and Necos (1990) reported that Hispanic-American mothers (both teen and adult) held more strict childrearing attitudes than African-American mothers. Similarly, Thomas and colleagues reported that adult Puerto Rican mothers living in New York City expected more strict adherence to their commands than Black or other non-Hispanic adult mothers (Thomas, Chess, Sillen, & Mendez, 1974). In contrast, Field and Widmayer (1981) found that Hispanic-American young mothers (from Puerto Rico and Cuba) experienced more positive parent–infant interactions than African-American young mothers of comparable age and SES. Little is known about the cultural context of teen parenting in the Hispanic community, particularly among Mexicans who recently immigrated to the United States. Such individuals make up a large percentage of the current sample.

Third, we sought to determine how and to what extent these qualities of adolescent mothers' parenting were related to children's behavioral outcomes. Similar to studies on adolescent parenting, most studies on the outcomes of the children of adolescent mothers have looked for differences in the social and cognitive development between children born to teenage mothers and children born to adult mothers. If differences are found, it is assumed that the mothers' parenting practices differed. Particularly in the case of teenage mothers, relationships between parental practices and child outcome are examined inferentially rather than directly (Brooks-Gunn & Furstenberg, 1986b). Research has given particularly scant attention to the links between the parenting qualities examined in this chapter (e.g., adolescent mothers' parenting attitudes, parenting confidence, parenting stress, and caretaking involvement) and children's behavioral adjustment. One note of caution, however, in interpreting the links between mothers' parenting and children's outcomes, because adverse social and economic conditions and teenage parenthood often co-occur, it is difficult to disentangle the relative effects on child outcome resulting from each condition (Brooks-Gunn & Furstenberg, 1986b; East & Felice, 1990; Panzarine, 1988). For example, most teenage mothers live in poor neighborhoods with few positive parenting role models and limited resources for nurturing their children. Such factors likely interact with the emotional immaturity associated with teenage motherhood and the less experienced mothering provided by teenage parents to exact a negative toll on children's development. Thus, in examining the links between young mothers' parenting qualities and their children's adjustment, it is likely that each is affected by the disadvantaged circumstances associated with teenage motherhood.

Before presenting the methods and results of this study, the parenting constructs examined in this chapter are discussed in greater depth.

## QUALITIES OF ADOLESCENT MOTHERS' PARENTING

### Parenting Attitudes

The parenting attitudes assessed in this study included the following: appropriateness of parental expectations of child, empathy toward child's needs, value of physical punishment, and parent–child role reversal. Each of these parenting values—that is, inappropriate expectations of children, lack of empathy toward children's needs, high value of physical punishment, and a belief in parent–child role reversal—has been found to be strongly linked with abusive and neglectful parenting (Aber & Cicchetti, 1984; Bavolek, 1984) and to be present within the childrearing styles of teenage parents (Bavolek, Kline, McLaughlin, & Publicover, 1979; Fox et al., 1987). For example, in regard to appropriateness of child expectations, adolescents have been found to have difficulty understanding the particular stages of their children's development and to both overestimate (Vukelich & Kliman, 1985) and underestimate (Field, Widmayer, Stringer, & Ignatoff, 1980) their children's abilities, often having unrealistically high or low demands and expectations of their children's behavior. Frequently, in the area of language, expectations are too low, whereas in other areas of development the adolescent expects her baby to behave in an adult manner, such as to not cry if hurt and to sit quietly for extended periods of time (Bierman & Streett, 1982). Unrealistic developmental expectations most likely stem from a lack of familiarity with children and a lack of understanding of normative child development, characteristics perhaps understandable among adolescents who have had less formal education and possibly fewer opportunities for informal childrearing experiences than adult women (Field et al., 1980). Unrealistic expectations may also reflect a transference of the unrealistic expectations placed on the teen mother herself: Just as the teen mother must appear more mature, so should her baby (Bierman & Streett, 1982).

Another parenting attitude linked with teenage parenting is the inability to be empathically aware of their children's needs and to respond to those needs in an appropriate fashion. Due to teenagers' relative cognitive and psychosocial immaturity, and given that many teenagers still possess a degree of egocentric thinking (Erikson, 1963), they may have a lack of understanding and sensitivity of their children's needs and wants (Bavolek, 1984; Elster et al., 1983). Often teenagers are unable to separate their own feelings and needs from the needs of their children because they themselves are trying to resolve individuation issues (Blos, 1962). For example, as described by Bierman and Streett (1982), teenage mothers typically have difficulty comforting their babies during pediatric visits when an inoculation is necessary, often abandoning their babies on the examining table: "It is as if the teenager feels it is she who is on the table getting the shot. This identification with her baby does not allow her to function as the baby's mother to comfort her child and allay his anxieties ... [and] is preventing her from seeing him/her as a separate individual with his/her own needs, fears, and feelings" (Bierman & Streett, 1982, p. 413).

Adolescent mothers have also been described as more reliant on physical means of discipline when compared to adult mothers (Garcia-Coll et al., 1986), and are more likely to engage in aggressive and inappropriate behaviors, such as poking and pinching their babies, behaviors rarely displayed by adult mothers (Elster et al., 1983). Adolescent mothers are also likely to report that physical punishment is an acceptable and important means of child control and discipline, beliefs not typically shared by nonabusive adult mothers (Bavolek et al., 1979). Such punitive attitudes are thought to stem from adolescents' self-centeredness and immaturity, high life stress, punitive parenting role models, and a lack of social support (Crockenberg, 1987a; Garcia-Coll, Hoffman, & Oh, 1987).

Teenage mothers are also more likely than adult mothers to ascribe to the belief that the child should comfort and nurture the parent, an attitude Bavolek (1984) called *parent–child role reversal*. Bavolek et al. (1979) discussed this parent–child role reversal expectation among adolescents whereby teenagers, being disappointed in others, bear children with the expectation that their children will love them and meet their needs. Frequently, teenagers who become pregnant have not had someone to parent them, thus, they have a child thinking that the child will be the parent. Sometimes, teen mothers even refer to their baby as "my mommy" or "my daddy" (Bierman & Streett, 1982). Coupled with this belief is the conviction that the teenage parent is the helpless one in need of nurturing—not the child—beliefs seldom shared by nonabusive adult mothers (Bavolek, 1984). Such beliefs likely derive from adolescent self-centeredness, narcissism, and inappropriate resolution of dependence–independence issues (Bierman & Streett, 1982).

## Parenting Confidence

In this chapter, *parenting confidence* refers to a mother's feelings of self-confidence in her mothering ability and parenting effectiveness and includes the following four dimensions: confidence in one's caretaking ability, confidence in the mothering role, acceptance of her child, and expected relationship with her child (Shea & Tronick, 1988). These dimensions of parenting confidence are believed to be clinically meaningful factors of maternal self-esteem that either mitigate or hinder women's adaptation to motherhood, particularly under conditions of adverse physical or medical maternal and infant health (e.g., in situations of difficult pregnancy or labor, low infant birthweight, prematurity, or the presence of infant physical anomalies or deformities). For example, a mother's belief that she can successfully nurse and calm her baby is important for her feelings of maternal self-competence. Mothers who feel, however, that by nursing their infants they might harm them (e.g., mothers of severely premature infants), report a sense of distrust in and a low self-confidence about their caretaking abilities (Kaplan & Mason, 1969).

Shea and Tronick (1988) described maternal self-esteem as correlating with—but distinct from—one's general self-esteem, or the sense of self that is a relatively stable, enduring, and core characteristic of the person. In contrast to general self-esteem, maternal self-esteem is thought to be highly specific to the domain of parenting, with a woman's feelings about her mothering ability and effectiveness based solely on her evaluation of her performance in child caretaking tasks. Because maternal self-esteem is thought to depend largely on a mother's success in interacting with and caring for her infant, the infant's behavioral and physical characteristics necessarily contribute to an adolescent's sense of parenting confidence (Lamb & Easterbrooks, 1981). Maternal self-esteem is also believed to be highly significant for both adolescents' initial and long-term adaptation to the maternal role. For example, teens whose parenting confidence is undermined by any of a host of biosocial factors may become less effective with their infants and, consequently, develop less secure attachments with them. Such insecure parent–infant bonds are likely to eventually disturb subsequent parent–child relations.

There are no studies that we are aware of that address adolescents' sense of parenting confidence in the way described here. There are studies, however, that describe adolescents' adjustment to parenting as influenced by the characteristics she brings to parenting tasks, such as her individual personality attributes, her general self-esteem, and her coping and problem-solving abilities. This literature suggests that adolescents with positive psychosocial adjustment prior to pregnancy (i.e., those with high self-esteem, effective coping skills, and a sense of maturity) show the most optimum parenting postpartum (Hamburg, 1986; and reviewed by Schellenbach et al., 1992). In addition, we know of no studies to date that have linked adolescent mothers' sense of parenting confidence to their children's behavioral outcomes. Research on adult mothers has also been sparse, with Shea and Tronick (1988) reporting that favorable maternal self-esteem correlated with mothers' parity, perceived lack of infant fussiness and maternal sensitivity when interacting with her baby.

## Parenting Stress

Most research on the significance of stress for parenting has analyzed either contextual sources of stress (e.g., divorce, poverty, single parenting) or major stressful life events that have occurred in the lives of parents (e.g., moving, a change in jobs, etc.; Shapiro & Mangelsdorf, 1994) as opposed to the stress associated with parenting itself. *Parenting stress*, as assessed in this chapter, refers to the latter meaning or "the irritating, frustrating, annoying, and distressing demands that (occur) ... within the specific context of parent–child relationships" (Crnic & Greenberg, 1990, p. 1629). *Parenting stress*, as defined here, among adult mothers has been found to correlate with children's behavioral problems, children's social incompetence, greater overall maternal distress, and less satisfied parenting (Crnic & Greenberg, 1990). Less is known about parenting stress among adolescent mothers, although it is likely that parenting stress would be high within such a population given the developmental and ecological sources of stress associated with early parenthood (Garcia-Coll et al., 1986; Ketterlinus, Lamb, & Nitz, 1991). For example, given that teenage mothers—in contrast to adult mothers—are more likely to have less effective coping strategies, to be less mature, and to have less established social support networks, they may be at risk of high stress associated with parenting (Garcia-Coll et al., 1986; Garica-Coll, Hoffman, & Oh, 1987). In this chapter, we describe the frequency and perceived intensity of parenting stress among adolescent mothers, and we explore their relations with other qualities of mothers' parenting, mothers' involvement with their children's care, and children's behavioral outcomes.

## Parenting Knowledge

A goal of many parenting programs for teenage mothers is to enhance their parenting and child development knowledge, with the underlying assumption that accurate knowledge contributes to skilled and sensitive parenting behavior and practices (Klerman, 1993; Panzarine, 1988). Although this link remains to be empirically documented, adolescent mothers do appear to be less knowledgeable about child developmental milestones than older mothers, even when social class and parity are controlled (DeLissovy, 1973; Field et al., 1980; Klerman, 1993). As stated previously, adolescents have been found to both overestimate (Vukelich & Kliman, 1985) and underestimate (Field et al., 1980) children's abilities. Adolescents also tend to have limited knowledge of typical infant behavior (e.g., the amount of time infants cry, sleep, are alert, etc.), and of desirable caregiving techniques (Field et al., 1980). Using the same developmental milestone scale as that used by Field et al. (1980), Seymore and colleagues, however, reported no differences between adolescent mothers and adult mothers in knowledge of child development or knowledge of effective caregiving techniques (Seymore, Frothingham, MacMillan, & DuRant, 1990). In addition, Parks and Smeriglio (1983) found no differences in the parenting knowledge of primiparous teenage mothers and primiparous adult mothers of equivalent educational level. Parenting knowledge in the Parks and Smeriglio study was assessed as the awareness that parenting behavior influences infants' current and future well-being. Thus, adolescent mothers appear to be sensitive to this component of parenting knowledge and are not less aware than are adult mothers. The instrument used in the current study assessed knowledge of infant and child developmental milestones, health and safety practices, and effective childrearing strategies.

## Parenting Commitment

Commitment to the parenting role is a relatively new construct within the parenting literature, deriving from the sociobiological concept of parental investment (Lancaster et al., 1986). *Parenting commitment* has been defined as the psychological significance that an individual attaches to the parenting role, and is conceptualized as including "the centrality of parenting to the self, the salience of parenting in relation to other activities, and aspirations to perform well as a parent" (Greenberger & O'Neil, 1993, p. 183). Parenting commitment has been most recently studied among employed mothers with the expectation that simultaneously high commitments to both parenting and work roles would create conflict that would ultimately hinder adaptive parenting and child development (Greenberger & Goldberg, 1989; Greenberger & O'Neil, 1993). Results revealed, however, that high commitments to both parenting and work were associated with optimal authoritative parenting among employed mothers, positive parenting beliefs, and favorable child adjustment (Greenberger & Goldberg, 1989). Similarly, Greenberger and O'Neil (1993) reported that high parental commitment among adult mothers correlated with parenting satisfaction, high spousal and neighbor support, and high marital commitment. Thus, high parental commitment, or one's desire and ability to allocate extensive time and energy to parenting, appears to be an advantageous parenting quality, one associated with optimal parenting socialization practices and favorable child development.

This aspect of parenting has not, as far as we are aware, been studied among adolescent mothers. It is plausible that adolescents would not be particularly highly committed to the parenting role given adolescents' relative psychosocial immaturity and still-emerging identities. Moreover, given competing demands to continue their education or to work to support their babies, adolescents may not be able to invest heavily in the parenting role. Adolescents may also be unwilling to devote extensive time to child-care responsibilities when activities with friends and peers become available.

## Maternal Involvement With Child Care

Mothers' involvement with child care is a frequently overlooked aspect of teenage mothering. Interventions focusing on teenage parenting typically use outcomes of mothers' sensitivity and responsivity during structured parent–infant interaction tasks or unstructured home observation (e.g., Crockenberg, 1981; Field et al., 1980; Field, Widmayer, Greenberg, & Stoller, 1982; and reviewed by Panzarine, 1988). Such interventions assume that adolescent mothers are primarily involved in their children's care. Oftentimes, however, this is not the case. Typically, it is the grandmother or a female relative who spend the majority of time looking after the teen's child (Crockenberg, 1987b; Furstenberg, 1980; Smith, 1975; and as is discussed further in chapter 5). Lack of maternal involvement in the child's caretaking may not be adaptive as this is the primary context through which patterns of mother–infant interaction, turn-taking, and communication are learned. Particularly over the child's first years of life, caretaking tasks of feeding, dressing, and bathing comprise most of the time mother and baby spend together and provide the opportunity for maternal infant stimulation, infant growth-inducing experiences, and shows of affection. Moreover, in so far as the mother will ultimately assume the role of primary attachment figure for her child, lack of consistent involvement in her infant's daily care may be disadvantageous for the development of a secure mother–child attachment bond. In this chapter, we examine the extent and regularity of adolescent mothers' involvement in their children's daily care as a dimension of teenage parenting and how it might covary with other parenting qualities (e.g., adolescents' parenting stress, perceived parenting competence, and parenting knowledge) and children's behavioral adjustment.

# METHODS

## Subjects

This chapter focuses on 119 of the 208 adolescent mothers (57%) who participated in The UCSD Teen OB Follow-Up Study and who were willing to complete an additional survey packet at the time of their regularly scheduled semi-annual interview. The 119 subjects who chose to complete these questionnaires did not differ from the 89 subjects who chose not to complete them with regard to demographic characteristics such as mothers' age, race, parity, or child's age or gender. Of the 119 subjects, 52 received postpartum case management and 67 did not. There were no differences between the case-managed group and the nonmanaged group on any of the parenting or child behavior measures included in this chapter.

The mean age of the 119 adolescent mothers at the time they completed the questionnaires was 20.2 years, with an age range between 17.1 and 22.6 years. Their mean age at delivery was 17.2 years, with an age range at delivery between 14 and 18.8 years. Subjects were predominantly Hispanic (50%), with 27% Black, 17% non-Hispanic White, and 6% Other. At the time the questionnaires were completed, most mothers were unmarried (76%) and Gravida 1 (87%); 12% had one other living child and one mother had two living children.

Each mother completed the parenting questionnaires with regard to how she parented the child resulting from the pregnancy for which she was inducted into the study. This child is referred to as the *target child,* and is not to be confused with any children the mother may have had previously or subsequently to the target child. The mean age of the target children (at the time the parenting questionnaires were completed) was 37.5 months (ranging from 12 to 50 months) and 50% of the children were boys.

## Measures

Subjects completed a packet of five parenting questionnaires that assessed their parenting attitudes, parenting confidence, parenting stress, parenting and child development knowledge, and their children's behavior. In addition, mothers rated (via interview) their involvement in their children's daily care and their commitment to parenting. The scale mean was the score used in analyses (unless otherwise indicated), and the score range was the possible scale range. All questionnaires are described further here.

*Parenting Attitudes.* Subjects' parenting attitudes were assessed by the Adult–Adolescent Parenting Inventory (AAPI; Bavolek, 1984; Fox et al., 1987), which is a 32-item questionnaire designed to index the following four parenting attitudes and values: (a) developmental expectations of child ("Children should be expected to talk before the age of 1 year"), (b) empathy toward child's needs

("Parents who are sensitive to their children's feelings and moods often spoil their children"), (c) value of physical punishment ("Children are more likely to learn appropriate behavior when they are spanked for misbehaving"), and (d) parent–child role reversal ("Young children should be expected to comfort their mother when she is feeling blue"). Response options ranged from 1 (*strongly agree*) to 4 (*strongly disagree*) with high scores reflecting, respectively, appropriate developmental expectations of child, high empathy toward child's needs, low value of physical punishment, and low expectations of the child taking a parenting role. Thus, high scores reflect favorable parenting attitudes and low scores reflect unfavorable parenting attitudes, or those found to be correlated with child abuse and neglect (Bavolek, 1984; Fox et al., 1987). The inventory was carefully developed and normed on more than 2,000 adults and 6,500 adolescents, including separate samples of abusive parents. All four subscales successfully discriminated between nonabusive and abusive parenting samples (Bavolek, 1984). Using adolescent mother samples, internal reliabilities for the four subscales ranged from .70 to .82 and the overall test–retest reliability was .76 (Bavolek, 1984). Using the current sample, the Cronbach alphas ranged from .69 (developmental expectations of child) to .84 (value of physical punishment).

*Parenting Confidence.* The Maternal Self-Report Inventory (MSRI; Shea & Tronick, 1988) was used to assess the following four dimensions of maternal self-esteem or mothers' feelings of confidence and competence in the mothering role: (a) confidence in caretaking ability ("I am not very good at calming my child"), (b) confidence in mothering role ("I think that I am a good mother"), (c) acceptance of child (assessed by a mother's love for her child, whether or not she was disappointed with the sex of her child, and whether or not she believes that her child will develop normally); and (d) expected relationship with child ("I am confident that I will have a close and warm relationship with my child"). For purposes of this study, the 26-item short form was used and the word "baby" was changed to "child." In addition to having good face validity, the MSRI has good concurrent validity (e.g., it correlates highly with clinical ratings of the mother and general self-esteem scores of the mother), and good construct validity (Shea & Tronick, 1988). Using the current sample, all Cronbach alphas of the short form exceeded .81 except for expected relationship with child which had an alpha of .66. Response options ranged from 1 (*really false*) to 4 (*really true*) with high scores indicating high confidence in one's caretaking ability, high confidence in oneself in the mothering role, high acceptance of child, and positive expectations for the mother–child relationship.

*Parenting Stress.* To assess the stress experienced with parenting, the Parenting Daily Hassles scale (PDH; Crnic & Greenberg, 1990) was used. The PDH lists 15 typical, yet stressful, everyday events in parenting and parent–child interactions (e.g., "I was nagged, whined at, or complained to by my kids"). In response to each item, using a 4-point scale, mothers were instructed to rate the frequency of occurrence of the event (*not at all, sometimes, a lot, constantly*) and the intensity of how hassled they felt by the event (*no hassle, a little hassle, kind of a big hassle, a big hassle*). Using the current sample, the internal reliabilities (Cronbach alpha) were .81 for the frequency scale and .90 for the intensity scale.

*Child Development and Parenting Knowledge.* The Knowledge of Infant Development Inventory (KIDI; MacPhee, 1981) was used to assess mothers' knowledge of infant and child development, health and safety practices, and effective childrearing strategies. Twenty-one representative questions in the areas of developmental milestones in infant physical, cognitive, and social development (8 items), health and safety issues (4 items), and parenting strategies (9 items) were chosen from the 75-item scale. Exemplar items are: "A 2-year-old is able to reason logically, much as an adult would" (assessing cognitive development); "You must stay in the bathroom when your toddler is in the tub" (assessing health and safety) and "A baby should not be held because this will make the baby want to be held all the time" (assessing parenting techniques). Possible responses were *agree, disagree,* and *not sure*. Correct answers were coded as 1 and all other choices, including *not sure*, were coded as 0. Scores were derived by summing the codes of all items. The possible score range for the total instrument was 0 to 21, with higher scores indicating greater knowledge. MacPhee (1981) reported an average Cronbach alpha of .82 for all subscales and test–retest reliability as .92. MacPhee and Fabio (1992) also reported good instrument concurrent validity, with knowledge scores correlating highly with extent of direct experience with children. Using the current sample, the Cronbach alpha of all items was .77.

*Parenting Commitment.* Six items from the 17-item Commitment to Parenting Scale (Greenberger & Goldberg, 1989) were used to assess mothers' sense of commitment to the parenting role. A typical item reads, "I give up personal pleasures, such as extra sleep or seeing my friends, to be with my child." Respondents indicated in an interview format their degree of agreement or disagreement with each item on a 4-point Likert scale, with high scores indicating greater commitment. The scale yields good internal reliability (Cronbach $\alpha = .71$) and shows relations to authoritative parenting style and favorable child outcomes (Greenberger & Goldberg, 1989). Using the current sample, the internal reliability (Cronbach alpha) of the six items was .71.

*Involvement With Child's Caretaking.* Mothers' involvement in their children's caretaking was assessed via interview at the 2-year follow-up only and was indexed as the extent and regularity with which the teen participated in the following six activities with the target child: bathes, feeds, puts to bed, dresses, reads to, and plays with. Response options were 0 (*never*), 1 (*sometimes*), 2 (*fairly often*), and 3 (*regularly*). The adolescent responded, via interview, about her involvement over the last month. Scores were summed across the six activities so that possible responses ranged from 0 to 18, with low scores indicating minimal involvement with children's caretaking and high scores indicating regular and extensive involvement in the child-care activities just cited. The Cronbach alpha of the six items was .74.

*Child Outcomes.*    Mothers rated 10 items on the social withdrawal and aggressiveness subscales of the Behavior Problem Checklist (Achenbach & Edelbrock, 1983). These two subscales were chosen because much of the literature on the outcomes of children of adolescent mothers has included similar indices of children's behavior (see, e.g., reviews by Brooks-Gunn & Furstenberg, 1986b; Furstenberg et al., 1987b). The five social withdrawal items were: is too shy, cries a lot, is withdrawn, feelings easily hurt, and doesn't like to be with other children. The five aggression items were: fights with others, throws temper tantrums, hits others, hurts others without meaning to, and has angry moods. Response options were: 0 = *not true*, 1 = *somewhat or sometimes true*; and 2 = *very true or very often*. The checklist was developed for children as young as 3 years of age (Achenbach & Edelbrock, 1983) and may not have been well suited to the youngest children in the sample (e.g., as young as 1 year). In the current sample, there were nine children between 1 and 2 years of age, and 14 children between 2 and 3 years of age. For items in which the behavior described was inappropriate for the age of the child, the mother was instructed to keep that item blank. Scores were derived by summing across all answered items and dividing by the number of items included in the total. This was done separately for each scale. Thus, the possible scale range was 0 to 2. Achenbach and Edelbrock (1983) reported high mother–father agreement for both scales and that both scales reliably discriminated between clinical and nonclinical child samples. Using the current sample, the internal reliabilities (Cronbach alphas) were .81 and .86 for the withdrawal and aggression subscales, respectively. The mean total withdrawal score was 0.50 (SD = 0.33) and the mean aggression score was 0.75 (SD = 0.58). Boys and girls did not differ significantly in their social withdrawal or aggression scores.

## Procedure

Time and method of assessment of each variable studied in this chapter are shown in Table 4.1. Mothers' parenting attitudes, parenting confidence, and parenting stress were assessed via questionnaire when the target child was between 12 and 50 months, with the mean month of assessment 37.5 months postpartum. The questionnaires were administered to mothers at their regularly scheduled interview at their convenience and in their place of residence. In addition to completing these questionnaires, mothers rated their children's behavioral outcomes by questionnaire. Mothers' parenting commitment and involvement in caretaking were assessed via interview at the regularly scheduled 2-year follow-up, and mothers' child development and parenting knowledge was assessed via questionnaire at the 2-year follow-up.

A social worker or nurse, known to subjects through their previous participation, described the instructions for completing the questionnaires and was available to answer any questions regarding word definitions and to look after the mothers' children. All subjects were assured of the confidentiality of their responses. An average of 10.2 weeks after the first assessment, 102 mothers (86%) completed the parenting questionnaires a second time.

Table 4.1
Time and Method of Assessment of Each Variable

| Assessment of | Time of Assessment | Method |
|---|---|---|
| Parenting attitudes | 12–50 months postpartum (M = 37.5 months) | Questionnaire |
| Parenting confidence | 12–50 months postpartum (M = 37.5 months) | Questionnaire |
| Parenting stress | 12–50 months postpartum (M = 37.5 months) | Questionnaire |
| Child development and parenting knowledge | 24 months postpartum | Questionnaire |
| Parenting commitment | 24 months postpartum | Interview |
| Involvement in caretaking | 24 months postpartum | Interview |
| Children's behavioral problems | 12–50 months postpartum (M = 37.5 months) | Questionnaire |

Note. Analysis for this chapter involved 119 young mothers and their children.

# RESULTS

The analyses that form the core of this chapter examined the interrelations and potential sources of within-group variation of several qualities of adolescent mothers' parenting. We also investigated how such dimensions of mothers' parenting were linked to their children's behavioral adjustment.

## Descriptive Data Associated With Parenting Qualities

The means and standard deviations of the (Time 1) parenting scores are shown at the bottom of Table 4.2. The Time 1 means of the four parenting attitude scales averaged 2.80 (score range = 1–4), the four parenting confidence scales averaged 3.44 (score range = 1–4), and the two parenting hassles scales averaged 1.85 (score range = 1–4). Mothers scored an average of 16 correct answers out of the 21 items on the KIDI (or 76% correct) with almost half of the mothers getting 81% correct or better. The adolescent mothers were most knowledgeable about health and safety issues, with 75% of teens answering all such items correctly (in contrast to 17% who answered all developmental milestone items correctly and 10% who answered all parenting technique items correctly). The mean of the parenting commitment scores was 3.42 on a possible 4-point scale, and the mean child-care involvement score was 15.60 on a scale range of 0 to 18. Thus, the mothers in this study had only moderately favorable parenting attitudes, but had high confidence in their parenting, perceived relatively low stress associated with their daily experiences of parenting and, were very knowledgeable about children's health and safety issues. The young mothers were also quite committed to the parenting role and were highly involved in their children's daily care.

Normed data were available only for the parenting attitudes inventory (Bavolek, 1984). Compared to the norms for nonabusive White and non-White adolescent mothers, the current sample had significantly lower—that is, less favorable—parenting attitude scores for all four indices. The current sample deviated significantly, however, from the norms derived using abusive teenage and adult mothers.

The test–retest reliabilities for the parenting scores (except for child development knowledge and parenting commitment, which were assessed only once) are shown in the last row of Table 4.2. Results indicated that all parenting scores were moderately stable across the 10-week period (M $r$ = .58). Confidence in the maternal role showed the highest stability, whereas child expectations and expected relationship with child showed the least stability over the time period studied.

## Interrelations Among Parenting Qualities

Results of the intercorrelations among all of the (Time 1) parenting scores (shown in Table 4.2) indicated that almost all of the subscales of parenting attitudes, parenting confidence, and parenting stress were highly intercorrelated. (Bonferroni-adjusted probability values were used to gauge statistical significance in efforts to protect against obtaining significant probability values by chance. Results using Time 2 parenting scores were comparable to those shown in Table 4.2.) Regarding the relations between mothers' parenting attitudes and parenting confidence, favorable parenting attitudes correlated significantly with high confidence on all indices of mothers' parenting except for acceptance of child. Thus, a mother's acceptance of her child does not appear to be associated with any of the parenting values assessed in this study. Neither mothers' parenting attitudes nor parenting confidence correlated significantly with frequency of parenting stress, but mothers who reported high parenting stress intensity also reported low confidence in themselves as mothers ($r$ = −.36, $p$ < .001), low confidence in their caretaking abilities ($r$ = −.26, $p$ < .05), and low child acceptance ($r$ = −.23, $p$ < .05). High knowledge of infant and child development was significantly associated with favorable parenting values and a strong commitment to the parenting role ($r$ = .33, $p$ < .01). Interestingly, however, accurate knowledge of developmental milestones was associated with high parenting stress ($r$ = .32 for stress frequency and $r$ = .30 for stress intensity, $p$ < .01), and awareness of health and safety issues was associated with frequent parenting stress ($r$ = .25, $p$ < .05). Thus, the more mothers knew about normal infant and child development and infant safety issues, the more stressed they felt about parenting. Mothers' commitment to the parenting role correlated significantly with mothers' high confidence in their caretaking abilities ($r$ = .22, $p$ < .05), high confidence in the mothering role ($r$ = .25, $p$ < .05), and a positive expected relationship with their children ($r$ = .28, $p$ < .05). Mothers' involvement in caretaking correlated significantly only with high intensity of parenting stress ($r$ = .28, $p$ < .05).

## Table 4.2
### Intercorrelations Among (Time 1) Parenting Qualities

| | 1 | 2 | 3 | 4 | 5 | 6 | 7 | 8 | 9 | 10 | 11 | 12 | 13 | 14 | 15 |
|---|---|---|---|---|---|---|---|---|---|---|---|---|---|---|---|
| **Parenting Attitudes** | | | | | | | | | | | | | | | |
| 1. Child expectations | — | .64*** | .56*** | .63*** | .36*** | .28* | .17 | .27* | -.01 | -.05 | .23* | .16 | .20 | .10 | .04 |
| 2. Empathy of child's needs | | — | .59*** | .69*** | .34*** | .37*** | .15 | .32** | -.09 | -.21 | .28* | .15 | .46*** | .11 | .20 |
| 3. Punishment value | | | — | .51*** | .36*** | .39*** | .13 | .36*** | -.15 | -.16 | .18 | .21 | .26* | .09 | -.06 |
| 4. Role reversal | | | | — | .32** | .29** | .03 | .32** | -.03 | .11 | .34*** | .13 | .38*** | .15 | -.02 |
| **Parenting Confidence** | | | | | | | | | | | | | | | |
| 5. Confidence in caretaking | | | | | — | .52*** | .39*** | .48*** | -.16 | -.26* | .11 | -.02 | .16 | .22* | .01 |
| 6. Confidence in role | | | | | | — | .37*** | .51*** | -.20 | -.36*** | .04 | .01 | .16 | .25* | .15 |
| 7. Acceptance of child | | | | | | | — | .32** | -.16 | -.23* | -.02 | -.08 | .08 | .13 | .12 |
| 8. Relationship with child | | | | | | | | — | -.03 | -.09 | .00 | -.11 | .14 | .28* | -.03 |
| **Parenting Stress** | | | | | | | | | | | | | | | |
| 9. Hassle frequency | | | | | | | | | — | .76*** | .32** | .25* | .21 | .15 | .10 |
| 10. Hassle intensity | | | | | | | | | | — | .30** | .17 | .18 | .05 | .28* |
| **Knowledge of Child Development/Parenting** | | | | | | | | | | | | | | | |
| 11. Developmental milestones | | | | | | | | | | | — | .13 | .46*** | .33** | -.14 |
| 12. Health and safety | | | | | | | | | | | | — | .09 | .19 | -.03 |
| 13. Parenting techniques | | | | | | | | | | | | | — | .32** | -.06 |
| 14. Parenting commitment | | | | | | | | | | | | | | — | -.10 |
| 15. Child care involvement | | | | | | | | | | | | | | | — |
| Mean | 2.91 | 2.85 | 2.70 | 2.75 | 3.01 | 3.46 | 3.77 | 3.54 | 2.03 | 1.66 | 5.98 | 3.70 | 6.51 | 3.52 | 15.60 |
| Standard deviation | 0.41 | 0.44 | 0.40 | 0.41 | 0.64 | 0.41 | 0.30 | 0.54 | 0.44 | 0.49 | 1.56 | 0.58 | 1.61 | 0.56 | 3.14 |
| Range | 1–4 | 1–4 | 1–4 | 1–4 | 1–4 | 1–4 | 1–4 | 1–4 | 1–4 | 1–4 | 1–8 | 1–4 | 1–9 | 1–4 | 0–18 |
| Time 1–Time 2 r | .45 | .68 | .48 | .60 | .55 | .70 | .49 | .46 | .51 | .66 | — | — | — | — | — |

*Note.* Bonferroni-adjusted probability values were used to gauge statistical significance in efforts to protect against obtaining significant probability values by chance. High scores indicate favorable parenting attitudes and more of the described quality (e.g., high parenting confidence).

*p < .05.   **p < .01.   ***p < .001.

## Relations Between Parenting Qualities
## and Mothers' Age and Age of Child

Table 4.3 presents the correlations between mothers' parenting scores and mothers' age at delivery, mothers' age at the time of the study, and children's age at the time of the study. (As in Table 4.2, Bonferonni-adjusted probability values were used to gauge statistical significance.) These correlations were computed to examine how qualities of adolescent mothers' parenting may be related to their age at delivery and their current age. Recall that, because mothers completed the parenting questionnaires at various times postpartum (ranging from 1 year to over 4 years), mothers' current age reflects both their age at delivery and the age of their child. Results showed that mothers' age at delivery was significantly related to acceptance of child ($r = .25, p < .01$) and parenting commitment ($r = .24, p < .01$), with younger mothers reporting lower acceptance of their children and less commitment to parenting. Similarly, mothers who were younger at the time of the study were less accepting of their children ($r = .22, p < .05$) and felt less committed to the parenting role ($r = .29, p < .01$). However, older mothers (at the time of the study) also tended to place more value on physical punishment ($r = -.25, p < .01$) and felt less confident about their caretaking abilities ($r = -.20, p < .05$).[1]

The correlations discussed above examined relations between mothers' age and their parenting qualities. However, because a mother's age at the time of the study was naturally correlated with her child's age (e.g., in this sample, $r = .30, p < .01$), we also computed partial correlations between all parenting scores and mothers' current age while controlling for the age of her child. These coefficients reflect associations between mothers' current age and their parenting qualities independent of the effects of the age of their children. Only 2 of the 14 partial correlations were statistically significant (all $rs < .14$; not shown in Table 4.3): mothers' current age correlated significantly with acceptance of child ($r = .25, p < .01$) and with parenting commitment ($r = .29, p < .01$), such that younger mothers were likely to have low acceptance of their children and low parenting commitment independent of the effects of their children's ages.[2]

Only 2 of the 14 parenting scores correlated significantly with child's age. Mothers who had older children placed greater value on physical punishment ($r = -.25, p < .01$) and were less involved in their children's daily care ($r = -.24, p < .01$). (Recall that endorsement of physical punishment was coded such that high scores indicate low value of physical punishment.)

---

[1]A MANOVA contrasting the parenting qualities of older (age 17 and older at delivery; $n = 69$) versus younger mothers (age 16.9 or younger at delivery; $n = 50$) showed that, similar to the correlations, mothers who were younger at delivery had lower child acceptance [$F (1, 118) = 5.50, p < .05$] and lower parenting commitment [$F (1, 118) = 4.77, p < .05$].

[2]Because mothers' current age did not correlate significantly with punishment value or caretaking confidence while controlling for the effects of child's age, it can be assumed that age of child inflated the correlations between mothers' current age and the value of physical punishment and between mothers' current age and

Table 4.3
Correlations Among (Time 1) Parenting Qualities
and Mothers' Age and Age of Child

| | Mothers' Age at Delivery | Mothers' Current Age | Age of Child |
|---|---|---|---|
| **Parenting Attitudes** | | | |
| Expectations of child | .06 | .02 | −.06 |
| Empathy of child's needs | .04 | .02 | −.03 |
| Value of physical punishment | −.11 | −.25** | −.25** |
| Parent–child role reversal | −.04 | −.12 | −.16 |
| **Parenting Confidence** | | | |
| Confidence in caretaking ability | −.11 | −.20* | −.18 |
| Confidence in mothering role | .03 | −.06 | −.15 |
| Acceptance of child | .25** | .22* | .03 |
| Expected relationship with child | −.03 | −.12 | −.16 |
| **Parenting Stress** | | | |
| Parenting hassle frequency | .14 | .12 | .02 |
| Parenting hassle intensity | .03 | .03 | .01 |
| **Child Development Parenting Knowledge** | | | |
| Developmental milestones | −.02 | .11 | .12 |
| Health and safety | .06 | −.04 | −.07 |
| Parenting techniques | .04 | −.02 | −.03 |
| **Parenting Commitment** | .24** | .29** | .12 |
| **Child-Care Involvement** | .14 | .11 | −.24** |

Note. Bonferroni-adjusted probability values were used to gauge statistical significance in efforts to protect against obtaining significant probability values by chance. High scores indicate favorable parenting attitudes and more of the described quality (e.g., high parenting confidence).
$*p < .05.$   $**p < .01.$

## Effects of Mothers' Parity and Marital Status and Gender of Child on Mothers' Parenting

There were no significant parity or gender of child effects for any of the parenting scores at either time of assessment. As previously reported, 76% of subjects were unmarried ($n = 90$) at the time the parenting questionnaires were completed. (Eighty-six subjects had never been married and four subjects were separated or divorced.) Using only subjects who were married or unmarried, marital status was found not to be associated with any of the Time 1 or Time 2 parenting scores. Marital status was also not associated with mothers' race: of those who were married there were equivalent percentages of Hispanic (23%), Black (23%), and White (25%) women [$\chi^2 (2) = 0.03$].

## Variations in Parenting By Mothers' Race

To investigate whether adolescent mothers' parenting qualities varied by race of mother, we conducted a multivariate analysis of variance using mothers' race (Hispanic, Black, or non-Hispanic White) as the independent variable and the 14 parenting scores (at Time 1) as the dependent variables. No racial differences were evident for the Time 1 scores [multivariate $F$ (28, 110) = 1.42, ns]. However, there was an association between mothers' race and their Time 2 parenting scores [multivariate $F$ (20, 96) = 2.32, $p$ < .01]. (Mothers' developmental knowledge, parenting commitment, and child care involvement were not assessed at Time 2 and, thus, were not part of this MANOVA.)

The means, standard deviations, and univariate $F$ values associated with each of the 10 (Time 2) parenting scores by mothers' race are shown in Table 4.4. As shown in this table, racial differences were evident in aspects of parenting attitudes and parenting confidence but were not found for either of the parenting stress subscales. White mothers were more likely to have parenting values favorable to the child (i.e., more appropriate expectations of child, greater empathy of child's needs, less value of physical punishment, and lower expectations regarding the child's nurturing role) than either Black or Hispanic mothers. Black mothers reported significantly greater confidence in their caretaking abilities than did Hispanic mothers and greater acceptance of their children than either White or Hispanic mothers (the individual contrasts were significantly different at $p$ < .05). Thus, Hispanic mothers appear not to have the benefit of positive parenting values, as compared to White mothers, nor high parenting confidence or high child acceptance, as compared to Black mothers.

Table 4.4
Mean Scores and F Values Associated With (Time 2)
Parenting Scores by Mothers' Race

| | Hispanic (n = 60) | Black (n = 32) | White (n = 20) | F (df = 2,110) |
|---|---|---|---|---|
| Parenting Attitudes | | | | |
| Expectations of child | 2.96[a] | 2.89[b] | 3.38[ab] | 6.38** |
| Empathy of child's needs | 2.83[a] | 2.89[b] | 3.36[ab] | 7.85*** |
| Value of physical punishment | 2.70[a] | 2.72[b] | 3.01[ab] | 3.13* |
| Parent–child role reversal | 2.83[a] | 2.80[b] | 3.26[ab] | 5.71** |
| Parenting Confidence | | | | |
| Confidence in caretaking ability | 3.01[c] | 3.56[c] | 3.35 | 5.99** |
| Confidence in mothering role | 3.57 | 3.60 | 3.61 | 0.07 |
| Acceptance of child | 3.79[c] | 3.91[b,c] | 3.74[b] | 2.63+ |
| Expected relationship with child | 3.55 | 3.72 | 3.75 | 1.38 |
| Parenting Stress | | | | |
| Parenting hassle frequency | 1.97 | 2.10 | 1.97 | 0.73 |
| Parenting hassle intensity | 1.69 | 1.73 | 1.68 | 0.04 |

Note. Means with the same letter superscript in the same row are significantly different.
[a]Hispanic–White contrast.
[b]Black–White contrast.
[c]Hispanic–Black contrast.
+$p$ < .10. *$p$ < .05. **$p$ < .01. ***$p$ < .001.

## Associations Between Qualities
## of Mothers' Parenting and Child Outcomes

To determine how mothers' parenting qualities were related to their reports of their children's outcomes, correlations were computed between the 14 qualities of mothers' parenting assessed in this study (at Time 1) and the child outcomes of social withdrawal and aggression. Results of the correlations (shown in Table 4.5) indicated that all aspects of mothers' parenting attitudes and parenting confidence were significantly related to their children's social withdrawal, with unfavorable parenting values and low maternal confidence associated with high child social withdrawal. High intensity of parenting stress, but not high frequency of stress, was also related to high social withdrawal in children. Regarding children's aggression, mothers' low acceptance of child, high perceived stress associated with parenting (both stress frequency and intensity), and accurate knowledge of developmental milestones and of effective childrearing strategies were significantly related to high child aggression. Mothers who were minimally involved in their children's care also rated their children high on aggression.

Regression analyses were also computed using the six domains of mothers' parenting as predictors (attitudes, confidence, stress, knowledge, commitment, and involvement) and children's behavioral scores as the dependent variables, while controlling for mothers' current age and the age of child. Domain of parenting scores were derived by summing the various subscales per parenting quality. For example, the domain score of parenting stress was derived by adding the scores for stress intensity and stress frequency. Domain scores were used to reduce the number of predictors in the regression analyses. Scores were coded such that high scores indicate favorable parenting attitudes and more of the described quality (e.g., high parenting confidence, etc.). None of the intercorrelations among the domain scores exceeded .44 and, thus, multicollinearity was not a problem.

Results of the multiple regressions for children's social withdrawal indicated that mothers' parenting attitudes ($\beta = -.34$) and parenting confidence ($\beta = -.24$) each made unique contributions to the variance in children's withdrawal, contributing 12% ($p < .01$) and 7% ($p < .05$), respectively. All of the parenting predictors cumulatively accounted for 21% of the variance associated with children's social withdrawal [$F (8, 111) = 3.54, p < .01$].

In the parallel analysis for children's aggression, only mothers' parenting stress made a unique contribution to children's aggression, contributing 26% of the variance in aggression ($\beta = .42; p < .001$). All six parenting scores contributed cumulatively 32% of the variance associated with children's aggression [$F (8, 111) = 6.37, p < .001$].

## DISCUSSION

The psychological qualities of adolescent and young adult mothers' parenting examined in this study showed meaningful patterns of convergence and within-group variation. Specifically, mothers who had low confidence about their parenting

Table 4.5
Correlations Between Mothers' Parenting Qualities
and Children's Outcomes at Mean Age of 3 Years

|  | Child Withdrawal | Child Aggression |
|---|---|---|
| Parenting Attitudes | | |
| Expectations of child | −.31*** | −.05 |
| Empathy of child's needs | −.40*** | −.11 |
| Value of physical punishment | −.20* | .04 |
| Parent–child role reversal | −.20* | .00 |
| Parenting Confidence | | |
| Confidence in caretaking ability | −.22** | −.04 |
| Confidence in mothering role | −.29** | −.10 |
| Acceptance of child | −.20* | −.28** |
| Expected relationship with child | −.30*** | −.15 |
| Parenting Stress | | |
| Parenting hassle frequency | .11 | .38*** |
| Parenting hassle intensity | .20* | .42*** |
| Child Development, Parenting Knowledge | | |
| Developmental milestones | −.02 | .22* |
| Health and safety | −.03 | .12 |
| Parenting techniques | −.14 | .18* |
| Parenting commitment | −.15 | .00 |
| Child-care involvement | −.01 | −.18* |

*p < .05.  **p < .01.  ***p < .001.

abilities also had unfavorable parenting attitudes such as inappropriate developmental expectations of their children, low empathy for their children's needs, high value of physical punishment, and high expectations regarding their children's nurturing role. Similarly, mothers who reported high intensity of parenting stress had low confidence in the mothering role and in their caretaking abilities and had low acceptance of their children. Intensity of parenting stress was more important for mothers' parenting values and parenting confidence than frequency of parenting stress, which correlated significantly only with high knowledge of infant and child development and with high knowledge of health and safety issues. As a whole, these interrelations indicate that inappropriate parenting values, low parenting confidence, and high parenting stress are likely to co-occur within mothers. Mothers who possess these parenting qualities are, based on previous research, at high risk for neglectful, punitive, and rejecting parenting (Frommer & O'Shea, 1973; Main & Goldwyn, 1984; Mash & Johnston, 1983), qualities that portend unfavorable child outcomes (Crockenberg, 1985; Main & Goldwyn, 1984). This issue is discussed further later.

Results regarding mothers' developmental knowledge indicated that accurate knowledge about children's developmental milestones was related to favorable parenting attitudes yet, also, to high parenting stress. What could explain this latter result? One possibility of this seemingly counterintuitive finding is that one's knowledge base of infant and child development is formed, in large part, by a person's experiences and interactions with children (MacPhee, 1981). It could be, then, that mothers who provide primary, direct care to their children on a consistent basis benefit from those interactions in terms of large amounts of knowledge but, nonetheless, also feel stressed and harried from such constant exchanges. This is partially substantiated by the significant relationship found between high involvement in child care and high intensity of parenting stress. Another interpretation is that mothers who are sensitive to children's developing competencies may be constantly assessing how their children are faring in comparison to developmental norms. Thus, high developmental knowledge may bear a cost of high stress to the mother.

High developmental knowledge did not correlate, however, with mothers' confidence in their parenting. Although the mothers in this sample scored quite well on the infant development items, they apparently are not aware of just how much they know. The fact that mothers' knowledge level was high runs counter to previous claims of deficient parenting knowledge by adolescents (see Klerman, 1993, for a review). It is possible, however, that mothers' level of knowledge was enhanced by the prenatal care educational services they received (which was standard protocol at both prenatal care recruitment sites). It is also possible that a self-selection factor biased mothers' knowledge scores in the upward direction: The mothers who volunteered to participate in this study may represent those most experienced with children and/or those most motivated to be knowledgeable mothers. In any case, other researchers report comparably high parenting knowledge scores by adolescent mothers (Parks & Smeriglio, 1983), suggesting that teenage mothers, as a group, are not necessarily unknowledgeable about children's health and safety practices and effective parenting strategies.

Regarding the within-group variation of adolescent mothers' parenting due to mothers' age and age of child, mothers who were younger at delivery and younger at the time of this study had low acceptance of their children and low commitment to the maternal role. Recall that both these findings held up independent of the effects of child's age. Several researchers have cautioned that the association between young maternal age and poor parenting is confounded by the finding that younger mothers are more likely to be from lower socioeconomic families (e.g., Conger et al., 1984; Elster et al., 1983; Klerman, 1993; McAnarney et al., 1986). This was not the case with the current sample. Younger mothers were not of lower SES, as indexed by adolescents' mothers' highest level of education: maternal age at birth correlated with adolescents' mothers' highest level of education .11 (ns). Even when partially out teenagers' socioeconomic status (i.e., teen's mother's educational level), young maternal age continued to be associated with low child acceptance ($r = .26, p < .01$) and low commitment to parenting ($r = .29, p < .01$). Moreover, SES was unlikely to confound these findings because all subjects were from low-income backgrounds.

Thus, within this sample of former adolescent mothers, the variability associated with maternal age appears to have clinical significance vis-à-vis child acceptance and commitment to parenting, independent of its relation to mothers' SES. This finding is important because it may reflect the inability of the very young teenager to psychologically commit to the role of "mother" and to adjust her expectations and fantasies of the baby she "wished for" to the baby she actually "gets." The fact that younger mothers had low child acceptance when their children were as old as 3 years indicates that this is not a short-lived phenomenon. Perhaps very young pregnant adolescents would benefit from prenatal and long-term postpartum counseling in order to help them develop more realistic expectations of parenting and their children.

Results also indicated that mothers of older children were likely to advocate physical punishment as a means of discipline. This result suggests that, as their children reach toddlerhood and are striving for physical and emotional autonomy, adolescent and young adult mothers were enforcing physical punishment as a control strategy. Programs may be especially warranted for young parents of toddlers that endeavor to increase parents' capabilities of setting limits and enforcing rules within a nurturant, warm, and understanding environment (Bavolek, 1984). In addition, programs that foster social support have been shown to be especially promising for adolescent mothers who have harsh and punitive discipline styles (Crockenberg, 1987b; Garcia-Coll et al., 1987; Weintraub & Wolf, 1983).

The parenting measures used in this study were also sensitive to cultural/racial differences among mothers. Whereas Black and Hispanic mothers shared similar parenting attitudes, White mothers held quite different parenting values. Moreover, Black mothers felt more confident about their caretaking abilities than did Hispanic mothers, and Black mothers had greater acceptance of their children than did either White or Hispanic mothers. Certainly, efforts to intervene with young mothers and their children should appreciate these cultural variations in parenting. However, it should be noted that the subsample of White mothers in this study was particularly small and the low power of such analyses may have precluded detection of significant differences across racial groups. Despite the relatively small subgroup sample sizes, however, differences nonetheless emerged among mothers of different racial backgrounds.

Results pertaining to the associations between mothers' parenting qualities and their children's outcomes showed that mothers' poor parenting attitudes (particularly low empathy for children's needs) and low parenting confidence were most closely linked with children's social withdrawal. These findings coincide with discussions in the attachment literature that emphasize that the trust and warmth experienced within the mother–child relationship act as a secure base from which the child can establish healthy relationships with others outside the family (Ainsworth, Blehar, Waters, & Wall, 1978). Interestingly, the items indexing low empathy of children's needs parallel quite well mother–infant attachment behavior (e.g., "Parents spoil their children by picking them up and comforting them when they cry" and "Children will quit crying faster if they are ignored"). Many attachment theorists claim that social timidity and anxiety are enhanced when children's needs are unreliably met and when children experience a sense of parental rejection. Such children are likely to develop attitudes of mistrust and to socially withdraw to protect against further rejection and social insecurity (Rubin, LeMare, & Lollis, 1990). Thus, it could be argued that lack of sensitivity in understanding children's needs and pessimistic views of the parent–child relationship are parenting characteristics that contribute to children's social withdrawal. Alternately, it is possible, of course, that children who are characteristically shy and withdrawn may promote such qualities in their parents. In either case, these results illustrate the particular importance of mothers' empathy and their expectations about the parent–child relationship as critical for their children's social well-being.

Other results of this study point to links between high child aggression and high maternal stress and between high child aggression and indices suggestive of maternal rejection (i.e., mothers' low involvement in their children's daily care and mothers' low acceptance of child). There is both conceptual and empirical justification for these findings. Mothers who are stressed are less tolerant of infant distress and child noncompliance, and stress may cause mothers to respond inappropriately and impulsively to their children (Ketterlinus et al., 1991). Patterson (1983) reported that minor daily hassles experienced by mothers predicted irritable responding to their children which, in turn, prompted aggressive child responding. Similarly, Dumas (1986) found that, on days when mothers experienced aversive social interaction with adults, they were more likely to respond adversely to their children than on other days. Thus, high maternal stress could certainly lead to children's aggressive behavior. It is also plausible, of course, that children who have aggressive tendencies create stress for their caregivers. The current findings are evidence only of associations between high parenting stress and child aggression, not to causal sequences of events.

Recall, too, that mothers who perceived their children as aggressive were less involved in their children's caretaking and had lower child acceptance. Parental nonacceptance has been discussed as a common correlate of children's aggression (Martin, 1975; Parke & Slaby, 1983). As Martin noted,

> parental rejection may have some aggression-producing qualities because it is associated with frustrations—the rejecting parent may ignore the young child's expressions of discomfort and thwart his needs for nurturance. … And on the other side of the coin—aggressive, disobedient children—are not as "likeable" as more well-behaved children and are likely to elicit more critical reactions. (p. 511)

Low child acceptance, particularly in combination with high punitiveness and low parental use of reasoning, has been found to be strongly related to children's aggression (reviewed by Parke & Slaby, 1983). Because teenage mothers appear especially vulnerable to possessing such parenting characteristics, their children may be vulnerable to being aggressive.

Further results of this chapter indicated that mothers' perceptions of their children's aggression were associated with mothers' knowledge of developmental milestones and knowledge of effective parenting techniques. These relations, though counterintuitive, may reflect the fact that perhaps mothers who have more parenting knowledge are also more sensitive to their children's behavior, even to their children's aggressive behavior. These relations may also reflect a tendency for knowledgeable mothers to more readily accept their children's natural aggressive tendencies, with less knowledgeable mothers not so willing to ascribe negative characteristics to their children. This link warrants further study particularly as it occurs among adolescent mothers.

Several limitations pertaining to these analyses warrant specific comment. As mentioned previously, the self-selection among study participants may limit the generalizability of the current findings. Women who completed the parenting questionnaires in addition to their regularly scheduled interview may have differed from nonparticipants on characteristics related to the quality of their parenting. In addition, the single occasion assessment of children's behaviors hindered this study's ability to draw causal links between mothers' parenting qualities and their children's outcomes. Other research points to circular and dynamic relations between parental stress created by and perpetuating child distress (Patterson, 1983). Longitudinal studies are needed to disentangle issues of causality. Finally, it should be noted that this study assessed mothers' perceptions of both their parenting qualities and their children's behavioral functioning. Thus, relations found among these domains may merely reflect associations of mothers' perceptions. However, Goodnow (1984) and others (East & Felice, 1990; Maccoby & Martin, 1983) argued that parents' perceptions of children's behavior have importance in their own right, and that perceived behavioral problems (whether corroborated by others, such as teachers) play a significant role in parents' parenting style. Parental perceptions of children's behavior problems may serve to validate unfavorable parenting attitudes, for example, or legitimize parenting stress. In any case, additional data on children's outcomes gathered from nonparent sources may have been revealing.

# Chapter 5

## The Role of Grandmothers in Adolescent Mothers' Parenting and Children's Outcomes

ಐ ✦ ೞ

Increased attention has recently been paid to the influence that the mothers of teenage mothers have on their daughters' parenting. This attention has grown out of speculation that the outcomes for children born to teenage mothers might be improved when grandmothers are involved in their grandchildren's care (Brooks-Gunn & Chase-Lansdale, 1991; Brooks-Gunn & Furstenberg, 1986a; Furstenberg, 1980; Furstenberg et al., 1987a, 1987b). Improved child outcomes would be expected for at least three reasons. First, due to age and experience, grandmothers' parenting is presumed to be of higher quality than that of their teenage daughters. Second, grandmothers presumably provide a positive modeling influence for their young daughters' parenting and, thus, high grandmother involvement offers more opportunity for positive role modeling (Chase-Lansdale et al., 1994; Oyserman, Radin, & Benn, 1993; Stevens, 1984; Tinsley & Parke, 1983). Third, by offering direct, hands-on child care, grandmothers provide significant amounts of social support that buffer their teenage daughters and their children from the stresses incurred from early parenting (Barrera, 1981; Cohler & Grunebaum, 1981; Colletta & Lee, 1983; Crockenberg, 1987b). But of the available literature, the evidence of grandmothers' influence on adolescent mothers' parenting is inconsistent. (The term grandmother here refers to the teen's child's grandmother and may be the maternal grandmother or the paternal grandmother.) Some findings reveal a positive relation between high grandmother child-care assistance and enhanced adolescent mothers' parenting sensitivity (Crockenberg, 1987b; Furstenberg & Crawford, 1978), child acceptance (Crockenberg, 1987a), and child stimulation (Cooley & Unger, 1991). Other studies, however, have found negative relations between grandmother-provided child care and children's outcomes, with extensive grandmother child assistance linked with angry and noncompliant child behavior at 2 years of age (Crockenberg, 1987a) and children's behavioral problems at 7 years of age

**64**

(Unger & Cooley, 1992). Moreover, Chase-Lansdale and colleagues (1994) found that grandmothers were not necessarily more effective parents than their teenage daughters. Many grandmothers were observed to have an authoritarian disciplinary style with their grandchildren and to be less engaged and less supportive with their grandchildren when living with them. Observation of such grandmother behaviors may enhance the development of unfavorable parenting patterns in young mothers. In contrast, others have found that the mothers of teenage mothers engage in nonpunitive, reciprocal, and responsive interchanges with their grandchildren (Stevens, 1984).

One of the difficulties in understanding grandmothers' influence on adolescent mothers' parenting and children's outcomes is that many adolescent mothers live with their families of origin (Furstenberg et al., 1987b; Hofferth & Hayes, 1987) and, thus, the true extent of grandmother child-care involvement may be unclear, underestimated, or undermined by the stresses incurred from coresidence. Analysis of the NLSY data collected in 1984 indicated that 74% of 15- to 19-year-olds with children were living as subfamilies in their parents' households, while the remainder maintained their own residence, usually with a partner (Hogan, Hao, & Parish, 1990). Adolescent mothers—whether living with a partner, living with parents, or living alone—reported that most of their support with childrearing derived from their families, particularly their mothers (Colletta & Lee, 1983; Crockenberg, 1987b; Furstenberg & Crawford, 1978; Furstenberg et al., 1987b; Lamb, 1988; Nitz, Ketterlinus, & Brandt, 1995; Parish, Hao, & Hogan, 1991; Spieker & Bensley, 1994). Furstenberg and colleagues (1987a) found that at 5 years postpartum, almost half of the Baltimore Study mothers reported that the maternal grandmother or another family member provided the primary child care or, at least, spent as much time as they did in caring for their child.

There is accumulating evidence, however, that the most positive circumstance for adolescent mothers and their children may be under conditions of high grandmother support but nonshared residence (Chase-Lansdale et al., 1994; Spieker & Bensley, 1994). It may be the case that when adolescent mothers live with parents and share child-care responsibilities, conflict results and negative outcomes ensue (Brooks-Gunn & Chase-Lansdale, 1991). To our knowledge, studies on grandmother–adolescent conflict have not yet been reported in the context of "shared" grandmother–mother parenting or grandmother–mother coresidence. It seems likely, however, that grandmother–adolescent conflict would result from prolonged grandmother child-care involvement and continued coresidence. The teen mother may, for example, be frustrated by the burden of caring for a young child but deeply resentful of her reliance on her parents for child care. This frustration may precipitate grandmother–adolescent conflict which, in turn, is likely to undermine both adolescent mothers' parenting and children's outcomes. Such negative outcomes associated with continued grandmother involvement should be considered given that so many adolescent mothers and their children continue to live as subfamilies in their parents' households for several years following delivery.

Researchers have also noted that, although initial help with child care often proves useful for the teen and her child, extensive and prolonged grandmother involvement leads to confusion about roles and lines of authority and may prevent the teen from developing adequate parenting skills and/or a secure relationship with her child (Brooks-Gunn & Chase-Lansdale, 1991; Furstenberg, 1980; Spieker & Bensley, 1994). Although social support is theoretically predicted to facilitate the teen's initial transition to parenting (Barrera, 1981; Colletta & Lee, 1983; Crockenberg, 1987b; Presser, 1989; Tinsley & Parke, 1983), continued grandmother child support may undercut young mothers' parenting confidence and ability to adopt the maternal role (Smith, 1975). Unger and Cooley (1992) found that as the number of years the grandmother lived in the child's household during the child's lifetime increased, adolescent mothers' cognitive stimulation to their children decreased. Mothers' parenting knowledge has also been shown to be less when grandmothers—as opposed to adolescent mothers—have the primary parenting responsibility of the children (Stevens, 1984). Moreover, when compared to adult mothers, adolescent mothers have been shown to be less involved in their children's care (Garcia-Coll et al., 1987). But whether this is induced by coresidence or extensive grandmother child involvement is not currently known.

Most studies of grandmothers' influence on teens' parenting have examined teen mothers' parenting sensitivity and responsiveness during either structured mother–child interaction tasks (Chase-Lansdale et al., 1994; Spieker & Bensley, 1994) or unstructured home observations (Cooley & Unger, 1991; Crockenberg, 1987a, 1987b; Unger & Cooley, 1992; Unger & Wandersman, 1988). No study that we are aware of has examined how grandmothers' coresidence and child-care assistance may be important for adolescent mothers' sense of confidence in their parenting, their commitment to the parenting role, or their involvement in their children's care. Such outcomes, however, may be crucial to understanding more directly how a strong grandmother presence may subvert teen mothers' parenting. High grandmother child-care involvement may, for example, engender feelings of maternal self-doubt and inadequacy, concerns already present for many adolescent parents (Shea & Tronick, 1988). Extensive grandmother child-care assistance may also be related to low child involvement by the teenage mother, and low commitment to the parenting role. Low parenting confidence, low child involvement, and low parenting commitment may also be associated with continued grandmother coresidence. These issues are the focus of this chapter.

In this chapter, we examine the relations among grandmothers' coresidence, grandmother-provided child-care assistance, and grandmother–adolescent conflict, and the links between these grandmother variables and adolescent mothers' parenting and children's outcomes. Indices of adolescent mothers' parenting include the parenting qualities examined in chapter 4: teen mothers' parenting attitudes, parenting confidence, parenting stress, parenting commitment, involvement with children's daily care, and knowledge of infant and child development. Indices of children's sociobehavioral adjustment included mother-rated assessments of children's social withdrawal and physical aggression. Specific effects related to maternal age and race were also investigated. For example, we considered whether grandmother coresidence, grandmother child-care assistance, and grandmother–adolescent conflict might vary by racial group or for younger versus older teenage mothers. Previous research has found that young Black mothers are almost twice as likely as White mothers to remain in their parents' home after delivery (Hofferth & Moore, 1979; Hogan et al., 1990; Mott, 1986; Unger & Cooley, 1992) and to receive child-care aid from extended family members (Parish et al., 1991). In addition, much has been written about the strong kin networks of African Americans and their beneficial effects for both parents and children (Jayakody, Chatters, & Taylor, 1993; Taylor, Casten, & Flickinger, 1993; Wilson, 1986), particularly for the poor, urban Black family (Hogan et al., 1990; Stack, 1974). In contrast, relatively little is known about the extent of grandmother support or coresidence for Hispanic teen mothers. A more accurate picture of the nature of grandmothers' influence on Hispanic adolescent mothers' parenting and their children's adjustment is essential for understanding the present status and future outlook for Hispanic young mother families. Regarding specific effects related to maternal age, younger teenage mothers have been shown to be more likely to live with their mothers but not more likely to receive greater grandmother support than older teenage mothers (Cooley & Unger, 1991; Spieker & Bensley, 1994). Moreover, grandmothers' coresidence was shown not to be more beneficial for the parenting of younger versus older teenage mothers (Chase-Lansdale et al., 1994). Chase-Lansdale et al. found, however, that in families involving a very young mother, the parenting of coresiding grandmothers was of higher quality than the parenting of noncoresiding grandmothers.

In this chapter, we tested the following six hypotheses; these are outlined in Table 5.1. First, it was expected that Black teens will be more likely to coreside with grandmothers and to receive greater grandmother child-care assistance than either White or Hispanic teens. Potential racial differences in grandmother–adolescent conflict were also investigated. It could be that because young Black mothers are more likely to live with their mothers, they have higher rates of grandmother–adolescent conflict. Second, it was expected that younger teenage mothers (i.e., age 16 or younger at delivery) will be more likely to live with their mothers but not necessarily more likely to receive greater grandmother child-care assistance than older teenage mothers (age 17 or older at delivery). Again, because younger mothers were expected to be more likely to live with their mothers, it was hypothesized that teenage mothers age 16 or younger would have more conflict with their mothers than teenage mothers age 17 or older. Third, it was expected that grandmothers' coresidence, grandmother-provided child-care assistance and grandmother–adolescent conflict will be positively interrelated, that is, that coresidence will be associated with high child-care assistance and high conflict and that high child-care assistance will be associated with high conflict. Fourth, it was expected that grandmother coresidence, high grandmother child-care assistance, and high grandmother–adolescent conflict will be related to poor adolescent mother parenting outcomes, such

Table 5.1
Hypotheses Addressed

1. Black teens will more likely coreside with grandmothers, receive greater grandmother child-care support, but also experience more grandmother–adolescent conflict, than White or Hispanic teens.

2. Younger teenage mothers will more likely live with their mothers and experience more conflict with them but will not necessarily receive greater child-care assistance from grandmothers than older teenage mothers.

3. Grandmothers' coresidence, high grandmother child-care assistance, and high grandmother–adolescent conflict will be positively interrelated.

4. Grandmother coresidence, high grandmother child-care assistance, and high grandmother–adolescent conflict will relate to poor adolescent mother parenting outcomes. Such effects may vary for mothers of different racial backgrounds and of different ages such that grandmother child-care assistance may benefit younger teenage mothers more than older teenage mothers vis-à-vis their parenting.

5. Grandmother coresidence, high grandmother child-care assistance, and high grandmother–adolescent conflict will be related to unfavorable children outcomes. Such outcomes may vary for children of different racial backgrounds and for children of younger versus older teenage mothers.

6. Nonshared residence and high grandmother child-care assistance will be related to low grandmother–adolescent conflict, favorable adolescent mothers' parenting, and positive children's behavioral adjustment.

as unfavorable parenting attitudes, low parenting confidence, high parenting stress, low parenting commitment, low child-care involvement, and low child development knowledge. Such effects may vary, however, for mothers of different ages, with younger mothers possibly benefiting more from grandmothers' coresidence and child-care involvement vis-à-vis their parenting outcomes than older teenage mothers (cf. Chase-Lansdale et al., 1994). It was also investigated whether grandmothers' coresidence and child-care assistance may be differentially beneficial for the parenting of mothers of different racial backgrounds. For example, grandmothers' coresidence and child care assistance may be more beneficial for the parenting of Black mothers than the parenting of White or Hispanic mothers (cf. Jayakody et al., 1993; Taylor et al., 1993). Or, put another way, grandmother coresidence may be more detrimental to the parenting of White teens than the parenting of Black teens, as found by Unger and Cooley (1992). Fifth, it was expected that grandmother coresidence, high grandmother child-care assistance, and high grandmother–adolescent conflict will be related to unfavorable children's outcomes, specifically to high child social withdrawal and high physical aggression (cf. Crockenberg, 1987a; Unger & Cooley, 1992). Such outcomes may vary for children of different racial backgrounds given that continued grandmother child care has been found to have negative effects for White children but positive effects for Black children (Unger & Cooley, 1992). Moreover, the children of younger teenage mothers might benefit more from grandmothers' coresidence and high child-care involvement than the children of older teenage mothers vis-à-vis their sociobehavioral adjustment. Sixth, it was hypothesized that coresidence status and grandmother child-care assistance will interact to predict grandmother–adolescent conflict, adolescent mothers' parenting, and children's behavioral adjustment such that nonshared residence and high grandmother assistance will be most closely linked with low grandmother–adolescent conflict, favorable adolescent mothers' parenting, and positive children's sociobehavioral adjustment. As observed by Spieker and Bensley (1994), living apart from grandmother but receiving high amounts of social support from her may diminish the conflict brought about from shared child-care arrangements, allow the adolescent to fully assume the parenting role and, thereby indirectly, positively influence children's sociobehavioral development.

For the sake of clarity, throughout this chapter the adolescent's mother will be referred to as the *grandmother* and the adolescent mother will be referred to as the *mother*. Unlike other studies (e.g., Chase-Lansdale et al., 1994), the grandmother in this chapter is the natural maternal grandmother, not a nonrelated grandmother figure or other maternal kin. Also, it should be recognized that although the presence of a male partner in the adolescent's life is an important issue for both mothers' parenting and children's outcomes, it is not the central focus of this chapter. Most of the young mothers in this sample were rearing their children without significant father involvement (see chapter 6), and in the majority of families, the grandmother provided significant assistance to the adolescent and her child. Finally, for the sake of clarity, coresidence implies living with the grandmother and noncoresidence implies not living with the grandmother and may indicate either living alone, living with other kin, or living with a partner. The measures used to assess grandmothers' coresidence, grandmother-provided child-care assistance, and grandmother–adolescent conflict are described here. The measures used to assess adolescent mothers' parenting (i.e., their parenting attitudes, parenting confidence, parenting stress, child-care involvement, parenting commitment, and knowledge of infant and child development) and child outcomes (social withdrawal and physical aggression) were described previously in chapter 4.

## METHOD

### Subjects

Subjects were 208 adolescent mothers (M age at birth = 17.18; SD = 1.03; range = 14–18.9) who were part of the UCSD Teen OB Follow-Up Study. Six infants did not live with their mother at any point of assessment. These families were deleted from all substantive analyses. (See chapter 1 for a description of the adolescent mother participants and chapter 4 for a description of the mothers' children.)

Assessments that are the focus of analyses for this chapter included the 6-, 12-, 18-, and 24-month follow-ups. Follow-up rates are shown in Table 1.5 and were not less than 77% at any time of assessment. Follow-up was not related to mothers' age nor race, with consistent percentages of all racial groups participating at each follow-up. As shown in Table 1.5, most assessments were conducted within 3 months of the scheduled follow-up and children's mean ages were at the scheduled time of follow-up.

## Table 5.2
### Time and Method of Assessment of Each Variable

| Measure | Time of Assessment | Method |
|---|---|---|
| Grandmother Variable | | |
| Grandmother coresidence | Intake, 6, 12, 18, and 24 months postpartum | Interview with teen |
| Grandmother provided child-care | 6, 12,18, and 24 months postpartum | Interview with teen |
| Grandmother–adolescent conflict | 6, 12, 18, and 24 months postpartum | Interview with teen |
| Adolescent Mothers' Parenting | | |
| Involvement in caretaking | 24 months postpartum | Interview with teen |
| Parenting commitment | 24 months postpartum | Interview with teen |
| Child development knowledge | 24 months postpartum | Questionnaire |
| Parenting attitudes[+] | 12–50 months postpartum (M = 37.5 months) | Questionnaire |
| Parenting confidence[+] | 12–50 months postpartum (M = 37.5 months) | Questionnaire |
| Parenting stress[+] | 12–50 months postpartum (M = 37.5 months) | Questionnaire |
| Child Outcomes | | |
| Social withdrawal[+] | 12–50 months postpartum (M = 37.5 months) | Questionnaire |
| Physical aggression[+] | 12–50 months postpartum (M = 37.5 months) | Questionnaire |

[+]Indicates that this measure was completed by a subsample of mothers (N = 119) at different points postpartum, ranging from 12 to 50 months with a mean of 37.5 months postpartum.

## Procedure

Time and method of assessment of each variable studied in this chapter are shown in Table 5.2. Grandmothers' coresidence, grandmother-provided child-care assistance, and grandmother–adolescent conflict were assessed by a structured interview with the teen at each point of follow-up. Adolescent mothers' involvement with the daily caretaking of the study child and their parenting commitment were also assessed by interview at the 2-year follow-up only. Mothers' knowledge of infant and child development was asked via questionnaire at the 2-year follow-up. Additional parenting assessments (of parenting attitudes, parenting confidence, and parenting stress) and child outcomes were assessed by questionnaires completed by the adolescent mothers at varying times postpartum and involved only a subset of mothers (n = 119). The 119 mothers who chose to complete the parenting questionnaires did not differ from the 89 subjects who chose not to complete them with regard to mothers' age, race, parity, and child's age or gender (see chapter 4). Most mothers who declined to complete the additional parenting questionnaires did so due to lack of time. The interviews and questionnaires were administered by a female professional specifically associated with this project. Unlike many studies that employ a trained research assistant, this project had trained professionals (e.g., a nurse or social worker) involved in data collection. All interviews and questionnaires were completed in the subjects' place of residence at a time of their convenience. The interview usually lasted about 45 minutes, with all questions asked in a caring and nonjudgmental fashion. The nurse or social worker described the instructions for completing the interview and the questionnaires and was available to answer any questions regarding directions or word definitions and to look after the mothers' children. All participants were assured of the confidentiality of their responses.

## Measures

Grandmother coresidence was assessed by adolescent interview at all points of assessment by the question, "Who do you currently live with?" The adolescent responded yes (coded as 1) or no (0) to 16 living arrangements (e.g., with mother only [the maternal grandmother], with father only, alone, with other relatives, etc.). Coresidence was defined as the adolescent living with the maternal grandmother regardless if other people were also present. Percentage of mothers coresiding at intake and at the 6-, 12-, 18- and 24-month follow-ups were: 42%, 40%, 37%, 29%, and 28%, respectively (see Table 5.3). Of the 40% coresiding families at the 6-month follow-up, 57% lived with their mothers only, 31% lived with both their parents, and 12% lived with their mother and a stepfather or common-law father. Of the 60% noncoresiding teens at the 6-month follow-up, 55% lived with the father of the baby, 18% lived with relatives other than the maternal grandmother, 9% lived with a girlfriend, and the remainder lived with their father only (7%), alone with their child (5%), in foster care (1%), or had no regular home (5%).

Grandmothers' child-care assistance was asked of the adolescent mothers at all points of assessment by the interview question, "What help during the day do you have with child care?". Response options were none (coded as 0), some (coded as 1), and a lot (coded as 2). This question was asked of the following: the maternal grandmother, the father of the baby, other relatives, neighbors/friends, nursery or day care, and any other source of child care. Mean scores of grandmother child-care assistance and all other child-care assistance providers for each assessment period are shown in Table 5.4. Grandmother-provided child-care assistance was the

### Table 5.3
Percentages of Coresiding Grandmothers and Mean Scores of Grandmother-Provided Child-Care Assistance and Grandmother–Adolescent Conflict at 6, 12, 18, and 24 Months Postpartum

| Grandmother | 6 Months | 12 Months | 18 Months | 24 Months |
|---|---|---|---|---|
| Coresidence | 40%[a, b] | 37%[c] | 29%[a] | 28%[b, c] |
| Child-care assistance | 0.79 | 0.83 | 0.89[e] | 0.75[e] |
|  | (.86) | (.84) | (.85) | (.84) |
| Conflict | 1.95[a,b] | 1.77[c,d] | 1.56[a,d] | 1.56[b,c] |
|  | (.88) | (.82) | (.76) | (.79) |

Note. Standard deviations are in parentheses. Percentages or means with the same letter superscript in the same row are significantly different (p < .05). Grandmother-provided child care assistance ranged from 0 (none) to 2 (a lot) and grandmother–adolescent conflict ranged from 1 to 4, with high scores indicating greater conflict.

Table 5.4
Mean Scores of Child-Care Assistance at Each Follow-Up

| | 6 Months | | 12 Months | | 18 Months | | 24 Months | |
|---|---|---|---|---|---|---|---|---|
| | M | (SD) | M | (SD) | M | (SD) | M | (SD) |
| Maternal grandmother | 0.79 | (.86) | 0.83 | (.86) | 0.89 | (.87) | 0.75 | (.87) |
| Father of baby | 0.58* | (.76) | 0.64 | (.81) | 0.66* | (.82) | 0.70 | (.89) |
| Other relatives | 0.64 | (.72) | 0.73 | (.82) | 0.81 | (.87) | 0.72 | (.81) |
| Neighbors/friends | 0.25* | (.57) | 0.11* | (.39) | 0.16* | (.47) | 0.23* | (.58) |
| Nursery/day care | 0.19* | (.54) | 0.23* | (.60) | 0.18* | (.53) | 0.29* | (.68) |
| Other | 0.13* | (.43) | 0.21* | (.51) | 0.26 | (.61) | 0.21* | (.57) |

*Indicates that the amount of child care provided by that source differed significantly from that provided by grandmothers for that assessment period.

highest of all listed providers at all points of assessment (see Table 5.4), as has been noted in other studies (e.g., Barrera, 1981; Crockenberg, 1987b; Furstenberg & Crawford, 1978; Jayakody et al., 1993).

Grandmother–adolescent conflict was assessed by a revised version of the Issues Checklist (IC; Prinz, Foster, Kent, & O'Leary, 1979), a measure designed to assess the frequency and intensity of conflict associated with 44 specific issues that might arise between a parent and an adolescent at home (e.g., getting low grades in school, how to spend free time, and talking back to parents). The questions used in the current study asked the adolescent (in interview format) about the intensity of discussion with her mother about the following seven topics within the last month: who the adolescent's friends are, coming home on time, getting poor grades in school, the adolescent helping around the house, the adolescent's boyfriend, the adolescent having sex with her boyfriend, and the adolescent's contraceptive use. (The last three items were added for the current study and were not part of the original IC.) Response options were: it was not discussed (coded as 0), it was a good, friendly discussion (coded as 1), both the adolescent and the mother were able to talk about it calmly (coded as 2), either the adolescent or the mother got annoyed (coded as 3), and either the adolescent or the mother got angry (coded as 4). Thus, if poor grades were not discussed (because the teen's grades were satisfactory or because the teen was not currently attending school), she was instructed to rate that topic as 0. Similarly, if another topic was not discussed over the last month, that item was coded as 0. All items that were not discussed within the last month were excluded from the conflict ratings. Eliminating those issues that were not discussed prevents a possible bias for higher conflict to occur within coresiding grandmother–adolescent dyads. For example, such topics as helping with housework and getting home on time are likely to be discussed only in coresiding families. Eliminating all nondiscussed items also makes the resultant scores reflect discussion intensity exclusively, void of discussion frequency. For example, mother–daughter pairs who do not talk often but, when they do, have angry discussions would receive high conflict scores. In contrast, mother–daughter pairs who have predominantly calm and friendly discussions, regardless of how often, would receive scores indicative of low conflict. All scores (except scores of 0) were averaged so that possible scores ranged from 1 to 4, with higher scores indicating greater conflict. The Cronbach alpha for all seven items was .68. Adolescents completed the conflict questions at each follow-up. The mean scores and standard deviations of grandmother–adolescent conflict at all follow-up points are shown in Table 5.3.

### Adolescent Mothers' Parenting and Child Outcomes.

Indices of adolescent mothers' parenting included teens' parenting attitudes, parenting confidence, parenting stress, involvement with child's caretaking, parenting commitment, and knowledge of infant and child development. All of the measures used to assess these parenting qualities were described previously in chapter 4. Measures were coded such that high scores indicate favorable parenting attitudes (e.g., low value of physical punishment), high parenting confidence (e.g., high confidence in caretaking ability), high parenting stress (e.g., high intensity and frequency of parenting stresses), regular and extensive involvement with the child's caretaking, high commitment to the parenting role, and accurate knowledge of normative child development. The subscales on the parenting attitudes, parenting confidence, and parenting stress measures were summed so as to provide one index of each domain. This was done to eliminate the number of dependent variables and, therefore, the complexity of analyses. Children's outcomes were assessed by mother ratings on a series of questions asking about her child's physical aggression and social withdrawal at varying points postpartum (M assessment point = 37.5 months. See chapter 4 for a further description of these scales). Questions were scored such that high scores indicate high aggression and high social withdrawal.

## RESULTS

Before presenting the substantive results related to grandmothers' role in adolescent mothers' parenting and children's outcomes, descriptive statistics related to the three grandmother variables are presented first.

### Stability and Change in
### Grandmother Variables Across Time

Adolescent mothers' residence status was quite stable over the 2 years studied, with the following percentage of subjects maintaining their residence status (whether coresiding or noncoresiding): from 6 to 12 months = 85%; from 12 to 18 months = 86%; and from 18 to 24 months = 78%. Coresidence was highest at intake (or when the teen was pregnant) at 42%, but tapered significantly by 18 months postpartum—when only 29% of adolescent mothers coresided with the grandmother (see Table 5.3 and Fig. 5.1; $t = 3.54$, $p < .01$, using a repeated measures ANOVA and coding noncoresiding as 0 and coresiding as 1). Also, significantly fewer teens lived with their mothers from 1 year to 2 years postpartum (from 37% to 28%; $t = 2.25$, $p < .05$).

In contrast, as shown in Fig. 5.1, grandmother-provided child-care assistance peaked at 18 months postpartum ($M = 0.89$) and dropped significantly at 2 years postpartum ($M = 0.75$; $t = 2.11$, $p < .05$, using a repeated measures ANOVA, see Table 5.3). Grandmother–adolescent conflict peaked at 6 months postpartum ($M = 1.95$) and declined significantly thereafter, with conflict at 2 years postpartum ($M = 1.56$) significantly less than conflict at 6 months ($t = 3.34$, $p < .001$) and at 1 year ($M = 1.77$; $t = 2.94$, $p < .01$, using a repeated measures ANOVA; see Table 5.3).

## Differences in Grandmother Variables by Mothers' Race

To test the hypothesis that Black teens were more likely to coreside with grandmothers and to receive greater grandmother child-care assistance than either White or Hispanic teens (cf. Hofferth & Moore, 1979; Hogan et al., 1990;

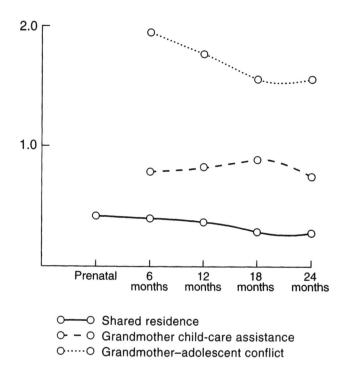

FIG. 5.1. Mean percentage of grandmother coresidence, and mean scores of grandmothers' child-care assistance and grandmother–adolescent conflict across time. The y axis represents the score range for grandmother child-care assistance and grandmother–adolescent conflict, and coresidence was plotted such that the 1.0 mark on the y axis represents 100%.

Unger & Cooley, 1992), chi-square analyses were performed on percent of Hispanic, Black, and White coresiding and noncoresiding grandmother–adolescent dyads. The number of adolescent mothers from the "other" racial group was deemed too small for analysis (n = 13 at 6 months postpartum) and, thus, these mothers were omitted from all analyses examining differences by mothers' race. Results, shown in Table 5.5, indicated no differences in percent of coresiding versus noncoresiding grandmothers for any of the racial groups at any time of follow-up. Black mothers had the highest coresidence rate at 6 months postpartum (at 48%) and White mothers had the highest coresidence rate at 12 months (45%), 18 months (41%), and 24 months postpartum (30%), but none of these differences were statistically significant.

Welfare receipt was also found to be significantly linked with coresidence status at 6 months [$\chi^2$ (1) = 9.63, $p < .01$] and 12 months postpartum [$\chi^2$ (1) = 9.44, $p < .01$], with those receiving welfare benefits more likely to live with family. At the 6-month follow-up, 58% of coresiding teens were receiving AFDC, as opposed to 66% of noncoresiding teens who were not receiving welfare. Similarly, at the 1-year follow-up, 63% of those coresiding were receiving AFDC, whereas 74% of those not coresiding with grandmother were not on welfare. Welfare receipt was not linked with coresidence at any other time postpartum. Welfare receipt was also not associated with grandmothers' assistance with child care nor to grandmother–adolescent conflict at any time postpartum.

To determine whether grandmother child-care assistance and grandmother–adolescent conflict differed by racial group, a multivariate analysis of variance (MANOVA) was calculated using grandmother child-care assistance scores and grandmother–adolescent conflict scores as the dependent variables and the three racial groups as the categorizing variable. Results indicated no differences in grandmother child-care assistance by maternal race at any time postpartum. However, conflict was significantly greater among Black grandmother–adolescent dyads than among White or Hispanic grandmother–adolescent dyads at 6 months [$F$ (2,142) = 4.63, $p < .05$] and at 12 months [$F$ (2,122) = 4.84, $p < .01$; shown in Table 5.5]. No differences by race were evident for conflict at 18 months or 24 months postpartum.

## Differences in Grandmother Variables
## for Older Versus Younger Adolescent Mothers

To examine whether younger teenage mothers (i.e., age 16 or younger at delivery) were more likely to live with their mothers than older teenage mothers (age 17–19 at delivery), chi-square analyses were computed for percent coresiding and noncoresiding for the two age groups. Seventy-eight subjects comprised the younger teenage mother group (at the 6-month follow-up; M age = 16.13 years; age range = 14–16.9 years) and 115 subjects comprised the older teenage mother group (at the 6-month follow-up; M age = 17.84 years; age range = 17–18.9 years). Results

## Table 5.5
### Grandmother Coresidence, Child-Care Assistance and Grandmother–Adolescent Conflict by Race of Mother

| | 6 Months | | | 12 Months | | | 18 Months | | | 24 Months | | |
|---|---|---|---|---|---|---|---|---|---|---|---|---|
| | H | B | W | H | B | W | H | B | W | H | B | W |
| Coresidence | 33% | 48% | 41% | 32% | 40% | 45% | 25% | 29% | 41% | 27% | 29% | 30% |
| Child-care assistance | 0.68 | 0.98 | 0.79 | 0.85 | 0.85 | 0.92 | 0.95 | 1.05 | 0.50 | 0.83 | 0.81 | 0.57 |
| | (.84) | (.85) | (.89) | (.88) | (.84) | (.81) | (.82) | (.87) | (.80) | (.81) | (.89) | (.84) |
| Conflict | 0.88[a] | 1.21[a,b] | 0.62[b] | 0.70[a] | 1.07[a,b] | 0.48[b] | 0.45 | 0.70 | 0.43 | 0.42 | 0.68 | 0.48 |
| | (.80) | (.99) | (.72) | (.75) | (.88) | (.72) | (.69) | (.83) | (.55) | (.60) | (.91) | (.65) |

Note. H indicates Hispanic; B indicates Black; and; W indicates White. Standard deviations are in parentheses. Means with the same letter superscript within the same follow-up assessment are significantly different.

[a]Hispanic–Black contrast.

[b]Black–White contrast.

indicated that, although more younger teenage mothers than older teenage mothers lived with grandmothers at all times of follow-up (except at 2 years postpartum), none of these differences were statistically significant (shown in Table 5.6). To determine whether grandmother child-care assistance and grandmother–adolescent conflict differed for older versus younger teenage mothers, $t$ tests were computed for all grandmother-provided child care and grandmother–adolescent conflict scores. Results showed no significant differences between the two age groups for either of these variables at any point postpartum.

When mothers' age at the birth of the study child was used as a continuous variable and correlations were computed between mothers' age at delivery and the three grandmother variables (i.e., coresidence, child-care assistance, grandmother–adolescent conflict) at all times of assessment, two associations were found (among 12 correlations computed). Subjects who were younger at delivery were more likely to live with the grandmother at 1 year postpartum ($r = -.15, p < .05$), and subjects who were younger at delivery reported receiving more child-care assistance from their mothers at 2 years postpartum ($r = -.18, p < .05$).

## Interrelations Between Grandmother Variables

To determine the extent to which grandmothers' coresidence, grandmother-provided child care, and grandmother–adolescent conflict were interrelated, correlations were computed between all grandmother variables within each time of assessment. Results, shown in Table 5.7, indicated that—consistent with our hypothesis—grandmother coresidence was associated with high grandmother-provided child-care assistance ($M r = .36$), coresidence was associated with high grandmother–adolescent conflict ($M r = .33$), and high grandmother child care assistance was associated with high grandmother–adolescent conflict ($M r = .27$). All variables were significantly intercorrelated at all times of assessment except at 6 months postpartum, when coresidence was not significantly correlated with conflict ($r = .08$).

Table 5.6
Grandmothers' Coresidence, Child-Care Assistance, and Grandmother–Adolescent Conflict for Older and Younger Adolescent Mothers

|  | 6 Months | | 12 Months | | 18 Months | | 24 Months | |
|---|---|---|---|---|---|---|---|---|
|  | Older | Younger | Older | Younger | Older | Younger | Older | Younger |
| Coresidence | 38% | 46% | 32% | 44% | 27% | 30% | 31% | 25% |
| Child-care assistance | 0.74 | 0.87 | 0.75 | 0.93 | 0.85 | 0.96 | 0.68 | 0.83 |
|  | (.82) | (.90) | (.80) | (.89) | (.81) | (.90) | (.82) | (.86) |
| Grandmother– adolescent conflict | 0.93 | 0.98 | 0.71 | 0.83 | 0.52 | 0.58 | 0.50 | 0.58 |
|  | (.83) | (.95) | (.74) | (.92) | (.82) | (.68) | (.72) | (.78) |

Note. Older teens were 17 to 19 years of age at delivery, and younger teens were 16.9 years of age or younger at delivery. Standard deviations are in parentheses.

Table 5.7
Within-Time Correlations Among Grandmothers' Coresidence,
Child-Care Assistance, and Grandmother–Adolescent Conflict
at 6, 12, 18, and 24 Months Postpartum

| | 6 Months | | 12 Months | | 18 Months | | 24 Months | |
| | Assistance | Conflict | Assistance | Conflict | Assistance | Conflict | Assistance | Conflict |
|---|---|---|---|---|---|---|---|---|
| Coresidence | .36** | .08 | .41** | .46** | .36** | .39** | .29* | .37** |
| Child-care assistance | | .21* | | .25** | | .29** | | .31** |

*p < .01. **p < .001.

To illustrate the mean level differences in grandmother child-care assistance and grandmother–adolescent conflict for coresiding and noncoresiding dyads, Figure 5.2 shows the mean scores of grandmother-provided child-care assistance and grandmother–adolescent conflict at each follow-up assessment for coresiding and noncoresiding families. Results of t tests indicated, and consistent with the correlations shown in Table 5.7, that grandmothers' child care assistance and grandmother–adolescent conflict were significantly and consistently higher in coresiding families than in noncoresiding families.

## Relations Between Grandmother Variables and Adolescent Mothers' Parenting

To investigate to what extent grandmother coresidence, grandmother-provided child care, and grandmother–adolescent conflict were related to adolescent mothers' parenting, correlations were computed between the three grandmother variables at each time of assessment and mothers' scores on parenting attitudes, parenting confidence, parenting stress, involvement in child's care, parenting commitment, and knowledge of infant and child development. Results are shown in Table 5.8. The pattern of correlations involving grandmothers' coresidence revealed few and modest associations: coresidence at 1-year postpartum related to mothers' negative parenting attitudes ($r = -.19$, $p < .05$), and coresidence at 18-months postpartum related to mothers' low parenting confidence ($r = -.23$, $p < .05$).

Regarding relations between grandmother-provided child-care assistance and qualities of adolescent mothers' parenting, all but one statistically significant correlation revealed that large amounts of grandmother-provided child care were associated with unfavorable mothers' parenting. For example, high grandmother child-care assistance at all times of follow-up was associated with mothers' poor parenting attitudes ($M r = -.24$), and high grandmother child care assistance at 2 years postpartum was related to teen mothers' low parenting confidence ($r = -.19$, $p < .05$). High grandmother child-care assistance at 12, 18, and 24 months postpartum was also significantly linked with low mother involvement in child care ($M r = -.30$), and high grandmother child-care assistance at 18 and 24 months

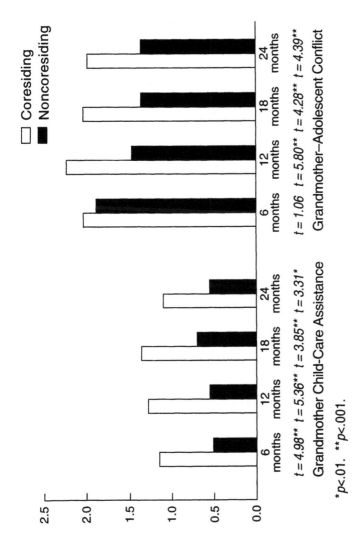

FIG. 5.2. Mean scores of grandmother child-care assistance and grandmother–adolescent conflict for coresiding and noncoresiding grandmother–adolescent dyads.

*p<.01. **p<.001.

postpartum was linked with low maternal knowledge about infant and child development (M $r$ = -.19). In addition, extensive grandmother child involvement at the 2-year follow-up was associated with adolescent mothers' low commitment to the parenting role ($r$ = -.16, $p$ < .05). The only favorable relation to emerge was that extensive grandmother child-care assistance at 18 months postpartum was associated with less parenting stress as perceived by teen mothers ($r$ = -.21, $p$ < .05).

Grandmother–adolescent conflict (at 12, 18, and 24 months postpartum) was, as expected, associated with teen mothers' unfavorable parenting attitudes (M $r$ = -.21), and grandmother–adolescent conflict at all times of assessment was linked with teen mothers' low involvement with their children's daily care (M $r$ = -.24). Conflict at any time postpartum was not, however, associated with teen mothers' parenting confidence, parenting stress, parenting commitment, or child development knowledge.

## Interaction Effects Between Maternal Age and Grandmothers' Child-Care Assistance for Adolescent Mothers' Parenting

As stated previously, it was hypothesized that the effects associated with grandmother child-care assistance for teen mothers' parenting might vary for mothers of different ages, with younger teenage mothers possibly benefiting more than older teenage mothers from grandmothers' high child-care involvement vis-à-vis their parenting outcomes. To address this possibility, two 2 × 2 MANOVAs were computed using high and low grandmother assistance groups and older versus younger teenage mother groups as the classification variables. High versus low grandmother child-care assistance groups were formed grouping the 2-year postpartum child-care assistance scores of 1 and 2 (*some* and *a lot*, respectively) to form the high assistance group ($n$ = 84) and using scores of 0 (*none*) to form the low assistance group ($n$ = 86). The 2-year grandmother child-care assistance scores were used because they were closest temporally to the assessment of some of the parenting outcomes (e.g., parenting attitudes, confidence, and stress—which were assessed, on average, at approximately 3 years postpartum). Younger and older teenage mother groups were formed using mothers' age at delivery, with mothers in the younger group age 16 or younger at delivery ($n$ = 70 at the 2-year follow-up) and mothers in the older group age 17 to 19 at delivery ($n$ = 101 at the 2-year follow-up).

One MANOVA was computed using scores for parenting attitudes, parenting confidence, and parenting stress as the dependent variables, and one MANOVA was computed using scores for mothers' child care involvement, parenting commitment, and child development knowledge as the dependent variables. This was done because only a subsample of mothers completed the surveys on parenting attitudes, parenting confidence, and parenting stress, whereas all participating mothers completed surveys on their child care involvement, parenting commitment, and

Table 5.8
Relations Between Grandmother Variables (at 6, 12, 18,
and 24 Months Postpartum) and Adolescent Mothers' Parenting

| Adolescent Mothers' Parenting | 6 Months | 12 Months | 18 Months | 24 Months |
|---|---|---|---|---|
| | | Grandmothers' Coresidence | | |
| Attitudes | −.15 | −.19* | −.16 | .04 |
| Confidence | .14 | −.04 | −.23* | −.17+ |
| Stress | .10 | .04 | .12 | .05 |
| Child-care involvement | .03 | .08 | −.08 | .06 |
| Commitment | −.11 | −.03 | −.02 | −.07 |
| Child development knowledge | −.07 | .02 | .01 | −.12 |
| | | Grandmothers' Child-Care Assistance | | |
| Attitudes | −.18* | −.18* | −.26** | −.34*** |
| Confidence | .12 | .07 | .12 | −.19* |
| Stress | .06 | −.07 | −.21* | .09 |
| Child-care involvement | −.03 | −.34*** | −.20** | −.35*** |
| Commitment | .08 | −.09 | −.06 | −.16* |
| Child development knowledge | .02 | −.07 | −.16* | −.21** |
| | | Grandmother–Adolescent Conflict | | |
| Attitudes | .04 | −.25** | −.19* | −.18* |
| Confidence | −.03 | −.13 | −.14 | .05 |
| Stress | .04 | .08 | .03 | .15 |
| Child-care involvement | −.21** | −.31*** | −.28*** | −.16* |
| Commitment | .07 | .08 | −.01 | −.02 |
| Child development knowledge | .11 | −.09 | .04 | .01 |

Note. Grandmothers' coresidence was coded as 0 = *does not live with teen mother*; 1 = *currently lives with teen mother*. Grandmother-provided child-care assistance was coded such that high scores indicate greater support. Grandmother–adolescent conflict scores were coded such that high scores indicate greater conflict. Adolescent mothers' parenting scores were coded such that high scores indicate favorable parenting attitudes, high parenting confidence, high parenting stress, extensive involvement with child care, high parenting commitment, and accurate knowledge of infant and child development.
+p < .06. *p < .05. **p < .01. ***p < .001.

child development knowledge. Thus, two MANOVAs were computed to best utilize the available data.

The results of the MANOVA on parenting attitudes, parenting confidence, and parenting stress scores revealed a significant maternal age by grandmother child care assistance interaction [the multivariate $F$ (3, 109) for the interaction = 2.98, $p$ < .05]. The results of the univariate analyses indicated that only parenting confidence and parenting stress had significant maternal age × grandmother child-care assistance interaction effects. The results of the MANOVA on child-care involvement, parenting commitment, and child development knowledge scores also revealed a significant maternal age by grandmother child-care assistance interaction [the multivariate $F$ (3, 165) for the interaction = 3.43, $p$ < .05]. The results of the univariate analyses indicated that only mothers' child-care involvement and child development knowledge had significant maternal age × grandmother assistance interaction effects.

The means, standard deviations, and univariate F values associated with mothers' parenting confidence, parenting stress, child-care involvement, and child development knowledge by mothers' age and grandmothers' child-care assistance are shown in Table 5.9. Individual contrasts were then computed using Newman-Keuls tests and $p < .05$ level of significance to control for the number of contrasts. Contrasts were computed comparing young teenage mothers who had high versus low grandmother child-care support, and comparing old teenage mothers who had high versus low grandmother child-care support. These contrasts were computed horizontally within Table 5.9, with significant differences denoted as a superscript "h." Results of the contrasts on young mothers (shown in the top half of Table 5.9) indicated that, compared to young mothers who had high grandmother child-care assistance, young mothers who had low grandmother child-care assistance had significantly less parenting confidence, less involvement with their children's care, and less accurate child development knowledge. When examining older teenage mothers (whose data are shown in the bottom half of Table 5.9), teens with high grandmother child-care assistance reported significantly more parenting stress than teens with low grandmother child-care assistance.

Table 5.9
**Means and Standard Deviations of Mothers' Parenting Scores by Mothers' Age at Delivery and Grandmother-Provided Child-Care Assistance**

| | Grandmothers' Child-Care Assistance | | |
| --- | --- | --- | --- |
| | High | Low | Interaction Univariate F (df) |
| Young | | | |
| Parenting confidence | 3.75[h] | 3.41[h] | 5.39* (1,109) |
| | (0.43) | (0.68) | |
| Parenting stress | 1.71 | 1.95[v] | 5.19* (1,109) |
| | (0.41) | (0.60) | |
| Child-care involvement | 2.79[h] | 2.51[h,v] | 7.40** (1,165) |
| | (0.30) | (0.77) | |
| Child development knowledge | 17.72[h,v] | 15.61[h] | 4.10* (1,165) |
| | (2.07) | (2.74) | |
| Old | | | |
| Parenting confidence | 3.50 | 3.61 | |
| | (0.60) | (0.49) | |
| Parenting stress | 1.86[h] | 1.52[h,v] | |
| | (0.55) | (0.44) | |
| Child-care involvement | 2.74 | 2.92[v] | |
| | (0.29) | (0.22) | |
| Child development knowledge | 15.89[v] | 15.97 | |
| | (2.94) | (2.56) | |

Note. Standard deviations are in parentheses.
[h]Means in the same row are significantly different (a horizontal contrast).
[v]Means in the same column for the same parenting quality are significantly different (a vertical contrast).
*$p < .05$.   **$p < .01$.

Individual contrasts were also made comparing the parenting outcomes of younger versus older teenage mothers within high and low grandmother child-care support groups. These contrasts were performed vertically within the same column in Table 5.9, with significant differences denoted as a superscript "v." Results of these contrasts revealed three differences: when compared to old teenage mothers with low grandmother child-care assistance, young teenage mothers with low grandmother child-care assistance perceived significantly more stress associated with parenting and were significantly less involved in their children's caretaking, and; old teenage mothers with high grandmother support had lower child development knowledge scores than young teenage mothers with high grandmother support.

These results clearly point to one group most at risk for negative parenting outcomes: young teenage mothers with low grandmother child-care assistance. Specifically, mothers age 16 or younger at delivery who reported no grandmother child-care assistance had the lowest parenting confidence, the highest parenting stress, the lowest child-care involvement, and the lowest child development knowledge scores of all four groups shown in Table 5.9. The most optimal parenting was evidenced by young teenage mothers with high grandmother child-care assistance (for parenting confidence and child development knowledge) and by older teenage mothers with low grandmother child-care assistance (for parenting stress and child development involvement). Thus, teenage mothers age 16 or younger appear to benefit most from grandmothers' assistance with child care, whereas teenage mothers age 17 or older benefit least from high grandmother child-care involvement and, in fact, experience unfavorable parenting outcomes when grandmother involvement with child care is high.

## Interaction Effects Between Maternal Age and Grandmothers' Coresidence for Adolescent Mothers' Parenting

Results of the MANOVAs computed on coresiding versus noncoresiding grandmother–mother dyads (at 24 months postpartum) and younger versus older teenage mothers revealed no significant maternal age by grandmother coresidence interaction effects for any of the parenting outcomes examined in this study. Thus, grandmothers' co-residence does not appear to be particularly beneficial for the parenting of younger versus older teenage mothers.

## Interaction Effects Between Mothers' Race and Grandmothers' Child-Care Assistance for Adolescent Mothers' Parenting

It was also examined whether effects associated with grandmother child care assistance might vary for mothers of different racial backgrounds. To address this possibility, high versus low grandmother child-care assistance groups were formed using the identical criteria described earlier. Mothers' self-reported race was used to form three racial groups: Black ($n = 52$), Hispanic ($n = 77$), and White ($n =$

30). Two 2 × 3 MANOVAs were computed using high and low grandmother child-care assistance groups and mothers' race as the classification variables and mothers' parenting scores as the dependent variables. As explained previously, to best utilize the available data, one MANOVA was computed using scores for mothers' parenting attitudes, parenting confidence, and parenting stress as the dependent variables, and one MANOVA was computed using scores for mothers' child-care involvement, parenting commitment, and child development knowledge as the dependent variables.

Results of the MANOVA on parenting attitudes, parenting confidence, and parenting stress scores revealed a significant maternal race by grandmother child-care assistance interaction [the multivariate $F$ (6, 110) for the interaction = 2.30, $p < .05$]. The results of the univariate analyses indicated that only parenting confidence had a statistically significant maternal race by grandmother assistance interaction, and that parenting attitudes and parenting stress had marginally significant univariate $F$ values for the interaction ($p < .10$). The results of the MANOVA on mothers' child-care involvement, parenting commitment, and child development knowledge revealed a marginally significant maternal race by grandmother child-care assistance interaction [the multivariate $F$ (6,165) = 2.04, $p < .07$], with a statistically significant univariate $F$ value for mothers' child-care involvement only ($p < .05$).

The means, standard deviations, and univariate $F$ values of mothers' parenting attitudes, parenting confidence, parenting stress, and child-care involvement by maternal race and grandmother child-care assistance are shown in Table 5.10. Individual contrasts were computed using Newman-Keuls and $p < .05$ level of significance. Comparisons were first made between teen mothers who had high versus low grandmother child-care support within each racial group (i.e., contrasts were computed vertically within each column, with significant differences denoted as a superscript "v" in Table 5.10). These vertical contrasts test whether high grandmother child-care assistance is beneficial for the parenting of mothers within each racial group.

Results of the vertical contrasts indicated that high grandmother child care assistance was associated with negative parenting outcomes for mothers of all races, and that high grandmother involvement was related to specific outcomes for different-race mothers. For example, White mothers who had high grandmother child care assistance had significantly less favorable parenting attitudes and less parenting confidence than White mothers who had low grandmother child-care assistance. Hispanic mothers who had high grandmother child-care assistance were significantly less involved in their children's care than Hispanic mothers who had low grandmother child-care assistance, and Black mothers who had high grandmother child-care assistance were significantly more stressed in their parent–child interactions than Black mothers who had low grandmother child-care assistance. Thus, high grandmother child care involvement seems to "matter" differently for teen mothers of different racial backgrounds. In fact, in all of these cases the race-specific mother with high grandmother assistance had the least favorable parenting outcome of all groups shown in Table 5.10, and her same-race counterpart

Table 5.10
Means and Standard Deviations of Mothers' Parenting Scores by Mothers'
Race and Grandmother-Provided Child-Care Assistance

| | White | Hispanic | Black | Interaction Univariate F (df) |
|---|---|---|---|---|
| Low Grandmother Child-Care Assistance | | | | |
| Parenting attitudes | 3.37$^v$ | 2.72 | 2.87 | 2.77$^+$ (2,110) |
| | (0.27) | (0.50) | (0.19) | |
| Parenting confidence | 3.77$^v$ | 3.61 | 3.33 | 4.39* (2,110) |
| | (0.28) | (0.31) | (0.52) | |
| Parenting stress | 1.87 | 2.13 | 1.60$^v$ | 2.83$^+$ (2,110) |
| | (0.43) | (0.49) | (0.32) | |
| Child-care involvement | 2.13 | 2.69$^v$ | 2.41 | 4.34* (2,165) |
| | (0.83) | (0.49) | (0.73) | |
| High Grandmother Child-Care Assistance | | | | |
| Parenting attitudes | 2.50$^v$ | 2.88 | 2.69 | |
| | (0.45) | (0.32) | (0.42) | |
| Parenting confidence | 2.99$^{v,a,b}$ | 3.59$^a$ | 3.38$^b$ | |
| | (0.44) | (0.39) | (0.35) | |
| Parenting stress | 1.99 | 1.90$^c$ | 2.32$^{v,c}$ | |
| | (0.37) | (0.32) | (0.57) | |
| Child-care involvement | 2.50 | 2.12$^{v,c}$ | 2.58$^c$ | |
| | (0.71) | (0.71) | (0.65) | |

Note. Standard deviations are in parentheses.
$^v$Means in the same column for the same parenting quality are significantly different (a vertical contrast).
$^a$White–Hispanic contrast.
$^b$White–Black contrast.
$^c$Hispanic–Black contrast.
$^+p < .10$.  $^*p < .05$.

with low grandmother assistance had the most favorable parenting outcome of all groups shown in Table 5.10. This suggests that the presence of even moderate grandmother involvement in child care is quite disadvantageous for adolescent mothers' parenting.

Individual contrasts were also computed (using Newman-Keuls and $p < .05$ level of significance) across racial groups for all teens who received high grandmother child care assistance (i.e., contrasts were computed horizontally within each row only for those means in the bottom half of Table 5.10). These contrasts test whether high grandmother child-care assistance is differentially beneficial (or disadvantageous, whichever the case may be) for the parenting of White, Hispanic, and Black teen mothers.

Results of these horizontal contrasts indicated that, among teen mothers who had high grandmother child-care assistance, White mothers evidenced the least favorable parenting confidence, Black mothers reported the most parenting stress, and Hispanic mothers were least involved in their children's caretaking. Thus, similar to the results just reported, high grandmother child-care involvement seems to have unique negative effects for teen mothers of different racial backgrounds.

## Interaction Effects Between Mothers' Race and Grandmothers' Coresidence for Adolescent Mothers' Parenting

Results of the MANOVAs computed on coresiding versus noncoresiding grand-mother–adolescent dyads (at 24 months postpartum) for mothers of different racial backgrounds revealed no significant maternal race by grandmother coresidence interaction effects for any of the parenting outcomes examined in this study. Thus, coresiding with grandmother does not appear to be differentially advantageous for mothers of different races.

## Relations Between Grandmother Variables and Children's Sociobehavioral Adjustment

To investigate to what extent grandmothers' coresidence, grandmother-provided child care and grandmother–adolescent conflict were related to children's out-comes, correlations were computed between the three grandmother variables at each time of assessment and children's scores of social withdrawal and physical aggression. Recall that children's behavior scores were available for only a subset of the total sample ($n = 119$) and that such data were collected when the children were, on average, 3 years old. Boys and girls did not differ significantly in their social withdrawal or aggression scores, and equivalent percentages of boys and girls lived with their grandmothers as did not. Results of the correlations indicated that only grandmothers' coresidence (at 12, 18, and 24 months) was significantly correlated with high levels of children's aggression ($rs = .22, .25,$ and $.23$, respectively; $p < .05$). To indicate the magnitude of the difference for children's aggression for coresiding and noncoresiding families, the aggression mean for children who coresided with grandmother at 1 year postpartum was 0.93 ($SD = 0.42$; the possible score range was 0 to 2) and the aggression mean for noncoresiding children (at 1 year postpartum) was 0.67 ($SD = 0.46$; $t = 2.48, p < .05$). None of the correlations between grandmothers' child-care assistance or grandmother–adolescent conflict and children's behavioral adjustment were statistically significant.

## Interaction Effects Between Maternal Age, Maternal Race, and Grandmother Variables for Children's Sociobehavioral Adjustment

We also examined whether children's outcomes associated with grandmothers' influ-ence might vary for the children of younger versus older mothers and for children of different race mothers. To address these possibilities, four MANOVAs were computed on children's behavioral scores using the following sets of independent classification variables: coresiding and noncoresiding families and younger versus older teenage mothers (2 × 2), coresiding and noncoresiding families and teenage mothers of different racial backgrounds (2 × 3), high versus low grandmother child-care assistance and younger versus older teenage mothers (2 × 2) and, high versus low grandmother child care assistance and teenage mothers of different racial backgrounds (2 × 3). Results indicated two significant interactions: maternal race by grandmothers' coresidence for children's social withdrawal [the univariate $F$ (2, 105) for the interaction = 3.10, $p < .05$], and maternal age by grandmothers' coresidence for children's aggression [the univariate $F$ (1, 108) for the interaction = 7.54, $p < .01$].

Analysis of mean group differences for the maternal race by grandmothers' coresidence interaction (using Newman-Keuls and $p < .05$ level of significance) indicated that White children living with their grandmothers were perceived by their mothers as significantly more socially withdrawn ($M = 0.76, SD = 0.52$) than white children not living with their grandmothers ($M = 0.48, SD = 0.33; t = 5.69, p < .05$). However, for Black children, grandmothers' coresidence had a positive effect: Black children living with their grandmothers had significantly lower social withdrawal scores ($M = 0.29, SD = 0.28$) than Black children not living with their grandmothers ($M = 0.59, SD = 0.42; t = 3.76, p < .05$).

Analysis of mean group differences for the maternal age by grandmother coresidence interaction indicated that the children of young mothers who coresided with their grandmothers had significantly higher aggression scores ($M = 1.13, SD = 0.41$) than the children of young mothers who did not coreside with their grandmothers ($M = 0.57, SD = 0.46; t = 12.73, p < .001$). Thus, as far as mothers' perceptions of their children's behavioral adjustment is concerned, grandmothers' coresidence appears to be associated with negative outcomes for White children and for children born to young teenage mothers. In contrast, grandmothers' coresidence seemed to benefit Black children, with Black children who coresided with their grandmothers having the lowest social withdrawal mean score of any other group.

## Interactions Between Grandmothers' Coresidence and Grandmother-Provided Child-Care Assistance for Adolescent Mothers' Parenting and Children's Sociobehavioral Adjustment

It has previously been reported that living apart from grandmother but receiving high levels of child-care support from her is the optimal situation for a favorable parent–child attachment for adolescent mothers (Chase-Lansdale et al., 1994; Spieker & Bensley, 1994). This possibility of favorable parenting and children's outcomes being associated with nonshared grandmother coresidence and high grandmother child-care assistance was tested using the data from this study. Specifically, a 2 × 2 MANOVA was computed using grandmother coresidence status and high and low grandmother child-care assistance groups as the independent variables, and the following nine scores as the dependent variables: grandmother–adolescent conflict, adolescent mothers' parenting attitudes, parenting confidence, parenting stress, child-care involvement, parenting commitment, and child development knowledge, and children's aggression and social withdrawal. Results revealed a significant coresidence × child-care assistance interaction [$F$ (9,109) = 4.21; $p$ < .01].

Significant univariate $F$ values for the grandmother coresidence × grandmother child-care assistance interaction were associated with the following five outcomes (out of nine outcomes tested): mothers' parenting attitudes, parenting confidence, child-care involvement, parenting commitment, and child aggression. The means, standard deviations, and univariate $F$ values associated with these outcomes by grandmothers' coresidence status and grandmothers' child-care assistance is shown in Table 5.11. Results of individual contrasts (using Newman-Keuls and $p$ < .05 level of significance) indicated that, in all cases, the most favorable outcome was associated with grandmothers' noncoresidence and high grandmother child-care support. Also, for all but one outcome (mothers' child-care involvement), the least positive functioning was associated with shared grandmother coresidence and high grandmother child-care support. Mothers' child-care involvement was the lowest, however, for coresiding families in which there was low grandmother child care assistance. As a whole, these results confirm previous findings by Chase-Lansdale et al. (1994) and Spieker and Bensley (1994) that living apart from grandmother but receiving high amounts of child-care assistance from her allows the adolescent mother to best acquire appropriate childrearing attitudes and to develop a positive confidence about her parenting. This situation also appears to benefit the teen's child. Children who did not live with their grandmother but who received large amounts of caretaking from her had the lowest physical aggression of any other group.

## DISCUSSION

What may we conclude about grandmothers' role in adolescent mothers' parenting and children's outcomes? The results of this study show many noteworthy effects related to grandmothers' coresidence, grandmother-provided child-care assistance and grandmother–adolescent conflict. As a whole, living with the grandmother and receiving extensive grandmother child-care assistance were related to high levels of grandmother–adolescent conflict which, in turn, was associated with unfavorable and uninvolved adolescent mothering. Grandmothers' coresidence was also found to be associated with high levels of mother-rated aggression in children. These findings varied, however, depending on mothers' age and race. Grandmothers' child-care assistance, for example, seemed to be beneficial for the parenting of very young mothers, and grandmothers' coresidence appeared to be advantageous for the behavioral adjustment of Black children. Although relatively few teens changed their residential arrangement during the 2 years following delivery, living with grandmother showed enough variability to have significantly decreased across time. Coresiding with grandmother was highest at delivery (at 42%), but declined significantly at 18 months postpartum with 29% of teens living with grandmother. This changed very little at the 2-year follow-up. Very similarly, grandmother–adolescent conflict peaked at 6 months postpartum (the first assessment

Table 5.11
Means and Standard Deviations of Mothers' Parenting and Children's
Behavioral Adjustment by Grandmothers' Coresidence and
Grandmother-Provided Child-Care Assistance

| | Grandmothers' Child-Care Assistance | | |
| | High | Low | Interaction Univariate F (df) |
|---|---|---|---|
| Coreside | | | |
| Parenting attitudes | 3.47[h,v] | 3.87[h] | 4.90* (1, 110) |
| | (0.38) | (0.27) | |
| Parenting confidence | 3.03[v] | 3.25 | 4.02* (1, 110) |
| | (0.51) | (0.61) | |
| Child-care involvement | 2.48[h,v] | 2.12[h,v] | 8.20** (1, 165) |
| | (0.81) | (1.18) | |
| Parenting commitment | 3.17[h,v] | 3.62[h] | 6.62* (1, 165) |
| | (0.65) | (0.41) | |
| Child aggression | 1.02[v] | 0.86 | 6.09* (1,110) |
| | (0.50) | (0.43) | |
| Noncoreside | | | |
| Parenting attitudes | 3.89[v] | 3.79 | |
| | (0.20) | (0.29) | |
| Parenting confidence | 3.61[h,v] | 3.13[h] | |
| | (0.35) | (0.59) | |
| Child-care involvement | 2.78[v] | 2.74[v] | |
| | (0.25) | (0.48) | |
| Parenting commitment | 3.66[v] | 3.48 | |
| | (0.41) | (0.44) | |
| Child aggression | 0.38[h,v] | 0.88[h] | |
| | (0.31) | (0.43) | |

Note. Standard deviations are in parentheses.
[h]Means in the same row are significantly different (a horizontal contrast).
[v]Means in the same column for the same outcome are significantly different (a vertical contrast).
*$p < .05$. **$p < .01$.

period for which we have conflict data) and decreased steadily across the postpartum period, in line with the percentage coresiding. The level of grandmother child-care assistance, however, remained fairly consistent throughout the time period studied, with a slight peak occurring at the 18-month follow-up. These and other results are discussed here, as well as interpretations of the findings and the limitations of the current study.

## Similarities and Differences in Grandmother Variables by Mothers' Race and Age

The first finding of note was the striking similarity in grandmother coresidence and grandmother child-care assistance for teen mothers of different racial backgrounds. This runs counter to previous findings in which Black teen mothers have been found to be more likely to live with grandmother (Hofferth & Moore, 1979; Hogan et al., 1990; Mott, 1986; Unger & Cooley, 1992) and more likely to receive extensive child-care aid from her than White teen mothers (Hogan et al., 1990; Parish et al., 1991). Compared to other studies, the White teen mothers in the current sample had relatively higher coresidence rates and the Black teen mothers in the current sample had relatively lower coresidence rates. For example, in the current sample 43% of White teens lived with the grandmother within the first year postpartum. In contrast, Hogan et al. (1990) and Parish et al. (1991) reported that only 6% of their samples' White mothers lived in the same household as the maternal grandmother. Moreover, in the current sample, 44% of Black teens coresided with their mothers over the first year following delivery. This is in contrast to Unger and Cooley's (1992) report that nearly 80% of their Black teen mothers lived with the child's maternal grandmother at some point after the child's birth. In addition, far more White mothers were single at the time of delivery in the current sample (87%) than the White mothers studied by Hogan et al. (1990), at 14%, or Unger and Cooley (1992), at 12%. Given that marital status and residential patterns are invariably linked (Hogan et al., 1990), the greater number of White teens coresiding with family within the current sample is most likely related to their higher nonmarried status.

Recall, too, that in the current sample, 33% of all Black mothers were Gravida 2 or higher at the time of delivery of the target study child. It has been noted that as a teen's family size increases, the likelihood of the teen living with her mother declines (Furstenberg et al., 1987b). This is often the result of strong family pressures for the teen to set up an independent household, as well as the need within the adolescent mother herself to assert her independence from her family once she has had two or more children of her own (Furstenberg & Crawford, 1978; Furstenberg et al., 1987b). Thus, perhaps the Black teens in this sample were relatively more likely to establish a residence independent from their mothers because they were farther along in developing their own families.

The current results also show that, like their White and Black counterparts, fewer than 33% of Hispanic teen mothers lived with their mothers during the 2 years following the birth of their children and, most Hispanic teens received only moderate support with child care from their mothers. These findings are discrepant with prior research indicating that Latina grandmothers play a prominent and influential role within the extended family system and that they are commonly in charge of the childrearing of their daughters' children (de Anda, 1984). The inconsistency between our findings and those from prior studies may be due to the large percentage of Hispanic teens in the current sample who immigrated from Mexico to the United States. Seventy-five percent of this sample's Hispanics were not U.S. citizens at intake into the study (i.e., while pregnant). It is likely that for these Hispanic women, their parents and much of their family remain in Mexico and, therefore, are not readily available to provide assistance with child care. In addition, post hoc analyses revealed that the Hispanic mothers in this sample did not shift their reliance for child care onto extended relatives nor to the father of the baby. Hispanic mothers actually reported receiving significantly less child-care support from other relatives and from the father of baby than did Black mothers. Thus, this sample of Hispanic adolescents may be unique from Hispanic teens studied elsewhere in the United States in that, for many of them, their mothers may not live nearby and, therefore, may not be readily available to provide the levels of child care generally associated with the Latina culture (de Anda, 1984; Wasserman et al., 1990). These findings also reconfirm other descriptions of recently immigrated Mexicans (e.g., Keefe, 1980; Vega, 1990), with kinship patterns seriously disrupted as migrating individuals leave existing family networks behind.

Results of this study also showed that a young maternal age at the time of delivery tended to be associated with a greater likelihood of living with the grandmother at 1 year postpartum and of receiving extensive child-care assistance from the grandmother at 2 years postpartum. The former result is in keeping with findings of other studies, which have shown that the younger the mother is at the birth of her child, the more likely she is to remain in her mother's home (Cooley & Unger, 1991; Furstenberg et al., 1987; Spieker & Bensley, 1994). However, the latter finding of increased grandmother assistance for younger mothers runs counter to previously reported null findings of the relationship between grandmothers' child care assistance and mothers' age (Cooley & Unger, 1991; Spieker & Bensley, 1994). In the Spieker and Bensley study, however, grandmothers' child-care involvement was measured only up to 1 year postpartum. At that time of assessment in the current study, no significant association was apparent either. It was only at the 2-year mark that grandmothers' child-care assistance began to relate to the young age of the mother. Perhaps as the child reaches toddlerhood, the challenges of parenting for younger mothers become too stressful and additional support is sought. Younger mothers may have particular difficulty in coping with the constant testing and noncompliant behaviors of their 2-year-olds, behaviors less present in the child during the first year of life (Bierman & Streett, 1982; Crockenberg, 1987a).

In addition, as reported in this chapter, coresidence with family during the first year postpartum was linked with adolescents' receipt of public assistance, with more welfare recipients residing with grandmothers than nonrecipients. Welfare receipt was not, however, linked with coresidence beyond the first year postpartum. Thus, coresidence does not occur within a vacuum but, rather, is the result of some combination of the teen's financial motivations as well as her school, marital, gravida, cultural, and maturity status.

## Grandmother Variables Positively Interrelated

A second set of findings were that all three grandmother variables studied in this chapter were positively interrelated, a finding in agreement with our prediction. Grandmothers' coresidence was associated with greater grandmother-provided child care but also greater grandmother–adolescent conflict, and greater grandmother-provided child care was associated with higher grandmother–adolescent conflict. These findings are in accord with previous results that show a strong relationship between high family child-care assistance and shared living arrangements among teenage mother families (e.g., Furstenberg & Crawford, 1978; Parish et al., 1991). The current results also show an association between heightened grandmother–adolescent conflict under conditions of coresidence and extensive grandmother-provided child care. Nitz et al. (1995) also reported that conflict was more likely to occur for coresiding grandmother–adolescent mother households than in noncoresiding households. It appears that when the teen and the maternal grandmother live together in the postpartum period, the teen benefits by receiving additional grandmother-provided child care but at a cost of high grandmother–adolescent strain and tension. It may be that in the ongoing and complex negotiations of shared living and shared child care, the mother–daughter relationship suffers. In discussing the burdens and benefits associated with teenage childbearing, Furstenberg (1980) described this scenario as follows:

> like most social institutions, the family can be viewed as either a benevolent or an oppressive arrangement. For the adolescent mother, it clearly provides a series of invaluable services during the transition to parenthood. Nevertheless, it is possible that the same structure that nurtures and promotes the development of the young mother at one stage in her life may thwart and frustrate her growth at another. (p. 81)

Although it makes intuitive sense that grandmother–adolescent conflict would be high in situations requiring frequent and constant negotiation, such as when coresiding and when sharing child-care responsibilities, these findings run counter to many earlier conceptualizations of grandmother assistance as an important source of social support for adolescent mothers (e.g., Barrera, 1981; Colletta & Lee, 1983; Crockenberg, 1987b; Furstenberg & Crawford, 1978; Tinsley & Parke, 1983). We would argue that the grandmother is indeed providing valuable and multifaceted social support to her daughter in the form of hands-on child care and, often, childrearing advice and free room and board. However, it may be that this aid is provided only under specific conditions, such as with an explicit understanding that the teen finish school, not see the father of the baby, not become pregnant again, or work to partially repay the family's child-care support. Such provisos would likely be sources of tension and frustration to both grandmother and adolescent. Others have also recognized this apparent paradox of supportive social ties: Under conditions of high stress, support is offered but at a cost of immense interpersonal conflict (e.g., Belle, 1981; Furstenberg, 1980; Presser, 1989). These findings imply that, for young mothers who because of financial or schooling constraints are obliged to continue to live with their families of origin throughout the postpartum period, tense grandmother–adolescent relations may be unavoidable and may be intensified when the grandmother participates heavily in the grandchild's care.

## Relations Between Grandmother Variables
## and Mothers' Parenting

Central to this chapter were the links among the three grandmother variables and the qualities of adolescent mothers' parenting. When all adolescent mothers were considered, results revealed that grandmothers' help with child care and grand-mother–adolescent conflict were consistently linked with mothers' harsh and punitive parenting attitudes and mothers' low involvement in child care. Grand-mothers' help with child care was also related to low levels of mothers' knowledge about normal infant and child development. Grandmothers' coresidence was, however, only modestly and sporadically linked with mothers' unfavorable parenting attitudes and low parenting confidence. These findings are important because most previous studies of grandmother influence for teen mothers' parenting have focused solely on maternal behaviors observed during mother–child interaction tasks, with specific interactive behaviors as outcomes (e.g., number of times mother smiles to or looks to child, etc.; Crockenberg, 1987a, 1987b; Chase-Lansdale et al., 1994; Spieker & Bensley, 1994; Unger & Cooley, 1992). In contrast, the parenting outcomes examined in this study were thought to be more enduring and stable (Fox et al., 1987; Shea & Tronick, 1988), more centrally related to how the teen approaches and carries out the parenting role (East et al., 1994), and more directly related to the grandmother variables under investigation.

These current results suggest, then, that grandmothers' involvement with their grandchildren's caretaking over the first 2 years of the child's life may diminish the young mother's interest in or possibly responsibility for her child's care. Such low involvement may engender unfavorable parenting attitudes and beliefs like those assessed in this study, such as inappropriate child expectations, low empathy toward child's needs, and high value of physical punishment. Grandmothers' predominant participation in their grandchildren's care may also restrict opportunities for the teen mother to enhance her knowledge about normative infant and child development. The current results are similar to those found by Stevens (1984), who reported that teen mothers' knowledge of child development was less among adolescents whose mothers were the primary parent figure for their children. Thus, by performing a large majority of the grandchild's caretaking over the first 2 years of life, the grandmother likely impedes her daughter's learning about her child's development.

It should be emphasized that the pattern of correlations found in this study can not be used to infer causation. That is, all grandmother variables were assessed in this study at regular 6-month intervals for the first 2 years postpartum, while mothers' parenting qualities were assessed only once at either 2-years postpartum or at an average of approximately 3 years postpartum. Thus, we cannot conclude a specific direction of effects—from grandmother influence to mothers' parenting—simply because the assessment of grandmother variables preceded the assessment of mothers' parenting qualities. It is as plausible that grandmother–adolescent conflict thwarted adolescent involvement with her child as it is that the teen's negligence in her child-care duties precipitated grandmother–teen conflict. A similar caveat should be made of the relationship between extensive grandmother child-care assistance and adolescents' low involvement with child care: Grand-mothers may intervene more when adolescent mothers are uninvolved; alternately, teen mothers' involvement in child care may be inhibited when grandmothers participate heavily in the child's daily care. Both interpretations are plausible.

Lest the reader think that grandmother involvement is all bad, grandmother child-care assistance at 18 months postpartum did seem beneficial in reducing mothers' parenting stress, and in improving several parenting qualities of the younger mothers in this sample. Teenage mothers age 16 or younger with high grandmother support (regardless of living situation) reported significantly more parenting confidence, greater child-care involvement, and more accurate child development knowledge than did young teenage mothers with low grandmother child care support. What was perhaps most significant about these results was the suboptimal parenting experienced by young teenage mothers with low grandmother child-care assistance. These mothers reported the highest parent-ing stress, the lowest parenting confidence, the lowest child-care involvement, and the least accurate knowledge of children's development. It may be the combination of such factors that places these very young mothers with low grandmother support at such high risk for maladaptive parenting rather than any one characteristic in isolation.

Another somewhat surprising finding was that older teenage mothers (age 17–19) with high grandmother support appeared to benefit least from grand-mother child-care involvement and, in fact, experienced greater parenting stress than similar-age mothers who reported low grandmother child-care assistance. It may be that the high level of grandmother involvement in child care stifles the older teen parent and causes her to feel stressed and self-conscious in her interactions with her child. For example, Shapiro and Mangelsdorf (1994) found that older adolescents with high family support had difficulty interpreting their infants' emotional signals, whereas younger teenage mothers' sensitivity increased with high family support. This finding of heightened stress for older teenage mothers with high grandmother support runs contrary to previous findings of high grandmother support being associated with a more secure mother–child relation-ship (Spieker & Bensley, 1994). However, in that study, the assessment of grand-mother social support was very general and was not specific to assistance with child care per se. This may be an important distinction and should be considered in future research on grandmother support.

## Relations Between Grandmother Variables and Children's Behavioral Adjustment

Of major importance in the present investigation was the role of grandmothers' coresidence, grandmothers' child-care assistance, and grandmother–adolescent conflict in the behavioral adjustment of the children of teenage mothers. As stated at the beginning of this chapter, children's outcomes might be improved when grandmothers, as opposed to teenage mothers, are involved in their grandchildren's care. In general, findings from the present study did not support this contention, although effects varied by race. Results indicated that grandmothers' coresidence was associated with higher levels of mother-reported aggression for all children and with higher levels of mother-reported social withdrawal for White children. However, coresiding with grandmother was related to diminished social withdrawal for Black children. These findings are similar to the pattern obtained by Unger and Cooley (1992), who found that grandmothers' child-care involvement was related to a higher incidence of behavior problems for White children, but to higher vocabulary scores for Black children. These findings cannot be explained by the varying quality of mothering for different race mothers in coresiding and noncoresiding families. Results of this study indicated no significant maternal race by grandmother coresidence interaction effects for any of the parenting qualities examined in this study. Thus, children's different behavioral outcomes as a function of race and coresidence do not appear to be due to differences in mothers' parenting.

One interpretation of these findings is that coresidence with grandmother may be a proxy for factors related to father absence. Children who lack fathers show significantly greater vulnerability to adjustment problems than children whose fathers are present at least some of the time (Bachrach, 1983; Dubow & Luster, 1990; Hofferth, 1984a). This may be tempered for Black children, however, given the frequency of nonmarital childbearing and father absence within the Black community (Hofferth, 1984b; South, 1993) and the very protective and nurturing environment of the Black extended family (Burton, 1990; Stack, 1974; Wilson, 1986). Thus, perhaps Black children fare better than White children in extended family living situations because such arrangements are better accepted within that culture (Burton, 1990; Wilson, 1986) and, as such, do not pose a risk to Black children's development.

Results also indicated that the children of young teenage mothers (age 16 or younger) who coresided with their grandmothers had significantly higher levels of aggression than comparable children who did not reside with their grandmothers. Similar to the results previously discussed, these findings cannot be explained by the varying quality of parenting exhibited by different-age mothers in coresiding and noncoresiding families. Results of this study showed no significant maternal age by grandmother coresidence interaction effects for any of the parenting qualities examined in this study.

Results of post hoc contrasts did reveal, however, large differences in levels of grandmother–adolescent conflict for coresiding and noncoresiding young teenage mothers. Young coresiding teenage mothers (age 16 and younger) reported significantly greater levels of conflict with grandmother at 12 months ($p < .001$), 18 months ($p < .001$), and 24 months postpartum ($p < .001$) than noncoresiding young mothers. Moreover, among younger mothers only, grandmother–adolescent conflict at all times of follow-up was positively correlated with children's aggressive behavior (rs ranged from .31 to .34, p <.01). (No coresidence effect was found for grandmother–adolescent conflict for older teenage mothers, and post hoc analyses computed on the total sample revealed that grandmother–adolescent conflict at all times of assessment was not related to children's aggression [rs ranged from .05 to .17, ns].) These findings suggest, then, that young coresiding teenage mothers experience relatively frequent tension and friction with their mothers, and that this conflict appears to be detrimental to the behavioral adjustment of their children. It is also possible, of course, that the conflict between grandmothers and young teenage mothers contributed to mothers' perceptions of their children's frequent fighting, hitting, and angry moods. Why such effects were found only for younger teenage mothers and were not present for older teenage mothers or their children is open to speculation. Certainly, additional studies of the dynamics within coresiding and noncoresiding families of younger and older teenage mothers are warranted.

### Nonshared Residence and High Grandmother Child-Care Assistance Linked With the Most Optimal Mothers' Parenting and Children's Behavioral Adjustment

In line with our prediction, and similar to the findings of other studies (Chase-Lansdale et al., 1994; Spieker & Bensley, 1994), results of the current study indicated that the most positive parenting qualities were evidenced by noncoresiding teens who received high grandmother child-care support. In contrast, the least favorable parenting (except for mothers' child-care involvement) was associated with living with the grandmother and receiving extensive child-care support from her. Thus, adolescent mothers' parenting appears to be compromised in situations where the teen continues to live with the grandmother and the grandmother performs the majority of the grandchildren's caretaking. In such situations, grandmothers—perhaps in an effort to protect their daughters from the stresses and strains of parenting—actually hinder their teenage daughters from becoming optimally involved in their children's care and, consequently, from developing a sense of parenting confidence and competence. Certainly, an alternate interpretation that is equally plausible and cannot be ruled out given the cross-sectional assessment of many of this study's variables, is that teens who chose to continue to live at home and who allow the grandmother to take over their children's caretaking may be less mature and less willing to adopt the parenting role than teens who set up households independent from the maternal grandmother. In the former case, grandmothers may assume the role of primary caretaker only out of necessity.

The present study extends previous research on mothers' parenting by documenting that not living with grandmother but receiving high amounts of caretaking from her benefits the teens' children as well. Such children gain in two ways: first, they have mothers with favorable parenting qualities (e.g., positive parenting attitudes, high parenting confidence, extensive involvement with child care, and a high commitment to parenting) and, second, they receive extensive additional caretaking from grandmothers. Such advantages apparently promote healthy child development, as evidenced in this study by the relative absence of physical aggression among children who received a lot of caretaking from their grandmothers while not living with them.

## Limitations and Implications

Several limitations of the current study warrant specific comment. Perhaps the most significant limitation was the lack of information about the quality of grandmothers' parenting. Given that extensive grandmother child-care assistance was associated with mothers' unfavorable parenting qualities, and that grandmother coresidence was linked with high levels of aggression for all children, we could infer that the quality of grandmothers' parenting may have been less than optimal. But the findings in the literature are mixed and are not sufficiently conclusive to support such an assumption. For example, Chase-Lansdale et al. (1994) found that grandmothers were not particularly effective parents, and Oyserman et al. (1993) found that grandmothers were not especially nurturant or engaging. In contrast, Stevens (1984) found that grandmothers exhibited a nonpunitive and responsive parenting style with their grandchildren. Certainly a key link in the role of grandmothers for adolescent mothers' parenting and children's outcomes is the quality and style of grandmothers' parenting. Whether grandmothers' parenting varies by residential pattern (cf. Chase-Lansdale et al., 1994) or by levels of child care involvement would also be important contributions of future research.

We should also emphasize that this study assessed adolescents' perceptions of grandmother child-care support and did not systematically employ a more objective measure of grandmother assistance, such as the number of hours grandmother served as the grandchild's primary caretaker. As stated in the introduction to this chapter, in coresiding family situations grandmothers' child-care support may be unclear, underestimated, or undermined by the stresses incurred from coresidence. Moreover, as widely documented in the social support literature, perceived support does not necessarily correspond to that truly provided and often includes a satisfaction component (Barrera, 1981; Crockenberg, 1987b; Sarason, Shearin, Pierce, & Sarason, 1987). The current study did not have available information on adolescents' satisfaction with the extent of grandmother-provided child-care assistance or their satisfaction with their living arrangements. Certainly, the extent to which the teen is pleased with the level of grandmother child-care involvement and her current living situation would be important for many of the parenting qualities examined in this chapter.

Another limitation of the current study was the omission of assessment of the adolescent's development in areas of life other than her parenting. Several researchers have reported that although adolescent mothers who continue to live with their mothers are less involved initially in their children's care, they are more likely to finish school, to experience a future stable marriage, and to eventually hold down a better paying job (Cooley & Unger, 1991; Furstenberg, 1980; Furstenberg et al., 1987a; Spieker & Bensley, 1994). Young mothers who are relieved of much of the responsibilities of early childrearing may also be in a better position to achieve the critical developmental milestones of adolescence and, consequently, may be more likely to realize a healthy and adaptive adulthood. Such teens are also likely to be unencumbered to practice appropriate "young adult" roles surrounding work, school, and peer relationships that will better prepare them for a more productive adulthood (Hamburg, 1974). Thus, teenage mothers who continue to reside with family and who receive large amounts of family support in raising their children may ultimately have more positive life-course outcomes in contrast to teens who undertake the full responsibility of their children's caretaking. Whether such long-term benefits for the teenage mother extend to enriched children's outcomes is not known. More studies are needed that investigate the long-term costs and benefits of extensive child-care involvement for the teenager's life course and her child's well-being.

The findings of the current study have implications for policy and intervention. Continued shared residence with grandmother among teenage mothers was found to be associated with much tension and strain. Such conflict was related to mothers' negative parenting attitudes and mothers' low involvement with child care. Grandmothers' child-care assistance, in contrast, seemed beneficial to the parenting of teenage mothers age 16 and younger, and grandmother assistance with child care in nonshared living arrangements seemed advantageous to both mothers' parenting and children's outcomes. It appears, then, and similar to the results obtained in other studies (Chase-Lansdale et al., 1994; Spieker & Bensley, 1994; Unger & Cooley, 1991), that shared living conditions may be the sole harmful element precipitating negative grandmother effects. Thus, interventions that might most benefit adolescent mothers and their children would be ones that promote grandmothers' child-care support while simultaneously helping the teenager establish an independent residence, one optimally within a stable and nurturing environment. Living with nearby relatives wherein the expectation is that the teenager will be responsible for as much of the child's care as is possible may diminish the conflict brought about by shared grandmother–adolescent childrearing while offering a stable and supportive environment. Employment programs that facilitate grandmothers' ability to assist with child care, such as those that arrange for flexible working hours or working out of her home, may be particularly helpful for primary caregiving grandmothers. Presser (1989) also found that cash payment to grandmothers enhanced the time they spent in caring for their grandchildren. Thus, programs that reimbursed grandmothers for their time spent at child care would likely facilitate grandmother-provided child care and perhaps lessen grandmother–adolescent conflict. Grandmother child-care assistance should be particularly encouraged for very young teenage mother families.

In addition to being beneficial to the adolescent mother, nonshared residence with the teen's family of origin may also have positive consequences for the adolescent's siblings. Results of our research on the younger sisters of childbearing teens indicates that such sisters engage in many problem behaviors (drug use, truancy), are likely to be sexually active, and have disproportionately high rates of early childbearing themselves (East, 1996; East & Felice, 1992; East, Felice, & Morgan, 1993). Whether these behaviors result from exposure to a parenting sister or to shared, within-family risk factors is not currently known (East & Felice, 1992). It does seem intuitive, however, that siblings would be affected by a teenage sister's childbearing both directly, such as by needing to provide child-care assistance, and indirectly, such as by experiencing a decrease in family income or an increase in family stress. Certainly, the effects of a coresiding parenting teenager on her siblings' development deserves more attention than it has currently received.

A note of caution should be realized, however, before encouraging young mothers to set up residences separate from their parents. In reality, this separation from parents often turns into a flight toward greater dependency, especially if the teen plans to return to school or to become employed. In addition, given that teen parents who marry have a much higher than average chance of divorce and that most nonmarried but cohabitating relationships with the father of the baby dissolve within years of the baby's birth (Teti & Lamb, 1989), it is unlikely that an adult-like family arrangement with both parents present will be maintained for a reasonable length of time. Certainly, each situation should be evaluated individually and careful consideration should be given to what is best for both the mother and her children.

Finally, the findings of this study speak to the importance of including the immediate family context in analyzing the well-being of teenage mothers and their children. As evidenced from this study's results, grandmother influence for the parenting of teenage mothers and the adjustment of their children was pervasive throughout the time period studied. Nearly half of all teenage mothers in this sample lived with their mothers postnatally, and the maternal grandmother provided the most assistance with child care throughout the 2 years studied, more than that provided by the father of the baby, other relatives, neighbors, friends, or formal day-care centers. To have excluded an examination of grandmothers' role would have missed a critical influence for many key dimensions of adolescent mothers' parenting and their children's adjustment.

# Chapter 6

## The Partners of
## Adolescent Mothers

80  ◆  cg

For many years, the adolescent pregnancy literature focused exclusively on the female with little information on male partners. In fact, the partners of adolescent mothers were not even included in clinical investigations of teenage pregnancy until the late 1960s and early 1970s. Since the 1970s, there have been many reports on the fathers of babies born to teenage mothers, but some of this information must be interpreted cautiously. Some studies suffer from methodological deficiencies including retrospective data collection, data collection through the pregnant female and her family only, underrepresentative sampling procedures (e.g., using juvenile detention centers), lack of comparison groups, and information on teenaged fathers only (East & Felice, 1994; Hardy et al., 1989; Robinson, 1988). Although there is much we still need to learn about the male partners of adolescent mothers, we now know enough to dispel many myths including the stereotypical image that young fathers are all uncaring teenagers from urban areas and minority backgrounds. Data from many sources indicate that these young men are a heterogeneous group and although some avoid the responsibilities of parenthood, others are eager to accept the father role (Smollar & Ooms, 1987).

### REVIEW OF THE LITERATURE
### ON THE PARTNERS OF TEEN MOTHERS

Demographic Information

Information concerning fathers is not always completed on birth certificates of children born to mothers under the age of 19 (Smollar & Ooms, 1987), including basic information such as age and race. This is particularly true for nonmarital births, where young women and their families may be reluctant to provide data concerning the father. According to one data set (NCHS, 1994), information on

**100**

the age of fathers was missing from 42% of birth certificates of babies born to teen mothers (Landry & Forrest, 1995). From data that are available, it appears that less than 20% of the partners are teenagers themselves, 20% to 35% were 20 to 21 years of age, and 45 to 60% are 21 years of age or older (Children's Defense Fund [CDF], 1987a; Hardy et al., 1989; NCHS, 1987; Robinson, 1988). The partners of teen mothers, like teen mothers themselves, come from all racial, ethnic, and socioeconomic groups (Felice, Shragg, James, & Hollingsworth, 1988; Hollingsworth & Felice, 1986), but most data are limited to White, Black, or Latino populations. It is estimated that 7% of all young men have fathered a child while a teenager (Marsiglio, 1987), but this figure varies by race and ethnicity and by socioeconomic group. Based on one large study of men's responses to questions concerning paternity, the literature suggests that about 11% of Latino, 15% of Black, 12% of disadvantaged White, and 5% of nondisadvantaged White males fathered children as adolescents (Marsiglio, 1987). Adolescent men usually have sexual partners who are the same age or younger, thus most, if not all of those reported pregnancies would be to adolescent women. The same information is not available for men older than 20 because the age of the mother of the child was not asked when men reported their ages when they had children.

## Family Background and Characteristics

There is more information available on the psychosocial backgrounds of adolescent partners than adult partners of teenage girls and more written on unwed partners than on married partners, probably because this is an area of societal concern. However, it does appear that young men who father babies born to teenage mothers are more likely to come from poor backgrounds. For example, data from the National Longitudinal Study of Labor Force Behavior (NLS) suggest that if a young man's family received welfare in 1979, that was a strong predictor that he would be an unwed father by 1984 (Lerman, 1988). That data set also indicated that the higher a family's income, the less likely that a son would be an unwed father (Smollar & Ooms, 1987). These facts should be interpreted cautiously, however, because there may be underreporting of existing children among White, never married men from affluent families in the data set studied. Although most teen births are in urban centers, it is important to note that between 25% and 33% of teen births are in rural areas (NCHS, 1987) and hence involve rural youth of both genders.

Most unmarried fathers live with their family or family members, even fathers who are not adolescents. For example, in a group of 395 young unwed fathers, ages 15 to 19 years, 62.7% lived with a parent or other close relative (Sander, 1988). In the large NLS data set, 64% of unwed fathers, ages 19 to 26 years, reported that they lived with a parent or close relative (Lerman, 1988). This is probably a reflection of poverty.

Partners of teen mothers also are more likely to have a family history of out-of-wedlock childbearing (Dryfoos, 1988; Hanson, Morrison, & Ginsburg, 1989) than their nonfather peers. This includes both female and male relatives. For example, in a clinical study comparing 100 Black teenage fathers with 100 Black nonfather peers, Rivara, Sweeney, and Henderson (1985) found that only 39% of the fathers felt that their families reacted negatively to their paternity, whereas a significantly higher 62% of the nonfathers felt that their families would react negatively if their son fathered a child. Most notably, 77% of the mothers of the study group versus a significantly lower 53% of the mothers of the comparison group were parents themselves during their teenage years. Many studies indicate that teenage fatherhood, like teenage motherhood, is likely to be repeated from one generation to the next (Brown-Robbins & Lynn, 1973; Dryfoos, 1988; Rivara et al., 1985; Vaz, Smolen, & Miller, 1983).

## Personal Characteristics

As previously mentioned, the partners of teen mothers are a heterogeneous group of individuals, but clinicians and researchers alike have often questioned whether young men who become unwed fathers have characteristics that would distinguish them from those who do not become unwed fathers particularly in their adolescent years. Ideally, one would prefer to have pre- and postpregnancy data for comparison for such a study. However, because adolescent paternity is not usually a planned event, it is difficult to obtain baseline data about personality characteristics of young men before they become fathers. There is one early study that included prepregnancy psychological testing (Pauker, 1971). Out of a study sample of 11,329 ninth-grade males (age range 13–17 years) who had been tested with the MMPI in Minnesota in 1954, Pauker matched 94 boys who later fathered a child nonmaritally with 94 nonfather controls. The few MMPI scale scores that were significantly different suggest that out-of-wedlock fathers were less self-disciplined than the controls. Overall, the MMPI differences were minimal and certainly not striking enough to determine why one group became out-of-wedlock fathers and the other group did not. Pauker concluded that "it seems that boys will be boys, and some ... will be out-of-wedlock fathers" (p. 218 ). In their small retrospective study of youth who were wards of the California Youth Authority, Brown-Robbins and Lynn (1973) confirmed Pauker's findings that young unwed fathers had less self-discipline and less self-control than young unwed nonfathers. More recent studies suggest that differences between fathers and nonfathers may be present for White fathers but not necessarily for Hispanic or Black fathers. Specifically, in some reports, White young unwed fathers have been found to be more likely than their peers who are not fathers to have histories of drug use, truancy, and/or criminal behavior (Christmon & Luckey, 1994; Deardan, Hale, & Wooley, 1995; Elster, Lamb, Peters, Kahn & Tavare, 1987; Lerman, 1988). This does not mean that Black and Hispanic fathers do not have histories of drug use or criminal behavior, but rather that these factors do not differentiate fathers from nonfathers as clearly as the data describing White fathers (Smollar & Ooms, 1987).

Young fathers, like young mothers, are also likely to have a truncated educational achievement compared to nonfathers. Card and Wise (1978) collected data on 375,000 high school students starting in 1960 with follow-up at 1, 5, and 11 years. The follow-up questionnaires included data on schooling, occupational or job-related experiences, and such personal history items as marital status, family size, and community activities. All the men and women who did not have children before age 20 received a high school diploma; many teenage parents of both genders did not. These data were gathered in the 1960s, but poor school attendance and performance by fathers compared to nonfathers have been reported in the more recent literature as well (Hendricks, Robinson-Brown, & Gary, 1984; Marsiglio, 1986; Panzarine & Elster, 1983; Rivara et al., 1985; Rivara, Sweeney, & Henderson, 1986; Smollar & Ooms, 1987). It is unclear whether poor school performance is an antecedent or a consequence of early parenthood for young men, but there appears to be at least some evidence that young fathers have deficits in basic academic skills (Smollar & Ooms, 1987). Whether these deficits predate the pregnancy or are a result of the pregnancy because the young man drops out of school to support the baby, it is clear that this population of young men is generally educationally disadvantaged.

## Relationship to the Teen Mother and Baby

In uninformed circles, there is the misperception that pregnant teenagers and their partners have a "hit-and-run" relationship, particularly if the birth is out of wedlock. The literature does not support this opinion. Most young couples know one another for some time before conception and report a close, caring relationship (Elster, 1988; Hendricks & Montgomery, 1983; Hollingsworth, 1978; Sander, 1988; Sherline & Davidson, 1978). For example, in a descriptive study from Mississippi, nearly 50% of the couples knew one another for more than a year before conception and only 20% of the couples knew one another for less than 6 months (Sherline & Davidson, 1978). However, after delivery, the relationship usually changed with a steady decrease in postpartum contact for those couples who were not married (Felice et al., 1987; Hollingsworth, 1978; Lorenzi, Klerman, & Jekel, 1977). In one sample, the number of unmarried mothers seeing the fathers of their babies on a regular basis declined from 56% at 3 months to 23% at 26 months (Lorenzi et al., 1977). In some studies, this change in relationship is more striking for White couples than for Black couples (Hollingsworth, 1978).

In past decades, pregnancy has been the precipitating event for many teens to marry (Zelnik & Kantner, 1978). Whether or not a young couple marries in response to the pregnancy appears to be related to many factors including race and age. Data from the NLS data set indicate that White and Hispanic fathers are more likely to marry the mother than are Black fathers (Lerman, 1988), and that Hispanic couples are more likely to be married at conception or at least prior to the birth than are White or Black couples (Felice et al., 1987). Young couples, particularly if the father is not yet 18, are unlikely to marry (Furstenberg, 1976b). When couples do marry during adolescence, they are more likely to experience marital problems than couples who marry later and this is particularly true if the marriage takes place simply to keep the child from having an "illegitimate" label (Burchinal, 1965; Elster & Lamb, 1986; Furstenberg et al., 1987b; Morgan & Rindfuss, 1985; Teti & Lamb, 1989). Marriage is also influenced by cultural norms. Since the 1970s, it has become more common for women of all ages to have children outside of marriage and hence there may not be the societal pressure of former decades for young men to marry the mother of their child and young women may not feel compelled to marry as well. This may influence future data concerning relationships between teen mothers and their partners.

More than 80% of unwed fathers in their late teens or early 20s live away from their children (Hardy et al., 1989; Lerman, 1988). Between 33% and 50% of these fathers visit their children at least once a week (Hardy et al., 1989; Lerman, 1988). Reports concerning child support are quite variable with as few as 40% (Hollingsworth, 1978) to as many as 95% (Rivara et al., 1986) of fathers stating that they contribute financially to the support of their children. However, the definition of *child support* is not uniform and young men may believe that any amount of money given to the mother is child support, even if it is a very small amount. It is clear that young men who are provided with job training are more likely than others to contribute financially to the mother and baby (Klinman, Sander, Rosa, Longo, & Martinez, 1985). Realistically, with limited education and a depressed economy, many young men in their 20s do not earn enough to support a family of three (CDF, 1987b).

## Adolescent Versus Adult Partners

As noted previously, more than 50% of the partners of teen mothers are adult men over the age of 21 years. Large age discrepancies between partners may be more prevalent in some ethnic or racial groups (Felice et al., 1987, 1988) and not seen in other groups. For example, in a small report on Indochinese immigrant pregnant teens, the mean age discrepancy was 7.2 years (Felice et al., 1988), but in a sample of urban Baltimore teens who were mostly African American, the age differences were only 2 to 3 years (Hardy & Zabin, 1991).

Large age differences between teen mothers and their partners may signal cases of incest or rape and all clinicians should be wary of this possibility. Although it is worrisome that teenage girls may become pregnant by men who are older than they are through guile or victimization, it is not necessarily so. There have now been several investigations comparing younger and older partners of teen mothers with interesting results. In one study of new parents, couples were divided into three groups by age: (a) mother less than 17, father less than 20; (b) mother less than 17, father older than 20; and (c) mother and father both older than 20 (Nakashima & Camp, 1984). Data were collected from both partners on demographics, parenting attitudes, and measures of vocabulary and abstract thinking. The two groups of fathers who paired with adolescent women were more similar than the fathers who paired with adult women. The authors concluded that the older man who pairs with an adolescent girl is more like an adolescent father than he is like an older man who pairs with a woman his own age. In another study of adolescent mothers and their partners, couples were divided into three groups by intracouple age: those with an intracouple age discrepancy less than 1 year; those with an intracouple age discrepancy between 15 and 36 months; and those with an intracouple age discrepancy of more than 42 months (Lamb, Elster, & Tavare, 1986). The mean age of all the young mothers was 17 years. Couples with the largest age discrepancy had known one another for a shorter period of time and yet were more likely to have planned the pregnancy and responded to the pregnancy in a positive manner. Interestingly, the authors noted that there were more differences between the young mothers in the three groups than there were between the fathers. Wong, Morgan, and East (1993) found no differences in the quality of the relationship between teen mothers and adolescent versus adult fathers up to 18 months postpartum, with most couples reporting a warm and loving relationship. In another study, mother and infant health outcomes were actually better for pregnant teens paired with older partners compared to those paired with teen partners (Buhlmann et al., 1988). The authors concluded that having an older partner may be a way to identify a pregnant teen population at decreased risk for poor perinatal outcomes such as low birthweight and prematurity. In the Buhlmann et al. sample, having an older partner generally meant that the pregnant teenager was married to a man who was employed. This is an area that warrants further study, but it does appear that adult men who pair with teenage girls are not necessarily different from adolescent men who pair with teenage girls. Perhaps the differences are really between young women who choose older partners versus young women who choose same-age partners.

## Focus of This Chapter

The purpose of this chapter is fivefold:

1. To present descriptive data concerning the fathers of babies born to teen mothers using this racially diverse sample;
2. To determine whether selected intake variables of both the adolescent mother and the father of the baby were associated with the father's racial background;
3. To chart changes in the relationship between the teen mother and her partner over 3 years' time;
4. To compare adolescent and adult fathers in specific areas such as background characteristics and relationship to the mother and baby; and
5. To examine how fathers' financial commitment, relationship commitment to the teen, and child-care assistance were related to their children's behavioral outcomes as assessed at 3 years of age.

## METHOD

### Subjects

In this chapter, we present data gathered at intake and at each of the follow-up points of assessment on the fathers of the babies born to the adolescent women who participated in the UCSD Teen OB Follow-Up Study. Intake data were available only for the partners of those teens who presented for prenatal care at the UCSD Teen OB Clinic. Follow-up data on fathers were available for both the teens who went to the UCSD Teen OB Clinic and for teens who went to the outlying community clinics for their prenatal care. Of the 127 teenage girls who were registered for prenatal care at the UCSD Teen OB Clinic, one teen was not certain of the identity of the father and hence data concerning this father are not available.[1] Three other fathers died (all due to gunshot wounds) between the time of conception and the mother's first prenatal visit. When appropriate, we include information about these fathers in the analyses for a sample size of 126; otherwise the sample size is 123. Follow-up data include information on an additional 69 fathers from the outlying community clinics for a potential sample size of 192 (the sample size decreased with time from 192 to 145, an attrition rate of 25% over 3 years).

Information concerning the father was obtained at intake into the UCSD Teen OB prenatal clinic via interview with the father whenever possible and updated at each data collection point. However, because partners did not accompany the teen to prenatal care for 95% of the teen mothers, information about the father was obtained from the teenage mothers for almost all study participants. Information concerning the fathers from the outlying clinics was first obtained at the 6-month follow-up visit with the teen mother and updated at each succeeding follow-up visit. Information was verified by the fathers whenever possible, but in most instances, information was not able to be verified particularly if the couples were not living together. Hence, this study suffers from some of the same flaws mentioned previously. However, the information obtained about the fathers adds greatly to our understanding of teen parenting in this sample of young mothers and we present these data as best as possible with the limitations noted.

## RESULTS

### Information At Intake

Information was available on 123 fathers at intake; Table 6.1 summarizes the background information on these fathers. The racial backgrounds of the fathers were the same as the mothers in all but two pairs: One White pregnant teen had a Black partner and one White pregnant teen had a partner from the Other racial category.

The mean age of the fathers was 19.70 (SD = 3.20), with a range of 15 to 34 years. (The mean age of the teen mothers at intake was 16.5 years.) About 60% of the fathers were 19 years of age or younger and about 70% were 21 years or younger. Although there was one 15-year-old and one 34-year-old father, in reality, most of

---

[1] This group of 127 teens includes the 18 teens who were omitted from all prior analyses. These 18 teens participated in a special county-run program and received multiple intensive and individual prenatal and postpartum services. The 18 teen were included in analyses for this chapter because such services would not likely affect the variables chosen for study on their partners.

## Table 6.1
## Background Information on the Fathers of the Babies (N = 123–126)

| | M | SD | N | % |
|---|---|---|---|---|
| Age | 19.70 | 3.20 | | |
| Range | 15-34 | | | |
| Race | | | | |
| Black | | | 52 | 43 |
| Hispanic | | | 40 | 33 |
| White | | | 19 | 16 |
| Southeast Asian | | | 3 | 2 |
| Other | | | 9 | 7 |
| Education | | | | |
| Years completed | 10.93 | 1.75 | | |
| School Status | | | | |
| Student | | | 31 | 25 |
| Dropped out (before pregnancy) | | | 31 | 25 |
| Graduated high school/GED | | | 45 | 37 |
| Other | | | 16 | 13 |
| Level of Education | | | | |
| < High school | | | 48 | 50 |
| High school | | | 44 | 45 |
| > High school | | | 5 | 5 |
| Grade Point Average While in School[a] | 2.70 | 1.67 | | |
| History of Truancy | | | | |
| None | | | 37 | 30 |
| Yes,sometimes | | | 28 | 23 |
| Yes,frequently | | | 10 | 8 |
| Unknown | | | 48 | 39 |

| Drug Use | Mean Frequency of Use[a] | | Ever Used | |
|---|---|---|---|---|
| Alcohol | 1.29 | | 82 | 67 |
| Marijuana | 0.94 | | 44 | 36 |
| Speed | 0.12 | | 5 | 4 |
| Cocaine | 0.34 | | 13 | 11 |
| Crystal | 0.38 | | 16 | 13 |
| PCP | 0.16 | | 6 | 5 |
| Heroin | 0.02 | | 1 | 1 |
| Crack | 0.08 | | 2 | 2 |
| Father's Occupation | | | | |
| Unemployed/not in school | | | 24 | 19 |
| Military | | | 10 | 8 |
| Unskilled labor | | | 29 | 23 |
| Skilled labor | | | 27 | 22 |
| In school or training | | | 24 | 19 |
| Professional | | | 3 | 2 |
| Other | | | 6 | 5 |
| Deceased | | | 3 | 3 |
| Do Teen Mothers' Parents Know Father? | | | | |
| Not at all | | | 30 | 24 |
| Slightly | | | 33 | 27 |
| Very well | | | 60 | 49 |

[a] See text for coding

**107**

the fathers were in the age range of 16 to 24 years, that is, older adolescents and young adults. Most of the fathers were ethnic minorities (78%). As a group, the fathers had a mean educational level of nearly 11 years, but the range was 1 to 14 years of schooling. Forty percent of the fathers were 18 years of age or less but only 25% were students. About 33% of the fathers completed their graduate equivalency diplomas (GEDs) or finished high school and 25% dropped out of school before the pregnancy. The teen mothers were asked about the grades that the fathers received when they were in school. Fifty-six percent of the girls did not know their partners' grades, but the other girls reported that the fathers had a mean "grade score" of 2.70 (SD = 1.67) where 1 = mostly As, 2 = mostly Bs; 3 = Bs and Cs; 4 = Cs, and 5 = Ds or less. Nearly 40% of the mothers did not know if the fathers had a history of truancy when they were in school, but 50% of the remaining girls who did claim to know this information admitted that the fathers were truant at least sometimes when in school.

Nearly 75% of the fathers used alcohol or drugs at some time. The frequency of use is listed in Table 6.1 with the scale of 0 = never used, 1 = only rarely tried, 2 = occasionally or a few times, 3 = frequent use once or twice per month, and 4 = used weekly or daily. Alcohol was the substance used most often, but the teen girls reported that the fathers used alcohol only rarely or occasionally. This may be true or it may be denial or unawareness by the teenager. Marijuana was the second most frequently used substance.

At prenatal intake, the pregnant teens reported that 8% of the fathers were on active duty in the military (not surprising since San Diego is a military center for the Marines and Navy) and 47% were employed elsewhere. Only 20% were neither employed nor in school or training. In about 50% of the cases, the parents of the pregnant teen knew the father of the baby very well.

Table 6.2 summarizes information concerning the father's family. At intake, more than 50% of the fathers lived with family members (parents, relatives, etc.) and 75% of the pregnant teenagers claimed to know the father's family and to know them well in half the cases. On the opposite side, it is disconcerting that 25% of the girls did not know the father's family and did not know where the father lived. It appears that 70% of the fathers' parents were informed about the pregnancy and most of those informed appeared to be accepting of the pregnancy. This may be because at least 33% of the pregnant teens were aware that the fathers' families had a history of teen parenthood and/or out-of-wedlock childbearing. This figure may be higher, however, because about 50% of the girls reported not knowing about their partners' family history.

Table 6.3 shows data pertaining to the relationship between the teen mother and the father of the baby at intake. As noted in Table 6.3, 41% of the pregnant teens reported that they had a close relationship with the fathers of their babies prior to conception, either married (7%), living together (13%), engaged (1%), or going steady (20%), and nearly 75% of the pregnant teens knew their partners for at least 6 months before becoming pregnant. At the time of intake, 35% of the girls stated

Table 6.2
Information Concerning Father's Family at Intake

| | N | % |
|---|---|---|
| Fathers' Living Arrangements | | |
| Both parents | 26 | 21 |
| Mother only | 18 | 15 |
| Father only | 5 | 4 |
| Other relations | 15 | 12 |
| Friend | 6 | 5 |
| Teen mother | 20 | 16 |
| Alone | 6 | 5 |
| Other/unknown | 27 | 22 |
| Does Teen Mother Know Father's Family? | | |
| Not at all | 31 | 25 |
| Slightly | 34 | 28 |
| Very well | 58 | 47 |
| Are Father's Parents Informed? | | |
| Yes | 88 | 70 |
| No | 38 | 30 |

| Attitude of Father's Parents About Pregnancy | Mother | Father |
|---|---|---|
| Not informed | 27% | 35% |
| Pleased | 24% | 13% |
| Accepting | 27% | 14% |
| Indifferent | 3% | 29% |
| Ambivalent | 3% | 2% |
| Unhappy | 3% | 1% |
| Strongly disapprove/hostile | 1% | 1% |
| Don't know | 12% | 32% |
| History of Teen Parenthood in Father's Immediate Family | | |
| Yes | 38 | 31 |
| No | 39 | 32 |
| Don't know | 46 | 37 |
| History of Out-of-Wedlock Childbearing in Father's Immediate Family | | |
| Yes | 35 | 28 |
| No | 33 | 27 |
| Don't know | 55 | 45 |

number of girls who claimed that they had a close relationship with the father prior to conception (engaged, living together, or going steady). About 20% of the girls stated that they chose to end the relationship with the father. There was no way for us to verify whether this was the girl's or the father's decision.

Very few fathers denied or questioned their paternity, but about 10% of the fathers were not informed about the pregnancy at intake. We presume but we are

## Table 6.3
## Relationship Between Teen Mother and Baby's Father at Intake

|  | N | % |
| --- | --- | --- |
| **Father's Relationship to Teen Mother Prior to Conception** | | |
| Married | 6 | 7 |
| Living together | 16 | 13 |
| Engaged | 2 | 1 |
| Going steady | 25 | 20 |
| Dating often | 51 | 41 |
| Dating occasionally | 13 | 11 |
| Slight acquaintance | 4 | 3 |
| Not known before | 4 | 3 |
| Other | 2 | 1 |
| **How Long Partners Knew One Another Before Teen Became Pregnant?** | | |
| > 2 years | 35 | 28 |
| 1–2 years | 20 | 16 |
| 6 month–1 year | 34 | 28 |
| < 6 months | 22 | 18 |
| < 1 month | 12 | 10 |
| **Relationship to Teen Mother at Intake** | | |
| Married | 10 | 8 |
| Plan to marry | 44 | 35 |
| Continue dating, no plans to marry | 22 | 18 |
| Friendly but not dating | 14 | 11 |
| Patient ended relationship | 25 | 20 |
| Father of baby deceased | 3 | 2 |
| Other | 8 | 6 |
| **Father's Response to Allegation of Paternity** | | |
| Not informed | 13 | 10 |
| Admits | 101 | 82 |
| Denies | 4 | 3 |
| Questioned | 1 | 1 |
| Other | 4 | 3 |
| **Initial Attitude Toward Pregnancy Resolution** | | |
| Not informed | 13 | 11 |
| Does not care | 6 | 5 |
| Whatever patient wants | 20 | 16 |
| Wants her to keep baby | 67 | 54 |
| Wants her to adopt out | 0 | 0 |
| Wants her to abort | 11 | 9 |
| Other | 6 | 5 |
| **Father's Attitude Toward Financial Support of Baby** | | |
| Has offered money will support | 85 | 67 |
| Not willing to support | 11 | 9 |
| Wants to but not able | 6 | 5 |
| Not informed of pregnancy | 13 | 10 |
| Deceased | 3 | 2 |
| Other | 8 | 6 |

Very few fathers denied or questioned their paternity, but about 10% of the fathers were not informed about the pregnancy at intake. We presume but we are not certain that the 10% who were not informed are part of the 20% who were "dropped" by the pregnant teen at the time of intake. Upon being initially told about the pregnancy, more than 50% of the fathers wanted the girls to have and keep the baby; only about 10% wanted her to have an abortion; and, no father wanted her to give the baby up for adoption. This may be a selection site bias because this study was initiated in a prenatal clinic setting. Most of the fathers (72%) offered to support the baby financially when they were told about the pregnancy.

## Racial Differences and Similarities in Father Intake Variables

Analyses were undertaken to examine differences and similarities in intake variables as a function of fathers' race. Of the 123 fathers on whom we have intake data, 3 were Southeast Asian and 9 were of an other racial/ethnic background (e.g., Philipino, American Indian, Korean, etc.). These numbers were considered too small for statistical analyses. Hence, race differences were examined for Black, Hispanic, and Non-Hispanic White groups only. All of the variables listed in Tables 6.1, 6.2, and 6.3 were analyzed for race differences. Table 6.4 lists those few variables where statistical differences were observed: U.S. citizenship, total years of education, frequency of alcohol and crystal use, and family history of out-of-wedlock children.

**Table 6.4**
**Selected Intake Data by Race of Father of Baby (FOB)**

|  | Black (n = 52) | Hispanic (n = 40) | White (n = 19) | F (2,108) |
|---|---|---|---|---|
| FOB is U.S. Citizen[+] |  |  |  |  |
| Yes | 100%[a] | 22%[a,b] | 95%[b] | 105.1*** |
| No | 0% | 78% | 5% |  |
| Years of Education | 11.30[a] | 10.03[a,b] | 11.57[b] | 6.42** |
|  | (1.06) | (2.50) | (1.09) |  |
| Frequency of Crystal Use | 0.0[c] | 0.55[b] | 0.77[b,c] | 5.21** |
|  | (0.0) | (1.06) | (1.48) |  |
| Frequency of Alcohol Use | 1.01[c] | 1.40 | 1.88[c] | 4.98** |
|  | (1.05) | (1.03) | (0.93) |  |
| Family History of Out-of-Wedlock Child[+] |  |  |  |  |
| Yes | 66%[c] | 44% | 13%[c] | 4.33* |
| No | 34% | 56% | 87% |  |

*Note.* Means or percentages with the same letter superscript in the same row are significantly different from each other.

[+]"No" responses were coded as 0, and "yes" responses were coded as 1.

[a]Black–Hispanic contrast  [b]Hispanic–White contrast  [c]Black–White contrast

*p < .05.  **p < .01.  ***p < .001.

It is not surprising that the Hispanic fathers were less likely to be U.S. citizens and to have less formal education than the White or Black fathers because many of these fathers were either probably still residing in Mexico or were recent immigrants from Mexico. White fathers who used crystal reportedly did so more than Black or Hispanic fathers and those White fathers who were reported to drink alcohol did so more than Black fathers. However, these data were the perceptions of the pregnant teenager and were not verified with the fathers. Black fathers were more likely to have a family history of out-of-wedlock children than White fathers (66% vs. 13%). It is interesting to note, too, that nearly half of the Hispanic fathers also had a family history of out-of-wedlock children. None of the other demographic variables differed by father's race. Specifically, there were no differences among the three racial groups in fathers' mean age, occupation, living arrangements, marital status, relationship with the pregnant teen, or attitude toward support of the baby. In fact, the fathers from the three racial groups appear to be more alike, through the young mothers' eyes, than different.

## Postpartum Involvement of the Father of Baby

As noted previously, the teen mothers were interviewed at intake into the prenatal clinic and at 6-month intervals after birth for 3 years. These interviews included information concerning the father of the baby and his involvement with the mother and their child. Follow-up data were obtained on all of the fathers from the UCSD Teen OB Clinic site and 69 of the fathers whose partners were seen at the community clinics for a maximum number of 192 fathers at 6 months. In only 5% of the cases did the actual father of the baby provide the information himself. The sample number decreased to 145 at 36 months, a 75% follow-up rate over 3 years.

Table 6.5 shows data regarding fathers' postpartum involvement in three areas: (a) father's financial support to the teen mother; (b) father's relationship with the teen mother; and (c) the father's relationship with the baby, indexed by such factors as mother's report of father's attitude toward the baby, father's help with infant care, and whether the father lives with baby. In each of these areas, variables were subjected to a multivariate analysis of variance to detect differences due to father's race. When a race effect was found, this was noted as an R superscript in Table 6.5 and is discussed in the text.

*Fathers' Financial Support.*    Over the 3-year period, about 30% of the teen mothers reported that the father of the baby was her primary source of financial support as opposed to her parents being her primary source of financial assistance or relying primarily on AFDC. This figure was as high as 34% at 6 and 12 months postpartum and decreased only slightly to 29% by 36 months postpartum. There was a race effect in teens' primary source of support at all assessment points except the 3-year follow-up. Teens with Black partners were more likely to be dependent on AFDC for financial assistance than teens with White or Hispanic partners at 6 months ($p < .01$), 18 months ($p < .001$), 24 months ($p < .05$), and 30 months

Table 6.5
Postpartum Involvement of Father of Baby (FOB)

| | 6 Months (n = 192) | 12 Months (n = 167) | 18 Months (n = 162) | 24 Months (n = 172) | 30 Months (n = 163) | 36 Months (n = 145) |
|---|---|---|---|---|---|---|
| FOB is Primary Source of Teen's Financial Support | 34%[R] | 34%[R] | 29%[R] | 30%[R] | 30%[R] | 29% |
| Teen Mother Receives Some Income From FOB | 50% | 49% | 39% | 39% | 36% | 41% |
| FOB Pays Child Support | 2% | 4% | 7% | 5% | 8% | 7% |
| Teen Mother's Relationship With FOB | | | | | | |
|   Married | 20%[a] | 21%[R] | 22% | 21% | 25%[R] | 27%[R] |
|   Lives with/unmarried | 24% | 24% | 18% | 18% | 18% | 12% |
|   Sees regularly | 18% | 12% | 13% | 7% | 6% | 6% |
|   Sees occasionally or never | 32% | 37% | 34% | 49% | 50% | 49%[b] |
|   Other | 4% | 6% | 3% | 5% | 7% | 5% |
| Teen Living With | | | | | | |
|   FOB | 37% | 37% | 40% | 37% | 34% | 36% |
|   (Married) | (13%)[a] | (13%) | (22%) | (19%) | (22%) | (23%) |
|   (Unmarried) | (24%) | (24%) | (18%) | (18%) | (12%) | (13%) |
| Teen's Perception of FOB's Attitude Toward Child | | | | | | |
|   Warm and loving | 75% | 74% | 65% | 74% | 68% | 61% |
|   Unconcerned | 15% | 15% | 21% | 17% | 22% | 7% |
|   Hostile/negative | 1% | 4% | 4% | 3% | 2% | 0% |
|   Not applicable/Not see FOB | 4% | 1% | 6% | 1% | 3% | 18% |
|   Other | 5% | 6% | 4% | 5% | 5% | 14% |
| Teen's Report of FOB's Help With Child Care | | | | | | |
|   None | 58% | 57% | 52% | 54% | 66%[R] | 60% |
|   Some | 26% | 20% | 24% | 22% | 10% | 13% |
|   A lot | 16% | 23% | 24% | 24% | 24% | 27% |
|   FOB lives with infant | 48%[R] | 44%[R] | 47%[R] | 44%[R] | 41%[R] | 41% |

Note.[a] The discrepancy between teens married to the FOB at 6 months (20%) and teens married to and living with the FOB at 6 months (13%) reflects the fact that 7% of the teen mothers reported being married to but not currently living with the FOB.

[b]At the 3-year follow-up, this category was separated into "see only occasionally" (15%) or "never see" (34%).

[R]A race effect found based on race of father. See text for explanation.

postpartum ($p < .01$). Similarly, at 12 months postpartum, teens with Hispanic partners were more likely to report that their primary source of financial support was the father of the baby as compared to teens with Black partners or teens with White partners ($p < .05$). Half of the teen mothers reported that they were receiving at least some financial support from the father of the baby at 6 months postpartum and this figure decreased to 36% by 30 months. On the other hand, 2% of the mothers stated that the father of the baby was paying child support at 6 months postpartum and this figure increased slightly to 8% by 30 months. There were no race effects noted for either of these latter categories at any time postpartum.

*Father's Relationship With the Teen Mother.*    One fifth of the mothers were married to the baby's father at the 6-month follow-up (compared to 8% at intake and 7% prior to conception) and this figure increased to 27% by the 3-year follow-up. In all the other categories there was a decline in the mother–partner relationship so that by the time the baby was 3 years old, more than 50% of the couples rarely or never saw one another. The number of couples living together (married or unmarried) actually remained steady over the 3 years studied with more cohabitating couples married than unmarried starting at the 18-month follow-up date. There was a race effect observed in the teen mother–partner relationship in that Black fathers were less likely to marry the mother and more likely to see the mother only occasionally or never than White or Hispanic fathers at the 12-month ($p < .05$), 30-month ($p < .05$), and 36-month ($p < .01$) follow-up visits.

*Father's Relationship With Baby.*    Three fourths of the mothers reported that the fathers were warm and loving to the babies at the 6-month follow-up, with this figure decreasing to 61% by 3 years. But this still indicates that more than half of the fathers were perceived to be close to their infants over a sustained period of time. It is refreshing to see that very few mothers reported that the fathers were hostile or negative over time, but nearly 20% of the fathers rarely saw their children at 3 years of age. In the mothers' eyes, between 50% and 70% of the fathers provided no assistance with child care over the entire 3-year period. The percentage of fathers who helped care for the child essentially remained stable over the 3-year period. It appears that this pattern was set by the 6-month follow-up and did not change with time (or maturity of either parent!). Nearly half of the infants lived with their fathers at 6 months (and this figure corresponds with the figures for mother–partner marriages and living together) and this decreased with time to 41% at the 3-year follow-up. Although there were no race effects noted in the teen mother's perception of the father's attitude toward the child, there were race effects in fathers' help with child-care and living arrangements. White fathers were more likely than Black or Hispanic fathers to help with child care at the 30-month follow-up ($p < .05$). It is important to note, however, that White fathers provided on average only "some" help with child care and that they were not abundantly helpful with the child's caretaking. At all but the last follow-up point, Black fathers were less likely than the others to live with the infant ($p$ values ranged from $< .01$ to $< .05$).

*Fathers' Gang and Jail Activity.*    Because the relationship between the teen mother and the father of her baby appeared to deteriorate with time for those couples who were not married or living together, we explored the possibility that the father was simply not available because he was in jail. Table 6.6 summarizes mother-reported information concerning the fathers' gang and jail activity by the 3-year follow-up. As noted, 20% of the fathers had been in a gang at some time, nearly 33% of the fathers had been in jail at some time, and nearly 10% were in jail at the 3-year follow-up (as reported by the teen mothers). These data are limited in that we do not know when

Table 6.6
Father of Baby in Gang or Jail by the 3-year Follow-up
by Teen Mother's Report (N = 145)

| | |
|---|---|
| Ever in a Gang? | |
| Yes | 20% |
| No | 74% |
| Unsure | 6% |
| Currently in a Gang? | |
| Yes | 9% |
| No | 84% |
| Unsure | 7% |
| Ever Been in Jail? | |
| Yes | 31% |
| No | 64% |
| Unsure | 5% |
| Currently in Jail? | |
| Yes | 9% |
| No | 83% |
| Unsure | 8% |

the fathers were in jail, but it is conceivable that at least some of them, if not all of them, were in jail sometime during the pregnancy or soon after the birth. This may explain some of the estrangement between the couples and could also explain why at least some of the teen mothers chose to stop seeing the father of their baby. There were no race differences in these data.

## Adolescent Versus Adult Fathers

The partners of the 123 teenage mothers from the UCSD Teen OB Clinic were divided into two groups by age at the intake visit: those who were 18 years of age or younger (the adolescent father group), and those who were older than 18 years (the adult father group). There were 50 fathers in the adolescent group with a mean age of 17 years, and there were 73 fathers in the adult group with a mean age of 21.5 years. These two groups were then compared on background characteristics, relationship with the pregnant teen at intake and at postpartum follow-up visits at 6, 12, and 18 months.

Table 6.7 lists selected background characteristics between the adolescent and adult father groups. There were no significant differences between the two age groups in racial/ethnic backgrounds, place of birth, citizenship, military service, school grades, history of truancy when in school, or drug use. As would be expected, significantly more adult fathers than adolescent fathers (53% vs. 15%) had graduated from high school and more adolescent fathers than adult fathers (59% vs. 2%) were still in school. Adult fathers were far more likely to be working than adolescent fathers (67% vs. 35%), which also would be expected.

Table 6.7
Selected Background Characteristics of Adolescent
and Adult Partners of Teen Mothers[a]

| | Adolescent (n = 50) | Adult (n = 73) |
|---|---|---|
| Race | % | % |
|    Black | 52 | 37 |
|    Hispanic | 26 | 38 |
|    White | 14 | 15 |
|    Other | 8 | 10 |
| U.S. Citizen | 76 | 69 |
| School Status | | |
|    In school | 59 | 2* |
|    Not in school | 26 | 45 |
| Graduate High School | 15 | 53 |
| Grade Completed (M years) | 10.6 | 11.2 |
| History of Truancy | 54 | 53 |
| Drug Use | | |
|    Marijuana | 43 | 44 |
|    Speed | 2 | 8 |
|    Cocaine | 8 | 20 |
| Occupation | | |
|    Unemployed | 14 | 22 |
|    Working (incl. military) | 35 | 67* |
|    In school/training | 44 | 3 |

[a]Adapted from Wong (1993). Unpublished data.
*$p < .001$.

Other areas were also explored for potential age of father differences but are not depicted in Table 6.7. There were no differences between the two age groups in family history of teen parenthood, out-of-wedlock births, whether the teen mother knew the father's family, whether the teen's family knew the father, whether the father's family knew about the pregnancy, or whether the father's family was supportive of the pregnancy. Except for school and work, the two groups were remarkably similar in backgrounds.

The relationship characteristics between the father of the baby and the pregnant teen at intake are shown in Table 6.8 for older and for younger fathers. Most of the partners in both age groups knew one another for 6 months or more prior to conception, but the adult fathers appeared to have had a closer relationship with the teen mother than the adolescent fathers prior to conception, with more adult fathers (33%) than adolescent fathers (2%) married to, living with, or engaged to the pregnant teen before she became pregnant. More adult fathers were married or planning marriage to their partners at intake (53% vs. 33%), and more adult fathers than adolescent fathers were living with the pregnant teen at intake regardless of marital status (27% vs. 2%).

The close relationship between the adult fathers and the pregnant teen observed at intake did not continue over time. Table 6.9 shows the partner's relationship with the teen mother over an 18-month period for both age fathers. There were no differences between the two age groups from 6 months onward in the proportion of partners who had close versus distant relationships. At 6 months, more adult fathers than adolescent fathers were married to the teen mother (15% vs. 3%, $p < .05$), but this difference clearly dissipated by 12 and 18 months as more adolescent fathers married the teen mother. At all three follow-up points, there were more teen mothers of adolescent partners living with a parent compared to teen mothers of adult partners ($p < .05$).

When the baby was 1 year of age, more adult fathers than adolescent fathers were the teen mother's primary financial support (48% vs. 9%, $p < .05$), which is probably a reflection of the fact that more adult fathers than adolescent fathers were employed. This probably also explains the fact that at the 6- and 12-month follow-ups more teenage mothers with adolescent partners than teenage mothers with adult partners received income from their parents. But this finding also disappeared by 18 months as both the young mother and the adolescent father aged. Interestingly, there were no differences over time between the adolescent and adult fathers in the number of fathers who assisted the teen mother with child care.

Because there were so many similarities between the adolescent and adult fathers, we speculated that there may be differences between the young women. Hence, we compared the teen mothers who had adolescent partners with the teen mothers who had adult partners. Although the teen mothers with adolescent partners were significantly younger than the teen mothers with adult partners at the time of conception of the target pregnancy (15.6 years vs. 16.1 years, $p < .01$),

### Table 6.8
### Relationship of Father With Pregnant Teen at Intake[a]

|  | Adolescent (n = 50) | Adult (n = 73) |
|---|---|---|
| Length of Time Parnters Knew One Another Prior to Conception | % | % |
|   < 6 months | 34 | 23 |
|   ≥ 6 months | 64 | 77 |
| Relationship to Partner Prior to Conception |  |  |
|   Close (married to, living with, engaged) | 2 | 33** |
|   Other | 98 | 67 |
| Relationship to Partner at Intake |  |  |
|   Married/planning to marry | 33 | 53* |
|   Not married/dating/other | 65 | 42 |
| Living Arrangements at Intake |  |  |
|   Parents/relatives | 67 | 30** |
|   Pregnant teen | 2 | 27 |
|   Other | 28 | 42 |

[a] Adapted from Wong (1993). Unpublished data
*$p < .05$. **$p$ .001.

Table 6.9
Postpartum Relationship of Adolescent Mothers
and the Fathers of Their Baby Over Time[a]

| | 6 Months | | 12 Months | | 18 Months | |
|---|---|---|---|---|---|---|
| | Adolescent | Adult | Adolescent | Adult | Adolescent | Adult |
| | (n = 40) | (n = 65) | (n = 37) | (n = 62) | (n = 40) | (n = 62) |
| Relationship of Partners | | | | | | |
| Close (married, engaged, living with or sees regularly) | 66 | 60 | 52 | 61 | 42 | 61 |
| Distant (sees occasionally, never, divorced, or separated) | 34 | 40 | 48 | 39 | 58 | 39 |
| Married to Father of Baby | 3 | 15* | 8 | 22 | 10 | 18 |
| Currently Lives With | | | | | | |
| Father of child | 20 | 31 | 22 | 37 | 24 | 42 |
| (Married) | (3) | (11) | (3) | (13) | (14) | (18) |
| (Unmarried) | (17) | (20) | (19) | (24) | (10) | (24) |
| At least one parent | 60 | 34* | 57 | 29* | 44 | 21* |
| Primary Source of Support | | | | | | |
| Father of child | 8 | 22 | 9 | 48* | 15 | 20 |
| Other | 92 | 78 | 91 | 52 | 85 | 80 |
| Receives Income From | | | | | | |
| Child support | 6 | 2 | 9 | 3 | 12 | 5 |
| Husband/boyfriend | 43 | 44 | 38 | 49 | 35 | 37 |
| Own parents | 50 | 23** | 43 | 19* | 33 | 30 |
| Father Provides Some Help With Child Care | 53 | 53 | 41 | 49 | 39 | 53 |

[a] Adapted from Wong (1993). Unpublished Data
*$p < .05$. **$p < .01$.

this translates only to a 6-month age difference that may not be clinically significant. Otherwise, there were no significant differences between the two groups of young women in race, age at first intercourse, number of sexual partners, or number of girlfriends who also became pregnant. More teens who were partners with adult men than teens who were partners with adolescent men admitted to a history of truancy (49% vs. 22%, $p < .01$), but there were no differences between the two groups in grade level completed, repeating a grade, or grades while in school.

Table 6.10 shows data on the attitudes of the two groups of young women toward their pregnancies and the fathers of their baby at intake. Young women with adult partners compared to young women with adolescent partners were more likely to have become pregnant because they wanted a baby compared to an unplanned pregnancy (43% vs. 24%, $p < .05$). There were, however, no differences between the two groups in their plans concerning the pregnancy when they first learned that they were pregnant or at intake into the clinic (e.g., abortion, adoption, keep the baby, undecided). Most of the mothers in both groups kept their babies with no significant difference between the two groups at any time in percentage of mothers keeping the baby as compared to not keeping the baby (e.g., adopted out, foster care, kin raising baby). Of course, not all adoptions take place at birth.

More young women who were partners of adult men compared to young women who were partners of adolescent men were likely to be married to the father at intake (14% vs. 2%, $p < .05$), as would be expected from previous analyses. There were, however, no differences in how the young women described their relationships with their partners, with only about 60% of both groups feeling that they had a fair to excellent relationship.

## Relations Between Fathers' Financial Support, Relationship With the Teen Mother, and Child-Care Assistance and Children's Behavioral Outcomes at 3 Years of Age

Table 6.10
Pregnant Teen's Attitudes Toward Pregnancy and Relationship
With Father of Baby (FOB) at Intake[a]

|  | Adolescent Father (n = 50) | Adult Father (n = 74) |
|---|---|---|
| Reason for Pregnancy | | |
| Wanted a baby | 24 | 43* |
| Unplanned | 76 | 57 |
| Plans for Pregnancy When First Diagnosed | | |
| Abortion | 20 | 11 |
| Adoption | 4 | 2 |
| Keep baby | 70 | 86 |
| Undecided | 6 | 2 |
| Plans for Baby at Intake | | |
| Abortion | 0 | 1 |
| Adoption | 10 | 1 |
| Keep baby | 88 | 96 |
| Undecided | 2 | 1 |
| Marital Status | | |
| Single | 98 | 84* |
| Married to FOB | 2 | 14 |
| Attitude Toward Marriage | | |
| Married to/plans to marry FOB | 28 | 49** |
| Does not want to marry FOB | 64 | 34 |
| Relationship to FOB | | |
| Poor (none, hostile, or indifferent) | 41 | 41 |
| Good (fair, good, or excellent) | 59 | 59 |

[a] Adapted from Wong (1993). Unpublished data.
*p < .05. **p < .01.

We examined the relations between children's behavioral adjustment and fathers' postpartum financial support, father's relationship with the teen mother over the postpartum period, and fathers' postpartum child-care assistance. Child outcomes included mother ratings of children's social withdrawal and physical aggression (as described in chapters 4 and 5). Child ratings were available for 119 children between 1 and 4 years, with most children 3 years of age. Results showed no associations among any of the aforementioned variables. There was a slight trend, however, for those children whose fathers provided no financial support to the teen mother at 2 years postpartum to be perceived by their mothers as more socially withdrawn ($M = 0.80$) than children whose fathers provided financial support at 2 years postpartum ($M = 0.61, t = 1.89, p < .06$). But this finding is probably due to chance given the number of tests computed.

## DISCUSSION

The goals of this chapter were to present a descriptive picture of a multiracial group of young men who were the partners of teenage mothers, to explore racial differences among such men, to chart changes in the relationships of teen mothers and their partners over time, to compare adolescent fathers and adult fathers in their relationships with the teen mother and the support provided to the teenage mother and her baby, and to examine the relations between fathers' financial and child-care support and their relationship with the teen mother to their children's behavioral outcomes. The findings for the fathers in this sample were remarkably similar to other reports in the literature. Compared to other studies, there were fewer fathers over the age of 21 in the current sample; only 30% of the fathers were 21 years or older in the current sample, whereas in other clinical samples, as many as 45% to 60% are over the age of 21 years (Hollingsworth, 1978). Although the fathers had a mean education of 11 years, 25% reportedly dropped out of school before conception, which strengthens the observation of other researchers that young men who are fathers are educationally disadvantaged (e.g., Hendricks et al., 1984; Panzarine & Elster, 1983). And in this group, it is clear that the pregnancy was not the cause of the educational deficit and indeed may be a consequence of it. That is, if the young man is not in school and has a job, he may feel that he is capable of supporting a partner and child. Only 20% of this group of young men were not in school and not employed at intake.

As in other samples, more than 50% of the fathers were living with family members and, in half the cases, the girl's family knew him well. And clearly, the teen mothers and this group of fathers were not casual acquaintances. Nearly 75% of the teen mothers stated that they knew the father of the baby for at least 6 months prior to the conception, and 50% knew the father for more than 1 year. It is interesting to us, that 20% of the girls stated that they "dropped" the father of the baby. We did not ask why they dropped the father and stopped seeing him. However, conveniently we note that 20% of the fathers were not employed and not in school and 20% reportedly were in gangs at some time and 33% reportedly were in jail at some point. It is possible that these issues are interrelated and that there is a subgroup of young men who are viewed as an undesirable mate or partner. However, this is only speculative.

There were very few differences among the three racial groups in nearly all areas of comparison. Although the Hispanic fathers had less education and Blacks had an increased family history of out-of-wedlock births, there appeared to be more similarities than differences across racial lines.

As noted by others, the relationship between the teen mother and her partner, if unmarried, deteriorated over time so that more than 50% of the couples rarely saw one another by 3 years postpartum. In contrast, the percentage of couples who married also increased over time. Approximately 7% of the couples were married at conception, 8% at intake, 21% at 6 months, and 27% by 36 months. But in reality, the relationship was set by 6 months. Very few couples married after 6 months. As previously noted by others, Blacks were less likely to marry than Whites or Hispanics.

And finally, there were very few differences between adolescent and adult partners of the teen mothers. In fact, the major differences were related to having a job or being in school that could simply be a consequence of age. Although more adult father–teen mother couples were married at 6 months, even this difference disappeared by 12 months postpartum. The older fathers were more likely to be the primary source of financial support for the teen mother initially, but this difference also disappeared with the passage of time. It is disturbing that only 60% of the teen mothers in both father age groups felt good about their relationship with the fathers of their baby. Perhaps the initial financial support lends stability to the young family but is not enough to sustain them emotionally.

It is clear that the descriptions of fathers in this sample are not much different from other descriptions of partners of pregnant teens in the literature. There were few differences by race and few differences by age. The partners of pregnant teens do have specific needs however that should be addressed. For example, this is a group of young men who have difficulties with school. In fact, poor school performance may be a marker for paternity risk.

Prevention programs should be aware of this high-risk potential. At least some of these young men are involved in many high-risk behaviors including drugs, gangs, and criminal behavior, but many are not. Young fathers who have jobs are more than willing to contribute to the welfare of their children. Job training must be a component to teen father programs. And finally, more than 50% of the fathers did not participate in child care over the 3 years studied, even those who were close to the mother and baby. The reasons for this are not known and are from the perspective of the young mother. But if it is true, clinicians and program planners must develop innovative programs to help young fathers be better "hands-on" fathers to their children and not simply a source of financial support.

# Chapter 7

## Summary
## and Conclusions

ઠ૦ ◆ ૦ક

In this book, we presented information on the pregnancy and parenting characteristics of a multiracial urban sample of young, poor adolescent women who reside
in the U.S. southwest. Participants were studied prenatally to 3½ years postpartum.
Five major areas were addressed: (a) prenatal and postnatal maternal and infant
health; (b) predictors of repeat pregnancy by 18 months postpartum; (c) parenting
traits; (d) the role of the teen's mother (the baby's grandmother) in the teen's
parenting; and (e) characteristics of the fathers of the babies. One of the strengths
of this study is the racial and ethnic diversity of the sample and whenever it was
appropriate, we presented racial/ethnic differences or similarities.

We learned much from the young women who participated in this study and we
appreciate the information that they and their partners and families shared with us.
Some of the data presented are confirmatory of other data in the literature; other
information is new. As much as possible, we compared our findings with existing
studies, and suggested other areas of investigation for future research. In this final
chapter, we summarize our findings and present implications for program development and policy directions. We hope that the knowledge gained from this San Diego
experience will benefit future generations of adolescent mothers and their offspring.

### SUMMARY OF TOPIC AREAS

#### Prenatal and Postnatal Outcomes

In general, the mothers and infants in this sample fared well, although even within
the current sample one baby died at birth and one mother died due to complications
contracted during delivery. Only 6% of the babies weighed less than 2,500 grams at
birth and only 7% were delivered at 37 weeks gestation or less. Hispanic teens were
more likely to be married and to have lower socioeconomic backgrounds than the

others and more White teenagers were likely to use illicit drugs than the others. However, there were no significant differences between White, Black, or Hispanic teenagers in the number or types of major prenatal problems for the mother or postnatal problems of the infant, except that the birthweights of Black infants were less than the birthweights of White infants, a finding that is consistent with many other reports. Despite this statistically significant finding, it is noteworthy that compared to other studies, relatively few infants of all three racial/ethnic groups were low birthweight (only 5%–8%), including Black infants. Poor maternal prenatal weight gain was associated with poor neonatal outcome. Girls who gained less than 20 pounds during the pregnancy had smaller babies with lower Apgar scores and 25% of those babies were premature. These young women tended to be younger than the others and to have had fewer prenatal visits that contributed further to the poor neonatal outcome.

The use of multiple regression analyses to predict pregnancy and neonatal outcomes indicated that alcohol and marijuana use, few prenatal visits, young maternal age, and late prenatal care were positive predictors for pregnancy complications and poor infant outcome. In other words, the older adolescent who had frequent prenatal visits and abstained from drugs and alcohol fared best for herself and her baby.

## Predictors of Repeat Pregnancy

We investigated repeat pregnancies and their outcomes for all primigravidae in the study sample up to 18 months postpartum. Fifteen percent of the participants had a repeat pregnancy within 6 months postpartum; 21% had a repeat pregnancy between 6 months and 18 months postpartum; and 65% did not have a subsequent pregnancy within this time frame. None of the sociodemographic characteristics of the adolescents obtained at intake and none of the prenatal or baby characteristics were associated with the timing of a repeat pregnancy, but young women who had an immediate repeat pregnancy (i.e., within 6 months postpartum) were strikingly different from the others at 6 months postpartum. Results from logistic regression analysis indicated that teens who at 6 months postpartum had not returned to school, had dropped out of school, were living with a male partner, were receiving some form of governmental assistance, and reported a large amount of child care assistance from their mothers were more than twice as likely to be pregnant again by 6 months postpartum than other women.

Pregnancy resolution did not differ by timing of the repeat pregnancy, although the most common pregnancy resolution for teens who became pregnant within 6 months was to have an abortion (46%), whereas teens who became pregnant after 6 months postpartum most often chose to carry to term (55%). About 18% of the women who became pregnant within 6 months had a miscarriage. Overall, only 17% of all first-time mothers in this sample had a repeat birth. Unfortunately, those who became pregnant immediately, compared to those who became pregnant later, sought prenatal care significantly later, used more alcohol and marijuana during their second pregnancies, and had more pregnancies overall by 18 months postpartum. Clearly, those women who became pregnant within 6 months of giving birth to their first child were a special high-risk group. Unfortunately, we, like others, could not identify characteristics in advance that would enable us to discriminate which adolescents would have an early repeat pregnancy compared to those who would not.

## Qualities of Adolescent Mothers' Parenting

To examine adolescent mothers' parenting qualities, we used standardized questionnaires to examine the interrelations among the adolescent's parenting attitudes, parenting confidence, parenting stress, parenting knowledge, and commitment to the parenting role, and we assessed whether these qualities varied by maternal age, race, parity, marital status, and age and gender of the child and if these qualities were related to the child's social withdrawal or aggressiveness. Overall, the mothers in this study had only moderately favorable parenting attitudes, but had high confidence in their parenting abilities. We wonder if this is a reflection of youthful invincibleness. The mothers in this sample knew a lot about healthy child development, and were quite committed to their parenting role.

There are, however, pockets of concern. For example, young maternal age at delivery was associated with low child acceptance and low commitment to parenting independent of the effects of the children's ages. Older mothers tended to place more value on physical punishment and felt less confident about their caretaking abilities. In addition, those mothers who knew more about normal infant and child development reported favorable parenting attitudes but also more parenting stress.

Regression analyses indicated some associations between mothers' parenting and child outcome. Specifically, unfavorable parenting values and low maternal confidence were associated with high social withdrawal in children. High parenting stress was associated with high child aggression.

There were no significant parity, marital status, or gender of child effects for any of the parenting measures, but there were variations by race. White mothers had significantly more favorable parenting values (i.e., more appropriate expectations of child, greater empathy for child's needs, less value of physical punishment, and lower expectations regarding the child's nurturing role) than did Black or Hispanic mothers. Black mothers reported greater confidence in their caretaking abilities than did Hispanic mothers and greater acceptance of their children than did either White or Hispanic mothers. Thus, Hispanic mothers in this sample may be in triple jeopardy. They appear not to have the benefit of appropriate parenting values compared to White mothers, nor parenting confidence or high child acceptance as compared to Black mothers.

These results are not causal, but rather associative. It is clear, however, that all components of parenting attitudes, parenting confidence, and parenting stress were highly intercorrelated, and that knowledge about children alone is not sufficient in helping young mothers be effective as parents.

## Relationships Between Teen Mothers and Their Mothers

We examined the role of the grandmother in the adolescent mother's parenting qualities and her child's outcome. Specifically, we investigated issues related to grand-mother–adolescent coresidence, amount of grandmother child-care assistance, and grandmother–adolescent conflict. For the sake of clarity, we referred to the adolescent's mother as the *grandmother* and to the teen mother as the *teen* or *adolescent mother* throughout this book. We found that young teenage mothers (age 16 or younger at delivery) who reported no grandmother child-care assistance had the lowest parenting confidence, the highest parenting stress, the lowest child care involvement, and the lowest child development knowledge scores of all groups studied. However, older teenage mothers (17 years or older at delivery) experienced the most favorable parenting outcomes only when there was low grandmother child-care assistance.

High grandmother child-care assistance was associated with negative parenting outcomes for mothers in all three racial/ethnic groups but in different ways. For example, White mothers who had high grandmother child-care assistance had significantly less favorable parenting attitudes and less parenting confidence than White mothers who had low grandmother child-care assistance. Hispanic mothers who had high grand-mother child-care assistance were significantly less involved in their children's care than Hispanic mothers who had low grandmother child-care assistance, and Black mothers who had high grandmother child-care assistance were significantly more stressed about parenting than Black mothers who had low grandmother child-care assistance. In fact, in all three racial groups, the teen mothers who fared best in parenting outcomes were the ones with the least grandmother child-care involvement. This suggests that even moderate grandmother involvement in child care could be quite disadvantageous for adolescent mothers' parenting. Alternatively, grandmothers might provide more assis-tance to teen mothers who are having great difficulties in the parenting role.

When we investigated child outcomes and grandmother involvement with respect to mother's race and age, we again found some interesting results. Grandmoth-ers' coresidence was associated with poor behavioral outcomes for White children and for children born to young teenage mothers, at least as perceived by mothers. White children living with their grandmothers were perceived to be significantly more socially withdrawn than White children not living with their grandmothers, and the children of young mothers who coresided with their grandmothers had significantly higher aggression scores than the children of young mothers who did not coreside with their grandmothers. However, grandmothers' coresidence seemed to benefit Black children, with Black children who coresided with their grandmothers having the lowest social withdrawal mean score of any other group.

The most favorable outcomes of all were those situations in which the mother and child lived apart from the grandmother but still received high amounts of child-care assistance from her. In those cases, the teen mother was able to acquire appropriate childrearing attitudes, develop a positive confidence about her parent-ing, and become optimally involved in her child's caretaking. The children, too, fared well in these situations, showing low levels of aggression.

## The Fathers of the Babies Born to Teenage Mothers

The fathers of the babies in this sample were similar in sociodemographics to other samples of fathers in the literature. About 30% of the fathers were over the age of 21 years, which is less than some other reports. Only 20% of the fathers were neither employed nor in school or training, but their mean year of schooling was only 11 years and most who were employed had low-skilled jobs. More than 50% of the fathers lived with their family. Three fourths of the mothers stated that they knew the baby's father for at least 6 months before becoming pregnant. Only 7% of the partners were married at the time of conception. About 33% of the fathers had been in jail at some time and 10% were reported to have been in jail at the time of the 3-year follow-up. Over all, there were very few differences among the three racial groups in any demographic variable except education: Hispanic fathers had less formal education than the others, and Black fathers were more likely to have a family history of out-of-wedlock births than White fathers. But this information was almost always obtained from the teen mother and not directly from the fathers and, hence, may have been underreported or misreported.

Over the 3-year study period, about 30% of the teen mothers reported that the father of the baby was her primary source of financial support. By 6 months postpartum, about 20% of the partners were married and this figure increased to 27% by the 3-year follow-up. The number of couples living together (either married or unmarried) actually remained steady over the 3-year study period. Black fathers were less likely to marry the mother than White or Hispanic fathers. Three fourths of the fathers were involved with their babies at the 6-month follow-up visit, and 60% were still involved at 3 years. But very few fathers were actually engaged in child-care activities at any time in the study.

We compared fathers who were older than 18 years of age with fathers who were 18 years of age or younger and there were very few differences. In fact, the two groups were more similar than different in backgrounds. There were some differences in the mother–father relationships initially, with the older fathers in a more committed relationship with the young mother than younger fathers, but even these differences dissipated with time. Most of the partners in both age groups knew one another for 6 months or more prior to conception, but the adult fathers appeared to have had a closer relationship with the teen mother than the adolescent fathers prior to conception, with more adult fathers than adolescent fathers married to, living with, or engaged to the teen before she became pregnant. By 12 months, there were no differences between the two father groups. Initially, the older fathers provided more financial support, but this trend disappeared by 18 months. It appears that the fathers in this sample were remarkably similar to descriptions of fathers of babies born to teenage mothers in other reports. These similarities did not vary by age or race to any great degree. They were mostly poor and limited in education, but they tried to provide financial support to the mother and baby at least initially. Over time, contact with mother and child decreased.

# IMPLICATIONS FOR THE FUTURE

What have we learned from this experience? What would we do differently today? What concepts would we advise policymakers to address? Are there loopholes in services that even comprehensive programs do not meet? These are the issues over which we have struggled like others in the field. We recognize that there is no such thing as a perfect program and that what may work in one community may not work in another. We also appreciate the fact that adolescent pregnancy is a multifaceted problem that demands multidimensional solutions. Health care, even interdisciplinary health care as provided here, is only one small component in the list of needs that pregnant teens have. A colleague once noted that "teen pregnancy is a sociological problem with medical consequences" (Hollingsworth, 1982, p. 546), a sentiment with which we concur. Based on our experiences in this modest study, we offer some observations and recommendations.

## Prevention is Still the Best Medicine

We consistently found that the youngest teen mothers were most at risk for poor health and social outcomes either for themselves or their infants. They were clearly at increased risk for poor parenting skills. We strongly support efforts to delay childbearing until a young woman is mature enough to handle the demands of parenthood both physically and psychologically. We choose the phrase "delay childbearing" rather than the phrase "prevent pregnancy" because both phrases have different connotations. The emphasis on pregnancy prevention may mean "abstinence until marriage" to some readers or the use of contraception to others (Dryfoos, 1992). We would support any approach that is successful in delaying a young woman's childbearing years by even a short period of time by whatever method works in a given community, whether this is abstinence promotion (Howard, 1992) or school-based clinics (Zabin, Hirsch, Smith, Streett, & Hardy, 1986). Even a pregnancy delay by a few years would probably be beneficial to teen and infant.

## Prenatal and Postnatal Care
## Must be Comprehensive and Multidisciplinary

This program was based on a multidisciplinary model, namely that all participants received services from many professionals from a variety of disciplines including pediatrics, obstetrics, nursing, nutrition, social work, and education, to name a few. It has been well documented by many experts in the field that comprehensive services are essential for pregnant teens and their babies for optimal outcome for both mother and infant (Hardy & Zabin, 1991; Hayes, 1987; Klerman & Horwitz, 1992; McAnarney et al., 1978), but the essential ingredient of comprehensiveness may be lost in the current trend toward managed health care with barebone components. Many teen pregnancy programs that have fostered a comprehensive, multidisciplinary model in the past using same site services or closely monitored case management services may lose patients in the future to HMOs or managed care companies where rewards are not given for comprehensive services but rather for the use of the least number of services in the name of efficiency. If outcome is not monitored in such a system, there may be a rise in low birthweight infants born to teenage mothers.

In the San Diego program, dietician counseling and WIC services were important components in helping teens gain an appropriate amount of weight. Those girls who did not gain sufficient weight had the smallest babies. The social workers were aggressive in helping the teenagers address overwhelming social problems, such as drug use, alcohol use, and runaway behavior, which would have influenced infant and maternal outcome. Comprehensive programs were initially developed in the 1970s and 1980s to prevent or at least reduce maternal and neonatal problems among pregnant teens. If services for pregnant teens are curtailed in the name of health care reform, we may see a dramatic return to the perinatal problems associated with teen pregnancy that existed in the past. This would be an ironic twist to adolescent medicine history.

## The Pregnant Teenager is an Adolescent Who is Pregnant Not a Pregnant Woman Who is an Adolescent

Caring for pregnant and parenting adolescents is challenging. These young women are still young. They have the same developmental, social, and cognitive needs as other adolescents. Hence, care should be provided by professionals who understand the developmental needs of adolescents and enjoy working with youth. Services must be tailored accordingly.

For example, these young women are minors. They should be in school. Yet many pregnant teens drop out of school before or after the pregnancy. Staff must help pregnant teens return and/or stay in school when possible. Adolescents are often concrete thinkers. Patient education sessions require teaching by example as well as didactics. For example, we soon realized that in spite of our "lecture" about good nutrition, our patients were eating "junk food" while waiting to be seen for their appointments. After that observation, we provided nutritious snacks at each prenatal session and taught the girls how to make them. (It was sobering to us health care professionals to learn that our patients rarely had fresh fruits or vegetables in their homes although they lived in Southern California, which supplies fresh produce for the entire country.) Adolescents are social by nature. Develop support groups where teens can teach one another. And like all children, these young women need positive reinforcement for their successes. Publicly praise adolescents who are successful (e.g., graduating from high school).

### Pregnancy is Just *One* of Their Problems

It was clear to us that being pregnant or being a young unwed mother was just one of many (medical, psychological, social, educational, financial, legal) problems which these young women were experiencing in themselves, their partners, or their family members. There were times when we were overwhelmed with the number of issues to be addressed such as poverty, hunger, homelessness, drugs, violence, abuse, racism, and others. To provide routine prenatal care without attending to at least some of these social problems is a formula for poor outcome.

For example, we learned that rather than call patients noncompliant when they did not have their prescriptions filled, it was far better to explore the cause. Rarely, did adolescents not want to comply with our directions. Sometimes, they had to choose between enough money for food versus filling the prescription. Or, a relative was using the teen's welfare money for alcohol or drugs. Or, she ran away and left the prescription at her previous dwelling and was afraid to return and retrieve it.

Some of the pregnant teens were engaging in other high-risk activities besides unprotected intercourse that resulted in pregnancy. Issues related to sexually transmitted diseases, HIV infection, and cigarette, alcohol, and illicit drug use were not uncommon. The fact that at least 30% of the fathers were in jail at some time cannot be overlooked. All programs designed for pregnant teens must be prepared to address the myriad of high-risk adolescent behaviors and the full gamut of society's ills.

## It is Difficult to Teach Good Parenting Skills

This project included a prenatal educational component that emphasized infant and child development. A master's level health educator was part of the staff and directed the health education sessions. The nurses provided one-on-one patient education at each visit. Information was presented in several ways including demonstrations. The teen mothers scored high on questionnaires testing their knowledge about infant development but this did not translate into effective parenting attributes. In other words, knowledge alone did not influence behavior, an observation that has been documented clearly in sex education studies (Dryfoos, 1992; Oakley et al., 1995). In fact, the teen mothers who knew the most about child development had good parenting attributes but the highest parenting stress scores. Adolescent mothers, like adult mothers, learn parenting from many sources, including school, the media, observation of others, parenting by their parents, and other sources. The clinic is only one small fragment in their lives and we may simply not have been able to exercise as great an influence as necessary in such a short period of time.

In the future, we would probably utilize a full curriculum on parenting with sessions not only on infant care and development, but on discipline and the stress associated with parenting (Epstein, 1980). Moreover, we would have these sessions over a period of months (Butler, Rickle, Thomas, & Hendren, 1993). We would couple this program with intensive parenting instruction after the birth of the child either in support groups in the clinic or in home visiting as has been reported in other cities with much success (Center for the Future of Children, 1993; Field et al., 1982; Fraiberg, Shapiro, & Cherniss, 1980; Olds, Henderson, Chamberlin, & Tatelbaum, 1986). We would also support those programs in schools that formally address parenting skills before teens become parents. But as parents of all ages soon learn, it is only after a child is born that one actually realizes how hard it is to be a truly good parent.

### Fathers of the Babies Must be Included in All Teen Pregnancy Programs and They Need Practical Guidance to Learn How to Parent

In retrospect, we wish that we had been able to engage the fathers of the babies into the program more inclusively. We were not sufficiently aggressive in involving them in the program. There are now many successful father programs (Association of Maternal and Child Health Programs, 1991) and suggestions for establishing such programs (Carrera, 1992; Vera Institute of Justice, 1990). We would urge colleagues to include all the fathers of babies born to teen mothers in special programs not just teen fathers. Based on our experience and other reports, we believe that paternal age is not a discriminating factor in teen pregnancy.

We were surprised at how little fathers were involved in hands-on child-care, even those fathers who were living with teen mothers and the babies. This suggests that they were uncomfortable in that role. Innovative programs to help fathers of all ages and races be more comfortable with their children would be invaluable. A recent study by Cox and Bithoney (1995) showed that the fathers of children born to adolescent mothers were involved in their 2-year-old children's lives if they had attended prenatal visits, saw the newborn in the hospital, and reported a supportive relationship with the young mother's family at 2 weeks postpartum. Interventions that increase fathers' participation in the prenatal, neonatal, and immediate post-partum periods, then, may potentially result in long-term active parenting by fathers. Curricula that foster father involvement have recently become available (Association of Maternal and Child Health Programs, 1991; Ekulona, 1994) and we look forward to their widespread use and evaluation.

### Grandmother Involvement is Not Always Good for the Adolescent or the Baby

Except for the youngest teenagers, intensive grandmother involvement was associated with poor mother and child outcomes. This does not mean that grandmothers should be excluded from care. In fact, parenting teens and their children appeared to fare best when there was active involvement by the grandmother but the teen mother and child were not living with her. This finding was striking and reported by others before us (Chase-Lansdale et al., 1994; Spieker & Bensley, 1994). Despite this observation, there is a political movement among some to force all pregnant and parenting teenagers to live at home or else not be eligible to receive any governmental assistance (i.e., welfare and medicaid). We are opposed to such a recommendation because it could be detrimental to all concerned. Besides, such a short-sighted policy does not take into consideration the reasons why a young woman may have chosen not to live at home in the first place. As we recommend that parenting teens return to school to finish their educations at a time when there is inadequate day care for mothers of all ages, it would be ludicrous to exclude grandmothers from a positive role. We would advise future programs to explore innovative approaches to involve the mothers of parenting teenagers in their programs in such a way that it is beneficial to teenager, child, and the grandmother. This is an area that needs much work in the future so that grandmothers may be a positive influence in helping to address the prevention of precocious pregnancy in their daughters.

## Programs Must be Tailored to Racial and Ethnic and Cultural Needs

It is clear from the information presented in this study and many others that pregnant and parenting adolescents from different racial or ethnic groups have both similarities and differences. There are both medical and psychosocial issues to consider. Staff must be aware of and sensitive to those issues. This may be more likely to happen if the staff members themselves are racially or ethnically diverse.

When we first opened the UCSD Teen OB Clinic, there was very little information in the literature about pregnant and parenting teenagers who were Hispanic, or Indochinese, or Asian, or American Indian. Much of the existing data at that time had been reported from inner-city African-American teenagers or poor non-Hispanic White adolescents. So, initially, we simply learned from our patients. We would caution other health care providers that the information we report here may not apply to all groups of pregnant and parenting teens, even teens from similar racial or ethnic groups. Adolescent pregnancy must always be viewed in the context of the individual, her family, and the community.

## Comprehensive Care for Parenting Teenagers and Their Children Must Continue After the Birth

Just as the pregnant teen needs comprehensive services that are tailored to her needs, so too does the parenting teen. Unrealistically, we may expect teenagers to attend school, keep all infant appointments for her child, keep all appointments for her own primary health care, and maintain continuous uninterrupted contraception while at the same time removing the support services that were provided when she was pregnant. Many parenting teenagers find that all the supportive services that they had before delivery suddenly disappear after the birth of the child when she may need the most support and help and be least equipped to find such services on her own (Klerman & Horwitz, 1992). After the birth of the child, the teenager may be at most risk for stress, depression, and drug use (Barnet, Duggan, Wilson, & Joffe, 1995; Pletsch, 1988), which in turn can lead to child abuse. We would urge all programs to maintain comprehensive services for parenting teens until at least 2 years after the birth of the child. Ideally, such services should be done in such a way that the mother and child can both receive health care in the same site at the same time, services sometimes called Teen–Tot Clinics or Two Generation Services (Klerman & Horwitz, 1992). Such programs may also include educational efforts, GED classes, job training, and day care, but most important is continuing support and contact with the teen mother after the child is born.

## Many Teen Mothers Do Well

Despite the negative findings presented here and elsewhere, it is important to remember that many pregnant and parenting adolescents do very well, particularly with a little help. We learned to respect and admire many young women who managed to take care of their child, attend school, and keep their lives together in what seemed to us overwhelming odds against them. We observed many young mothers interacting with their children in loving and appropriate ways. And we learned that the script that we would write for our patients may not be the script that they would write for themselves. We noticed that some young women chose to drop out of school for a time and then return at a later date. Others informed us that being a good mother was more important to them than returning to school. We believed them.

It is only over time that one can observe the effect of the pregnancy on the lives of the teen and the child. The 20-year follow-up study of pregnant teens in the Young Mothers Program in New Haven indicates that 71% of the young mothers in that program had finished high school or received a GED certificate, 77% were employed, 82% had received no welfare support for at least 6 months, and 48% had incomes equal to or more than $15,000 a year (Horwitz, Klerman, Kuo, & Jekel, 1991). The 20-year follow-up of a Baltimore sample also found that many of the former teenage parents had become reasonably successful. In that group, 68% were employed, 71% had graduated from high school, and 47% had incomes equal to or more than $15,000 a year (Furstenberg et al., 1987b). It is important to note that both of the groups described had received comprehensive services in the late 1960s and in both reports, the authors credited the programs for the success of the young mothers in later life. We cannot guess how the teen mothers from this San Diego program will fare 20 years from now. We can only hope that they, too, will benefit from the services provided for them for many years to come.

## CONCLUSIONS

Teenage pregnancy and parenting are problems that have been in existence for many years and are unlikely to disappear soon. We must continue to design programs that help the teenager and her infant have optimal health outcomes while assisting her in being the best parent that she can be. Our efforts must include the fathers of the babies and the grandmothers and other family members as appropriate. Most importantly, our efforts must continue to be based on the needs of the young people we serve.

# References

❦ ◆ ❧

Aber, J. L., & Cicchetti, D. (1984). The socio-emotional development of maltreated children: An empirical and theoretical analysis. In H. Fitzgerald, B. Lester, & M. Yogman (Eds.), *Theory and research in behavioral pediatrics* (pp. 147–205). New York: Plenum.

Achenbach, T. M., & Edelbrock, C. (1983). *Manual for the Child Behavior Checklist.* Burlington, VT: T. M. Achenbach.

Ahmad, F. (1990). Unmarried mothers as a high risk group for adverse pregnancy outcomes. *Journal of Community Health, 15,* 35–44.

Ainsworth, M. D. S., Blehar, M., Waters, E., & Wall, S. (1978). *Patterns of attachment.* Hillsdale, NJ: Lawrence Erlbaum Associates.

Alan Guttmacher Institute. (1994a). Department of Health Services, Vital Statistics Section, 1995. Washington, DC: Senate Office of Research.

Alan Guttmacher Institute (1994b). *Sex and America's teenagers.* Washington, DC: Author.

Alo, C.J., Howe, H.L., & Nelson, M.R. (1993). Birthweight-specific infant mortality risks and leading causes of death: Illinois, 1980–1989. *American Journal of Diseases of Children, 147,* 1085–1089.

Association of Maternal and Child Health Programs. (1991). *Adolescent fathers: Directory of services.* Washington, DC: National Center for Education in Maternal and Child Health.

Atkin, L. C., & Alatorre-Rico, J. (1992). Pregnant again? Psychosocial predictors of short-interval repeat pregnancy among adolescent mothers in Mexico City. *Journal of Adolescent Health, 13,* 700–706.

Bachrach, C. (1983). Children in families: Characteristics of biological, step-, and adopted children. *Journal of Marriage and the Family, 45,* 171–179.

Baldwin, W., & Cain, V. S. (1980). The children of teenage parents. *Family Planning Perspectives, 12,* 34–43.

Barnet, B., Duggan, A., Wilson, M. D., & Joffe, A. (1995). Association between postpartum substance use and depressive symptoms, stress and social support in adolescent mothers. *Pediatrics, 96,* 659–666.

Barrera, M. (1981). Social support in the adjustment of pregnant adolescents: Assessment issues. In B. H. Gottlieb (Ed.), *Social networks and social support* (pp. 69–96). Newbury Park, CA: Sage.

Baumrind, D. (1978). Parental disciplinary patterns and social competence in children. *Youth and Society, 9,* 239–276.

Bavolek, S. J. (1984). *Adult–Adolescent Parenting Inventory.* Eau Claire, WI: Family Development Association Press.

Bavolek, S. J., Kline, D., McLaughlin, J., & Publicover, P. (1979). Primary prevention of child abuse: Identification of high risk adolescents. *Child Abuse and Neglect: The International Journal, 3,* 1071–1080.

Belle, D. (1981). *The social network as a source of both stress and support to low-income mothers.* Paper presented at the biennial meeting of the Society for Research in Child Development, Boston, MA.

Bierman, B. R., & Streett, R. (1982). Adolescent girls as mothers: Problems in parenting. In I. Stuart & C. Wells (Eds.), *Pregnancy in adolescence: Needs, problems, and management* (pp. 407–426). New York: Reinhold.

Blos, P. (1962). *On adolescence: A psychoanalytic interpretation.* New York: The Free Press.

Brindis, C. D., & Jeremy, R. J. (1988). *Adolescent pregnancy and parenting in California: A strategic plan for action* (Center for Population and Reproductive Health Policy). San Francisco: University of California Press.

Brooks-Gunn, J., & Chase-Lansdale, P. L. (1991). Children having children: Effects on the family system. *Pediatric Annals, 20,* 467–481.

Brooks-Gunn, J., & Furstenberg, F. F. (1986a). Antecedents and consequences of parenting: The case of adolescent motherhood. In A. Fogel & G. Melson (Eds.), *Origins of nurturance: Developmental, biological and cultural perspectives on caregiving* (pp. 233–258). Hillsdale, NJ: Lawrence Erlbaum Associates.

Brooks-Gunn, J., & Furstenberg, F. F. (1986b). The children of adolescent mothers: Physical, academic, and psychological outcomes. *Developmental Review, 6,* 224–251.

Brown, H. L., Fan, Y. D., & Gonsoulin, W. J. (1991). Obstetric complications in young teenagers. *Southern Medical Journal, 84,* 46–48.

Brown-Robbins, M. M., & Lynn, D. B. (1973). The unwed fathers: Generational recidivism and attitudes about intercourse in California youth authority wards. *Journal of Sex Research, 9,* 334–341.

Buhlmann, U., Felice, M. E., Shragg, G. P., & Hollingsworth, D. R. (1988). Mother–father age difference in school-age pregnancy: A way to identify lower risk groups. *Journal of Adolescent Health Care, 9,* 264 (abstract).

Burchinal, L. G. (1965). Trends and prospects for young marriages in the United States. *Journal of Marriage and the Family, 27,* 243–254.

Burton, L. (1990). Teenage childbearing as an alternative life-course strategy in multigeneration black families. *Human Nature, 1,* 123–143.

Butler, C., Rickle, A. U., Thomas, E., & Hendren, M. (1993). An intervention program to build competencies in adolescent parents. *The Journal of Prevention, 13,* 183–198.

California Department of Health Services. (1994). *Teenage birth statistics.* Unpublished data. San Francisco: Author.

Card, J. J., & Wise, L. L. (1978). Teenage mothers and teenage fathers: The impact of childbearing on the parents' personal and professional lives. *Family Planning Perspectives, 10,* 199–205.

Carrera, M. A. (1992). Involving adolescent males in pregnancy and STD prevention programs. *Adolescent Medicine: State of the Art Reviews, 3,* 269–281.

Center for the Future of Children. (1993). *The future of children: Home visiting* (Vol. 3). Los Altos, CA: The David and Lucile Packard Foundation.

Centers for Disease Control. (1993). Teenage pregnancy and birth rates: United States, 1990. *Morbidity and Mortality Weekly Report, 42,* 733–737.

Chase-Lansdale, P., Brooks-Gunn, J., & Zamsky, E. S. (1994). Young African-American multigenerational families in poverty: Quality of mothering and grandmothering. *Child Development, 65,* 373–393.

Children's Defense Fund. (1987a). *Child support and teen parents.* Washington, DC: Author.

Children's Defense Fund. (1987b). *Declining earnings of young men: Their relation to poverty, teen pregnancy, and family formation.* Washington, DC: Author.

Christmon, K., & Luckey, I. (1994). Is early fatherhood associated with alcohol and other drug use? *Journal of Substance Abuse, 6,* 337–343.

Cohler, B. J., & Grunebaum, H. U. (1981). *Mothers, grandmothers and daughters: Personality and childcare in three generation families.* New York: Wiley.

Colletta, N. D. (1983). At risk for depression: A study of young mothers. *Journal of Genetic Psychology, 142,* 301–10.

Colletta, N. D., & Lee, D. (1983). The impact of support for Black adolescent mothers. *Journal of Family Issues, 4,* 127–143.

Cooley, M. L., & Unger, D. G. (1991). The role of family support in determining developmental outcomes in children of teen mothers. *Child Psychiatry and Human Development, 21,* 217–234.

Conger, R. D., McCarty, J. A., Yang, R. K., Lahey, B. B., & Burgess, R. L. (1984). Mother's age as a predictor of observed maternal behavior in three independent samples of families. *Journal of Marriage and the Family, 46,* 411–424.

Cox, J. E., & Bithoney, W. G. (1995). Fathers of children born to adolescent mothers. *Archives of Pediatric and Adolescent Medicine, 149,* 962–966.

Crnic, K. A., & Greenberg, M. T. (1990). Minor parenting stresses with young children. *Child Development, 61,* 1628–1637.

Crockenberg, S. (1981). Infant irritability, mother responsiveness, and social support influences on the security of infant–mother attachment. *Child Development, 52,* 857–865.

Crockenberg, S. (1985). Toddlers' reaction to maternal anger. *Merrill-Palmer Quarterly, 31,* 361–363.

Crockenberg, S. (1987a). Predictors and correlates of anger toward and punitive control of toddlers by adolescent mothers. *Child Development, 58,* 969–975.

Crockenberg, S. (1987b). Support for adolescent mothers during the postnatal period: Theory and research. In C. Z. Boukydis (Ed.), *Research and support for parents and infants in the postnatal period* (pp. 3–24). Norwood, NJ: Ablex.

Darabi, K., Graham, E. H., & Philliber, S. G. (1982). The second time around: Birth spacing among teenage mothers. In I. Stuart & C. Wells (Eds.), *Pregnancy in adolescence: Needs, problems, and management* (pp. 427–437). New York: Van Nostrand Reinhold.

de Anda, D. (1984). Informal support networks of Hispanic mothers: A comparison across age groups. *Journal of Social Service Research, 7,* 89–105.

Deardan, K. A., Hale, C. B., & Wooley, T. (1995). The antecedents of teen fatherhood: A retrospective case-control study. *American Journal of Public Health, 85,* 551–554.

DeLissovy, V. (1973). High school marriages: A longitudinal study. *Journal of Marriage and the Family, 35,* 245–55.

Dempsey, J. J. (1972). Recidivism and post delivery school withdrawal: Implications of a follow-up study for planning preventive services. *Journal of School Health, 52,* 291–297.

Dryfoos, J. G. (1988). *Putting the boys in the picture.* Santa Cruz, CA: Newwork.

Dryfoos, J. G. (1992). School and community–based pregnancy prevention programs. *Adolescent Medicine: State of the Art Reviews, 3,* 241–255.

Dubow, E. F., & Luster, T. (1990). Adjustment of children born to teenage mothers: The contribution of risk and protective factors. *Journal of Marriage and the Family, 52,* 393–404.

Dubowitz, L,. Dubowitz, V., & Goldberg, C. (1970). Clinical assessment of gestational age in the newborn infant. *Journal of Pediatrics, 77,* 1–10.

Dumas, J. E. (1986). Indirect influence of maternal social contacts on mother–child interactions: A setting event analysis. *Journal of Abnormal Child Psychology, 14,* 205–216.

East, P. L. (1996). The younger sisters of childbearing adolescents: Their attitudes, expectations, and behaviors. *Child Development, 67,* 267–284.

East, P. L., & Felice, M. E. (1990). Outcomes and parent–child relationships of former adolescent mothers and their 12-year-old children. *Journal of Developmental and Behavioral Pediatrics, 11,* 175–183.

East, P. L., & Felice, M. E. (1992). Pregnancy risk among the younger sisters of pregnant and childbearing adolescents. *Journal of Developmental and Behavioral Pediatrics, 13,* 128–136.

East, P. L., & Felice, M. E. (1994). The psychosocial consequences of teenage pregnancy and childbearing. In R. Schenker (Ed.), *Adolescent medicine* (pp. 73–92). London: Harwood Academic Press.

East, P. L., Felice, M. E., & Morgan, M. C. (1993). Sisters' and girlfriends' sexual and childbearing behavior: Effects on early adolescent girls' sexual outcomes. *Journal of Marriage and the Family, 55,* 953–963.

East, P. L., Matthews, K. L., & Felice, M. E. (1994). Qualities of adolescent mothers' parenting. *Journal of Adolescent Health, 15,* 163–168.

Elster, A. B. (1988). *Adolescent fathers: Fact, fiction, and implications for federal policy.* Washington, DC: U.S. Government Printing Office.

Elster, A. B., & Lamb, M. E. (1986). Adolescent fathers: The under studied side of adolescent pregnancy. In J. B. Lancaster & B. A. Hamburg (Eds.), *School-age pregnancy & parenthood* (pp. 177–190). New York: Aldine de Gruyter Press.

Elster, A. B., Lamb, M. E., Peters, L., Kahn, J., & Tavare, J. (1987). Judicial involvement and conduct problems of fathers of infants born to adolescent mothers. *Pediatrics, 79,* 230–234.

Elster, A. B., McAnarney, E. R., & Lamb, M. E. (1983). Parental behavior of adolescent mothers. *Pediatrics, 71,* 494–503.

Epstein, A. (1980). *Assessing the child development information needed by adolescent parents with very young children.* Washington, DC: U.S. Department of Health, Education, and Welfare.

Erikson, E. (1963). *Childhood and society.* New York: Norton.

Erkan, K. A., Rimer, B. A., & Stine, O. C. (1971). Juvenile pregnancy: Role of physiologic maturity. *Maryland State Medical Journal, 20,* 50–52.

Ekulona, A. (1994). *A curriculum for male involvement in prenatal care* (Healthy Start Initiative). Baltimore, MD: The Baltimore City Health Department.

Felice, M.E., Granados, J.L., Ances, I.G., Hebel, R., Roeder, L.M., & Heald, F. P. (1981). The young pregnant teenager: Impact of comprehensive prenatal care. *Journal of Adolescent Health Care, 1,* 193–197.

Felice, M. E., Shragg, G. P., James, M., & Hollingsworth, D. R. (1986). Clinical observations of Mexican-American, Caucasian, and Black pregnant teenagers. *Journal of Adolescent Health Care, 7,* 305–310.

Felice, M. E., Shragg, G. P., James, M., & Hollingsworth, D. R. (1987). Psychosocial aspects of Mexican-American, White, and Black teenage pregnancies. *Journal of Adolescent Health Care, 8,* 330–335.

Felice, M. E., Shragg, G. P., James, M., & Hollingsworth, D. R. (1988). Adolescent pregnancy in Indochinese refugees in the United States. *International Pediatrics, 3,* 448–453.

Field, T., Healy, B., Goldstein, S., & Guthertz, M. (1990). Behavior-state matching and synchrony in mother–infant interactions of nondepressed versus depressed dyads. *Developmental Psychology, 26,* 7–14.

Field, T., & Widmayer, S. (1981). Mother–infant interaction among lower SES Black, Cuban, Puerto Rican and South American immigrants. In T. M. Field, A. M. Sostek, P. Vietze, & P. H. Liederman (Eds.), *Culture and early interactions* (pp. 41–62). Hillsdale, NJ: Lawrence Erlbaum Associates.

Field, T., Widmayer, S., Greenberg, R., & Stoller, S. (1982). Effects of parent training on teenage mothers and their infants. *Pediatrics, 69,* 703–706.

Field, T., Widmayer, S., Stringer, S. & Ignatoff, E. (1980). Teenage, lower-class, black mothers and their preterm infants: An intervention and developmental follow-up. *Child Development, 51,* 426–36.

Ford, K. (1983). Second pregnancies among teenage mothers. *Family Planning Perspectives, 15,* 268–272.

Fox, R. A., Baisch, M. J., Goldberg, B. D., & Hochmuth, M. C. (1987). Parenting attitudes of pregnant adolescents. *Psychological Reports, 61,* 403–406.

Fraiberg, S., Shapiro, V., & Cherniss, D. (1980). Treatment modalities. In S. Fraiberg (Ed.), *Clinical studies in infant mental health* (pp. 135–152). New York: Basic Books.

Fraser, A. M., Brockert, J. E., & Ward, R. H. (1995). Association of young maternal age with adverse reproductive outcomes. *New England Journal of Medicine, 332,* 1113–1117.

Friede, A., Baldwin, W., Rhodes, P. H., Buehler, P., Strauss, P., Smith, R., & Hogue, J.(1987). Young maternal age and infant mortality: The role of low birth weight. *Public Health Reports, 102,* 192–199.

Frommer, E., & O'Shea, G. (1973). Antenatal identification of women liable to have problems in managing their infants. *British Journal of Psychiatry, 123,* 149–156.

Furstenberg, F. F. (1976a). *The social consequences of teenage childbearing.* New York: The Free Press.

Furstenberg, F. F. (1976b). The social consequences of teenage parenthood. *Family Planning Perspectives, 8,* 148–164.

Furstenberg, F. F. (1980). Burdens and benefits: The impact of early childbearing on the family. *Journal of Social Issues, 36,* 65–87.

Furstenberg, F. F., Brooks-Gunn, J., & Morgan, S. P. (1987a). Adolescent mothers and their children in later life. *Family Planning Perspectives, 19,* 142–150.

Furstenberg, F. F., Brooks-Gunn, J., & Morgan, S. P. (1987b). *Adolescent mothers in later life.* New York: Cambridge University Press.

Furstenberg, F. F., & Crawford, A. G. (1978). Family support: Helping teenage mothers to cope. *Family Planning Perspectives, 10,* 322–333.

Garcia-Coll, C. T., Hoffman, J., & Oh, W. (1987). The social ecology of early parenting of caucasian adolescent mothers. *Child Development, 58,* 955–963.

Garcia-Coll, C. T., Vohr, B., Hoffman, J., & Oh, W. (1986). Maternal and environmental factors affecting developmental outcome of infants of adolescent mothers. *Journal of Behavioral and Developmental Pediatrics, 7,* 230–236.

Gillmore, M. R., Butler, S. S., Lohr, M. J., & Gilchrist, L. (1992). Substance use and other factors associated with risky sexual behavior among pregnant adolescents. *Family Planning Perspectives, 24,* 255–268.

Goldenberg, R. L., & Klerman, L. V. (1995). Adolescent pregnancy: Another look. *New England Journal of Medicine, 332,* 1161–1162.

Goodnow, J. (1984). Parents' ideas about parenting and development: A review of issues and recent work. In M. E. Lamb, A. L. Brown, & B. Rogoff (Eds.), *Advances in developmental psychology* (Vol. 3, pp. 193–242). Hillsdale, NJ: Lawrence Erlbaum Associates.

Greenberger, E., & Goldberg, W. A. (1989). Work, parenting, and the socialization of children. *Developmental Psychology, 25,* 22–35.

Greenberger, E., & O'Neil, R. (1993). Spouse, parent, worker: Role commitments and role-related experiences in the construction of adults' well-being. *Developmental Psychology, 29,* 181–197.

Haiek, L., & Lederman, S. A. (1989). The relationship between maternal weight for height and term birth weight in teens and adult women. *Journal of Adolescent Health Care, 10,* 16–22.

Hall, J. A., Henggeler, S. W., Felice, M. E., Reynosa, T., Williams, N. M., & Sheets, R. (1993). Adolescent substance use during pregnancy. *Journal of Pediatric Psychology, 18,* 265–271.

Hamburg, B. A. (1974). Early adolescence: A specific and stressful stage of the life cycle. In G. Coelho, D. Hamburg, & J. Adams (Eds.), *Coping and adaptation* (pp. 101–124). New York: Basic Books.

Hamburg, B. A. (1986). Subsets of adolescent mothers: Developmental, biomedical, and psychosocial issues. In J. B. Lancaster & B. Hamburg (Eds.), *School-age pregnancy and parenthood: Biosocial dimensions* (pp. 115–145). New York: Aldine DeGruyter.

Hanson, S. L., Morrison, D. R., & Ginsburg, A. L. (1989). The antecedents of teenage fatherhood. *Demography, 26,* 579–596.

Hardy, J. B., Duggan, A. K., Masynk, K., & Pearson, C. (1989). Fathers of children born to young urban mothers. *Family Planning Perspectives, 21,* 159–163.

Hardy, J. B., & Zabin, L. S. (Eds.). (1991). *Adolescent pregnancy in an urban environment: Issues, programs, and evaluation.* Baltimore, MD: Urban & Schwarzenberg Press.

Hayes, C. D. (Ed.). (1987). *Risking the future: Adolescent sexuality, pregnancy, and childbearing* (Vol. 1). Washington, DC: National Academy Press.

Hendricks, L. E., & Montgomery, T. (1983). A limited population of unmarried adolescent fathers: A preliminary report of their views of fatherhood and the relationship with the mothers of their children. *Adolescence, 18,* 201–210.

Hendricks, L. E., Robinson-Brown, D. P., & Gary, L. E. (1984). Religiosity and unmarried black adolescent fatherhood. *Adolescence, 19,* 417–424.

Henshaw, S. K. (1993). Teenage abortion, birth and pregnancy statistics by state, 1988. *Family Planning Perspectives, 25,* 122–126.

Henshaw, S. K., Kenney, A. M., Somberg, D., & Van Vort, J. (1989). *Teenage pregnancy in the United States: The scope of the problem and state responses.* New York: Alan Guttmacher Institute.

Hofferth, S. L. (1984a). Children's life course: Family structure and living arrangements in cohort perspective. In G. Elder (Ed.), *Life-course dynamics* (pp. 968–980). Ithaca, NY: Cornell University Press.

Hofferth, S. L. (1984b). Kin networks, race, and family structure. *Journal of Marriage and the Family, 46,* 791–804.

Hofferth, S. L., & Hayes, C. D. (Eds.). (1987). *Risking the future: Adolescent sexuality, pregnancy, and childbearing* (Vol. 2). Washington, DC: National Academy Press.

Hofferth, S. L., & Moore, K. A. (1979). Early childbearing and later economic well-being. *American Sociological Review, 44,* 784–815.

Hogan, D. P., Hao, L., & Parish, W. L. (1990). Race, kin networks, and assistance to mother-headed families. *Social Forces, 68,* 797–812.

Hollingsworth, D. R. (1978). The pregnant adolescent. In A. K. Kreutner & D. R. Hollingsworth (Eds.), *Adolescent obstetrics and gynecology* (pp. 67–77). Chicago: Year Book Publishers.

Hollingsworth, D. R. (1982). The pregnant adolescent: Sociologic problem with medical consequences. In G. N. Burrows & T. F. Ferris (Eds.), *Medical complications during pregnancy* (pp. 546–564). Philadelphia: W.B. Saunders.

Hollingsworth, D. R., & Felice, M. E. (1986). Teenage pregnancy: A multiracial sociologic problem. *American Journal of Obstetrics and Gynecology, 155,* 741–746.

Horwitz, S.M., Klerman, L. V., Kuo, H. S., & Jekel, J. F. (1991). School-age mothers: Predictors of long-term educational and economic outcomes. *Pediatrics, 87,* 862–868.

Howard, M. (1992). Delaying the start of intercourse among adolescents. *Adolescent medicine: State of the art reviews, 3,* 181–193.

Hughes, D., & Simpson, L. (1995). The role of social change in preventing low birth weight. In R. E. Behrman (Ed.), *The future of children* (Vol. 5, pp. 87–102). Los Angeles, CA: The David and Lucille Packard Foundation.

Institute of Medicine, Food and Nutrition Board. (1990). *Nutrition during pregnancy*. Washington, DC: National Academy of Sciences Press.

Jayakody, R., Chatters, L. M., & Taylor, R. J. (1993). Family support to single and married African-American mothers: The provision of financial, emotional, and child care assistance. *Journal of Marriage and the Family, 55*, 261–276.

Jekel, J. F., Harrison, J. T., Bancroft, D., Tyler, N., & Klerman, L. (1975). A comparison of the health of index and subsequent babies born to school age mothers. *American Journal of Public Health, 65,* 370–374.

Jekel, J. F., Klerman, L. V., & Bancroft, D. R. (1973). Factors associated with rapid subsequent pregnancies among school-age mothers. *American Journal of Public Health, 63,* 769–773.

Jones, E., Forrest, J., Goldman, N., Henshaw, S., Lincoln, J., Rosoff, C., Westoff, C., & Wulf, D. (1985). Teenage pregnancy in developed countries: Determinants and policy implications. *Family Planning Perspectives, 17,* 53–63.

Kaplan, D. N., & Mason, E. A. (1969). Maternal reactions to premature birth viewed as an acute emotional disorder. *American Journal of Orthopsychiatry, 30,* 539–552.

Keefe, S. E. (1980). Acculturation and the extended family among urban Mexican-Americans. In A. M. Padilla (Ed.), *Acculturation* (pp. 85–110). Boulder, CO: Westview.

Ketterlinus, R. D., Henderson, S. H., & Lamb, M. E. (1990). Maternal age, sociodemographics, prenatal health and behavior: Influences on neonatal risk status. *Journal of Adolescent Health Care, 11,* 423–431.

Ketterlinus, R. D., Lamb, M. E., & Nitz, K. (1991). Developmental and ecological sources of stress among adolescent parents. *Family Relations, 40,* 435–441.

Kinsman, S. B., & Slap, G. B. (1992). Barriers to prenatal care. *Journal of Adolescent Health, 13,* 146–154.

Klerman, L. V. (1993). Adolescent pregnancy and parenting: Controversies of the past and lessons for the future. *Journal of Adolescent Health, 14,* 533–561.

Klerman, L. V., & Horwitz, S. M. (1992). Reducing the adverse consequences of adolescent pregnancy and parenting: The role of service programs. *Adolescent medicine: State of the art reviews, 3,* 299–316.

Klinman, D. G., Sander, J. H., Rosa, J. L., Longo, K. R., & Martinez, L. P. (1985). *Reaching and serving the teenage father.* New York: Bank Street College of Education.

Koenig, M. A., & Zelnik, M. (1982). Repeat pregnancies among metropolitan-area teenagers: 1971–1979. *Family Planning Perspectives, 14,* 341–344.

Kokotailo, P.K., Adger, H., Duggan, A.K., Repke, J., & Joffe, A. (1992). Cigarette, alcohol, and other drug use by school-age pregnant adolescents: Prevalence, detection, and associated risk factors. *Pediatrics, 90,* 328–334.

Lamb, M. (1988). The ecology of adolescent pregnancy and parenthood. In A. R. Pence (Ed.), *Ecological research with children and families: From concepts to methodology* (pp. 99–121). New York: Teachers College Press.

Lamb, M., & Easterbrooks, A. (1981). Individual differences in parental sensitivity: Origins, components, and consequences. In M. Lamb & L. Sherrod (Eds.), *Infant social cognition: Empirical and theoretical considerations* (pp. 127–153). Hillsdale, NJ: Lawrence Erlbaum Associates.

Lamb, M. E., Elster, A. B., Peters, L. J., Kahn, J. S., & Tavare, J. (1986). Characteristics of married adolescent mothers and their partners. *Journal of Youth and Adolescence, 15,* 487–496.

Lamb, M. E., Elster, A. B., & Tavare, J. (1986). Behavioral profiles of adolescent mothers and partners with varying intracouple age differences. *Journal of Adolescent Research, 1,* 399–408.

Lancaster, J. B., Altmann, J., Rossi, A., & Sherrod, L. (Eds.). (1986). *Parenting across the life span.* New York : Aldine de Gruyter.

Landry, D. J., & Forrest, J. D. (1995). How old are U.S. fathers? *Family Planning Perspectives, 27,* 159–165.

Lerman, R. I. (1988). *A national profile of young unwed fathers: Who are they and how are they parenting?* Washington, DC: U.S. Government Printing Office.

Levine, L., Garcia-Coll, C. T., & Oh, W. (1985). Determinants of mother–infant interaction in adolescent mothers. *Pediatrics, 75,* 23–29.

Linares, L. O., Leadbeater, B., Jaffe, L., Kato, P., & Diaz, A. (1992). Predictors of repeat pregnancy outcome among Black and Puerto Rican adolescent mothers. *Journal of Developmental and Behavioral Pediatrics, 13,* 89–94.

Lorenzi, M. E., Klerman, L. V., & Jekel, J. F. (1977). School-age parents: How permanent a relationship? *Adolescence, 12,* 14–22.

Maccoby, E., & Martin, J. (1983). Socialization in the context of the family: Parent–child interaction. In P. H. Mussen (Series Ed.) & E. M. Hetherington (Vol. Ed.), *Handbook of child psychology: Socialization, personality, and social development* (pp. 1–101). New York: Wiley.

MacPhee, D. (1981). *Knowledge of Infant Development Inventory.* Unpublished manual, Colorado State University, Fort Collins.

MacPhee, D., & Fabio, C. (1992). *A question of match: Knowledge of child development and age-appropriate stimulation.* Paper presented at the American Psychological Association meeting, Washington, DC.

Main, M., & Goldwyn, R. (1984). Predicting rejection of her infant from mother's representation of her own experience: Implications for the abused–abusing intergenerational cycle. *Monographs of Child Abuse and Neglect: The International Journal, 8,* 203–17.

Marsiglio, W. (1986). Teenage fatherhood: High school completion and educational attainment. In A. B. Elster & M. E. Lamb (Eds.), *Adolescent fatherhood* (pp. 67–87). Hillsdale, NJ: Lawrence Erlbaum Associates.

Marsiglio, W. (1987). Adolescent fathers in the United States: Their initial living arrangements, marital experience and educational outcomes. *Family Planning Perspectives, 19,* 245–251.

Martin, J. A. (1975). Parent–child relations. In F. D. Horowitz (Ed.), *Review of child development research* (Vol. 4, pp. 503–566). Chicago: University of Chicago Press.

Mash, E. J., & Johnston, C. (1983). Parental perceptions of child behavior problems, parenting self-esteem, and mothers' reported stress in younger and older hyperactive and normal children. *Journal of Consulting and Clinical Psychology, 51,* 86–99.

Matsuhashi, Y., Felice, M. E., Shragg, P., & Hollingsworth, D. (1989). Is repeat pregnancy in adolescents a "planned" affair? *Journal of Adolescent Health Care, 10,* 409–412.

Maynard, R., & Rangarajan, A. (1994). Contraceptive use and repeat pregnancies among welfare-dependent teenage mothers. *Family Planning Perspectives, 26,* 198–205.

McAnarney, E.R., & Hendee, W.R. (1989). Adolescent pregnancy and its consequences. *Journal of the American Medical Association, 262,* 74–77.

McAnarney, E. R., Lawrence, R. A., Riccuiti, H. N., Polley, J., & Szilagyi, M. (1986). Interactions of adolescent mothers and their 1-year-old children. *Pediatrics, 78,* 585–589.

McAnarney, E.R., Roghmann, K.J., Adams, B.N., Tatelbaum, R. C., Kash, C., Coulter, M., Plume, M., & Charney, E. (1978). Obstetrical, neonatal, and psychosocial outcome of pregnant adolescents. *Pediatrics, 61,* 199–205.

McCarthy, J., & Hardy, J. (1993). Age at first birth and birth outcomes. *Journal of Research on Adolescence, 4,* 373–392.

McCormick, M. C., Shapiro, S. S., & Stanfield, B. (1984). High risk mothers: Infant mortality and morbidity in four areas in the United States 1975–1978. *American Journal of Public Health, 74,* 18–23.

Mecklenburg, M. E., & Thompson, P. G. (1983). The adolescent family life program as a prevention measure. *Public Health Reports, 98,* 21–29.

Meserole, L.P., Worthington-Roberts, B.S., Rees, J.M., & Wright, L.S. (1984). Prenatal weight gain and postpartum weight loss patterns in adolescents. *Journal of Adolescent Health Care, 5,* 21–27.

Moore, K. A. (1993). *Facts at a glance.* Washington, DC: Child Trends.

Moore, K. A., Hofferth, S. L., Wertheimer, R. F., Waite, L. J., & Caldwell, S. B. (1981). Teenage childbearing: Consequences for women, families, and government welfare expenditures. In K. G. Scott, T. Field, & E. G. Robertson (Eds.), *Teenage parents and their offspring* (pp. 35–54). New York: Grune & Stratton.

Moore, K. A., Simms, M. C., & Betsey, C. L. (1986). *Choice and circumstance: Racial differences in adolescent sexuality and fertility.* New Brunswick, NJ: Transaction Books.

Moore, K. A., & Waite, J. (1977). Early childbearing and educational attainment. *Family Planning Perspectives, 9,* 220–5.

Moore, K. A., Wenk, D., Hofferth, S. L., & Hayes, C. D. (1987). Trends in adolescent sexual and fertility behavior. In S. L. Hofferth & C. D. Hayes (Eds.), *Risking the future: (Vol. 2) Adolescent sexuality, pregnancy and childbearing* (pp. 353–503). Washington DC: National Academy Press.

Morgan, S. P., & Rindfuss, R. R. (1985). Marital disruption: Structural and temporal dimensions. *American Journal of Sociology, 90,* 1055–1077.

Mott, F. (1986). The pace of repeated childbearing among young American mothers. *Family Planning Perspectives, 18,* 5–12.

Nakashima, I., & Camp, B. W. (1984). Fathers of infants born to adolescent mothers: A study of paternal characteristics. *American Journal of Diseases of Children, 138,* 452–454.

National Center for Health Statistics (NCHS). (1987). *Advance report on final natality statistics, 1985. Supplement to the Monthly Vital Statistics Report* (Vol. 36, No. 4). Washington, DC: U.S. Government Printing Office.

National Center for Health Statistics (NCHS). (1993). *Advance report of final natality statistics, 1990. Supplement to the Monthly Vital Statistics Report* (Vol. 41, No. 9). Washington, DC: U.S. Government Printing Office.

National Center for Health Statistics (NCHS). (1994). *Advance report of final natality statistics, 1991. Supplement to the Monthly Vital Statistics Report* (Vol. 42, No. 3). Washington, DC: U.S. Government Printing Office.

Newcomb, M. D., & Bentler, P. M. (1989). Substance use and abuse among children and teenagers. *American Psychologist, 44,* 242–248.

Nitz, K., Ketterlinus, R. D., & Brandt, L. J. (1995). The role of stress, social support, and family environment in adolescent mothers' parenting. *Journal of Adolescent Research, 10,* 358–382.

Oakley, A., Fullerton, D., Holland, J., Arnold, S., France-Dawson, M., Kelley, P., & McGrellis, S. (1995). Sexual health education interventions for young people: A methodological review. *British Medical Journal, 310,* 158–162.

Olds, D. L., Henderson, C. R., Chamberlin, R., & Tatelbaum, R. (1986). Preventing child abuse and neglect: A randomized trial of nurse home visitation. *Pediatrics, 78,* 65–78.

Osofsky, J. D., Hann, D., & Peebles, C. (in press). Adolescent parenthood: Risks and opportunities for parents and infants. In C. Zeanah (Ed.), *Handbook of infant mental health.* New York: Guilford.

Oyserman, D., Radin, N., & Benn, R. (1993). Dynamics in a three-generational family: Teens, grandparents, and babies. *Developmental Psychology, 29,* 564–572.

Panzarine, S. (1988). Teen mothering: Behaviors and interventions. *Journal of Adolescent Health Care, 9,* 443–448.

Panzarine, S., & Elster, A. B. (1983). Coping in a group of expectant adolescent fathers: An exploratory study. *Journal of Adolescent Health Care, 4,* 117–120.

Parish, W., Hao, L., & Hogan, D. (1991). Family support networks, welfare, and work among young mothers. *Journal of Marriage and the Family, 53,* 203–215.

Parke, R. D., & Slaby, R. G. (1983). The development of aggression. In P. H. Mussen (Series Ed.) & E. M. Hetherington (Vol. Ed.), *Handbook of child psychology (Vol. 4): Socialization, personality, and social development* (pp. 547–641). New York: Wiley.

Parks, P. L., & Smeriglio, V. L. (1983). Parenting knowledge among adolescent mothers. *Journal of Adolescent Health Care, 4,* 163–167.

Patterson, G. (1983). Stress: A change agent for family process. In N. Garmezy & M. Rutter (Eds.), *Stress, coping, and development in children* (pp. 235–264). New York: McGraw-Hill.

Pauker, J. D. (1971). Fathers of children conceived out of wedlock: Pregnancy, high school, psychological test results. *Developmental Psychology, 4,* 215–218.

Phipps-Yonas, S. (1980). Teenage pregnancy and motherhood: A review of the literature. *American Journal of Orthopsychiatry, 50,* 403–431.

Pletsch, P.K. (1988). Substance use and health activities of pregnant adolescents. *Journal of Adolescent Health Care, 9,* 38–45.

Polit, D. F., & Kahn, J. R. (1986). Early subsequent pregnancy among economically disadvantaged teenage mothers. *American Journal of Public Health, 76,* 167–171.

Presser, H. B. (1989). Some economic complexities of child care provided by grandmothers. *Journal of Marriage and the Family, 51,* 581–591.

Prinz, R. J., Foster, S., Kent, R. N., & O'Leary, K. D. (1979). Multivariate assessment of conflict in distressed and nondistressed mother–adolescent dyads. *Journal of Applied Behavior Analysis, 12,* 691–700.

Rivara, F. P., Sweeney, P. J., & Henderson, B. F. (1985). A study of low socioeconomic status, black teenage fathers and their non-father peers. *Pediatrics, 75,* 648–656.

Rivara, F. P., Sweeney, P. J., & Henderson, B. F. (1986). Black teenage fathers: What happens when the baby is born? *Pediatrics, 78,* 151–158.

Robinson, B. E. (1988). Teenage pregnancy from the father's perspective. *American Journal of Orthopsychiatry, 58,* 46–51.

Rohner D. (1975). *They love me, they love me not: A worldwide study of the effects of parental acceptance and rejection.* New Haven, CT: Yale University Press.

Roosa, M. W., Fitzgerald, H. E., & Carlson, N. A. (1982a). A comparison of teenage and older mothers: A systems analysis. *Journal of Marriage and the Family, 44,* 367–377.

Roosa, M. W., Fitzgerald, H. E., & Carlson, N. A. (1982b). Teenage parenting and child development: A literature review. *Infant Mental Health Journal, 3,* 4–18.

Rubin, K., LeMare, L., & Lollis, S. (1990). Social withdrawal in childhood: Developmental pathways to peer rejection. In S. Asher & J. Coie (Eds.), *Peer rejection in childhood* (pp. 217–249). New York: Cambridge University Press.

Sander, J. (1988). *The teen father collaboration: A national research and demonstration project.* Washington, DC: U.S. Government Printing Office.

Sander, J. H., & Rosen, J. L. (1987). Teenage fathers: Working with the neglected partner in adolescent childbearing. *Family Planning Perspectives, 19,* 107–110.

Sarason, B. R., Shearin, E., Pierce G., & Sarason, I. (1987). Interrelations of social support measures: Theoretical and practical implications. *Journal of Personality and Social Psychology, 52,* 813–832.

Schellenbach, C. J., Whitman, T., & Borkowski, J. (1992). Toward an integrative model of adolescent parenting. *Human Development, 35,* 81–99.

Scholl, T. O., Hediger, M. L., Ances, I. G., & Cronk, C. E. (1988). Growth during early teenage pregnancies. *Lancet, 1,* 701–702.

Scholl, T. O., Hediger, M. L., & Belsky, D. H. (1994). Prenatal care and maternal health during adolescent pregnancy: A review and meta-analysis. *Journal of Adolescent Health, 15,* 444–456.

Seymore, C., Frothingham, T., MacMillan, J., & DuRant, R. (1990). Child development knowledge, childrearing attitudes, and social support among first-and second-time mothers. *Journal of Adolescent Health, 11,* 343–350.

Shapiro, J. R., & Mangelsdorf, S. C. (1994). The determinants of parenting competence in adolescent mothers. *Journal of Youth and Adolescence, 23,* 621–641.

Shea, E., & Tronick, E. Z. (1988). The maternal self-report inventory: A research and clinical instrument for assessing maternal self-esteem. In H. Fitzgerald, B. M. Lester, & M. W. Yogman (Eds.), *Theory and research in behavioral pediatrics* (pp. 101–139). New York: Plenum Press.

Sherline, D. M., & Davidson, R. A. (1978). Adolescent pregnancy: The Jackson, Mississippi experience. *American Journal of Obstetrics & Gynecology, 132,* 245–255.

Siegel, E., Thomas, D., Coulter, E., Tuthill, R., & Chipman, S. (1971). Continuation of contraception by low income women: A one-year follow-up. *American Journal of Public Health, 61,* 1886–1898.

Smith, E. W. (1975). The role of the grandmother in adolescent pregnancy and parenting. *The Journal of School Health, 65,* 278–283.

Smollar, J., & Ooms, T. (1987). *Young unwed fathers: Research review, policy dilemmas and options.* Washington, DC: Catholic University and Maximus.

South, S. J. (1993). Racial and ethnic differences in the desire to marry. *Journal of Marriage and the Family, 55,* 357–370.

Spieker, S. J., & Bensley, L. (1994). Roles of living arrangements and grandmother social support in adolescent mothering and infant attachment. *Developmental Psychology, 30,* 102–111.

Stack, C. (1974). *All our kin: Strategies for survival in a Black community.* New York: Harper & Row.

Stahler, G. J., & DuCette, J. P. (1991). Evaluating adolescent pregnancy programs: Rethinking our priorities. *Family Planning Perspectives, 23,* 129–133.

Stevens, J. H. (1984). Black grandmothers' and Black adolescent mothers' knowledge about parenting. *Developmental Psychology, 20,* 1017–1025.

Stevens-Simon, C., Parsons, J., & Montgomery, C. (1986). What is the relationship between postpartum withdrawal from school and repeat pregnancy among adolescent mothers? *Journal of Adolescent Health Care, 7,* 191–194.

Stevens-Simon, C., Roghmann, K. J., & McAnarney, E. R. (1990). Repeat adolescent pregnancy and low birth weight: Methods issues. *Journal of Adolescent Health, 11,* 114–118.

Stevens-Simon, C., Roghmann, K. J., & McAnarney, E. R. (1992). Relationship of self-reported prepregnant weight and weight gain during pregnancy and relationship to body habitus and maternal age. *Journal of the American Dietetic Association, 92,* 85–87.

Taylor, R. D., Casten, R., & Flickinger, S. M. (1993). Influence of kinship social support on the parenting experiences and psychosocial adjustment of African-American adolescents. *Developmental Psychology, 29,* 382–388.

Teberg, A. J., Howell, V. V., & Wingert, W. A. (1983). Attachment interaction behavior between young teenage mothers and their infants. *Journal of Adolescent Health Care, 4,* 61–66.

Teti, D. M., & Lamb, M. (1989). Socioeconomic and marital outcomes of adolescent marriage, adolescent childbirth, and their co-occurrence. *Journal of Marriage and the Family, 51,* 203–212.

Thomas, A., Chess, S., Sillen, J., & Mendez, O. (1974). Cross cultural study of behavior in children with special vulnerabilities to stress. In D. Ricks, A. Thomas, & M. Roff (Eds.), *Life history research in psychopathology* (Vol. 3, pp. 53–67). Minneapolis: University of Minnesota Press.

Tinsley, B. R., & Parke, R. D. (1983). Grandparents as support and socialization agents. In M. Lewis (Ed.), *Beyond the dyad* (pp. 161–194). New York: Plenum.

Trussell, J. (1988). Teenage pregnancy in the United States. *Family Planning Perspectives, 20,* 262–272.

Trussell, J., & Menken, J. (1978). Early childbearing and subsequent fertility. *Family Planning Perspectives, 10,* 209–218.

Unger, D. G., & Cooley, M. L. (1992). Partner and grandmother contact in Black and White teen parent families. *Journal of Adolescent Health, 13,* 546–552.

Unger, D. G., & Wandersman, L. P. (1988). The relation of family and partner support to the adjustment of adolescent mothers. *Child Development, 59,* 1056–1060.

United Way of San Diego County (1993). *San Diego County: Children's future scan.* San Diego, CA: Author.

Upchurch D. M., & McCarthy, J. (1989). Adolescent childbearing and high school completion in the 1980s: Have things changed? *Family Planning Perspectives, 21,* 199–202.

U.S. Bureau of the Census. (1988). The Hispanic population in the United States, March 1985. *Current Population Reports,* Series P-20, No. 422.

U.S. Bureau of the Census. (1990). United States population estimates by age, sex, race, and Hispanic origin: 1980–1988. *Current Population Reports,* Series P-25, No. 1045.

U.S. Bureau of the Census. (1992). *Statistical abstract of the United States: 1992.* Washington, DC: U.S. Government Printing Office.

Vaz, R., Smolen, R., & Miller, G. (1983). Adolescent pregnancy: Involvement of the male partner. *Journal of Adolescent Health Care, 4,* 246–250.

Vega, W. A. (1990). Hispanic families in the 1980s: A decade of research. *Journal of Marriage and the Family, 52,* 1015–1024.

Vera Institute of Justice: The Study Group on the Male Role in Teenage Pregnancy and Parenting. (1990). *The male role in teenage pregnancy and parenting: New directions for public policy.* New York: Author.

Vukelich, C., & Kliman, D. S. (1985). Mature and teenage mothers' infant growth expectations and use of child development information sources. *Family Relations, 34,* 189–196.

Wasserman, G., Rauh, V., Brunelli, S., Garcia-Castro, M., & Necos, B. (1990). Psychosocial attributes and life experiences of minority mothers: Age and ethnic variations. *Child Development, 61,* 566–580.

Wegman, M.E. (1993). Annual summary of vital statistics–1992. *Pediatrics, 92,* 743–754.

Weintraub, M., & Wolf, B. (1983). Effects of stress and social supports on mother–child interactions in single- and two-parent families. *Child Development, 54,* 1297–1311.

Westbrook, M. T. (1978). The effect of the order of birth on women's experience of childbearing. *Journal of Marriage and the Family, 40,* 165–172.

Wilson, M. (1986). The black extended family: An analytical consideration. *Developmental Psychology, 22,* 246–258.

Wong, C. (1993). *Paternal support provided by adolescent and adult fathers* (Independent Study Project undertaken in partial fulfillment for the Doctorate of Medicine). Unpublished data, University of California, San Diego School of Medicine, San Diego.

Wong, C., Morgan, M., & East, P. (1993). Paternal support provided by adolescent versus adult fathers. *Journal of Adolescent Health, 14,* 65.

Zabin, L. S., Hirsch, M. B., Smith, E. A., Streett, R., & Hardy, J. (1986). Evaluation of a pregnancy prevention program for urban teenagers. *Family Planning Perspectives, 18,* 119–126.

Zahn-Waxler, C., Kochanska, G., Krupnick, J., & McKnew, D. (1990). Patterns of guilt in children of depressed and well mothers. *Developmental Psychology, 26,* 51–59.

Zelkowitz, P. (1982). Parenting philosophies and practices. In D. Belle (Ed.), *Lives in stress: Women and depression* (pp. 154–162). Beverly Hills, CA: Sage.

Zelnik, M. (1980). Second pregnancies to premaritally pregnant teenagers, 1976 and 1971. *Family Planning Perspectives, 12*, 69–76.

Zelnik, M., & Kantner, J. F. (1978). First pregnancies to women aged 15–19: 1976 and 1971. *Family Planning Perspectives, 10*, 11–20.

Zlatnik, F. J., & Burmeister, L. F. (1977). Low "gynecologic age": An obstetric risk factor. *American Journal of Obstetrics & Gynecology, 128*, 183–186.

Zuckerman, B., Amaro, H., & Cabral, H. (1989). Validity of self-reporting of marijuana and cocaine use among pregnant adolescents. *Journal of Pediatrics, 115*, 812–815.

# Author Index

❧ ◆ ❧

# Subject Index

൭ ◆ ൫

www.ingramcontent.com/pod-product-compliance
Ingram Content Group UK Ltd.
Pitfield, Milton Keynes, MK11 3LW, UK
UKHW020429010325